SPECULUM ANNIVERSARY MONOGRAPHS

SIX

THE COMMUNE OF LUCCA UNDER PISAN RULE, 1342-1369

SPECULUM ANNIVERSARY MONOGRAPHS

SIX

THE COMMUNE OF LUCCA UNDER PISAN RULE, 1342-1369

CHRISTINE E. MEEK

THE MEDIAEVAL ACADEMY OF AMERICA   1980

The publication of this book was made possible by funds contributed to the Mediaeval Academy during the Semi-Centennial Fund Drive, and by an additional grant from the Grace Lawless Lee Fund, Trinity College, Dublin. The author wishes to thank the Grace Lawless Lee Fund, and the Twenty-Seven Foundation, which provided financial support for the archival research on which this study is based.

Contents

ABBREVIATIONS

Anz. Av. Lib.	Anziani Avanti la Libertà (series in Archivio di Stato, Lucca)
A.S.P.	Archivio di Stato (Pisa)
Inventario	*Inventario del R. Archivio di Stato in Lucca,* vols. 1–4 ed. S. Bongi (Lucca, 1872–88), vol. 5 ed. E. Lazzareschi (Pescia, 1946), vol. 6 ed. D. Corsi (Lucca, 1961)
Mancinelli, "Carlo IV"	G. Mancinelli, "Carlo IV di Lussemburgo e la repubblica di Pisa," *Studi storici* di A. Crivellucci 15 (1906), pp. 313–365, 445–502.
Memorie e documenti	N. Cianelli, *Memorie e documenti per servire all'istoria del principato lucchese,* 1 (Lucca, 1813)
Ragionieri	Ragionieri della Camera e del Commune (series in the Archivio di Stato, Lucca)
Regesto	L. Fumi, ed., *Regesto del R. Archivio di Stato in Lucca* (Lucca, 1903)
R.I.S.	Rerum Italicarum Scriptores
Sercambi	*Le chroniche di Giovanni Sercambi, Lucchese, pubblicate sui manoscritti originali a cura di Salvatore Bongi,* 3 vols. (Rome, 1892)

Introduction

WITH THE expansion of the more powerful Italian city-states, which was to lead to the emergence of a small number of regional states, it was the fate of many smaller cities to fall under the rule of their neighbours, some temporarily, but many permanently. One example of the temporary loss of self-rule is the Tuscan commune of Lucca, which in 1342 fell to its neighbour and long-term enemy, Pisa. Pisan rule lasted for over twenty-five years, until Lucca finally regained its independence in 1369.

The problem of the rule of one city over another has not gone entirely unstudied, and something is known in general about the internal organisation of regional states. Often the rule of one city over another was established very slowly and gradually; it may therefore be difficult to isolate the precise moment when the subject city ceased to enjoy effective independence.[1] Even after outside rule was firmly established, subject cities long maintained a degree of autonomy, retaining their own statutes and customs, the right to elect their own officials and councils, and the right to raise and administer their own taxes.[2] Even as powerful a state as that of the Visconti had something of the character of a federation of communes—each of which had independently accepted the same lord—rather than that of a unitary state.[3] Although there was some attempt, especially under Giangaleazzo Visconti, to impose a more uniform system of administration, traditions of local patriotism and municipal autonomy worked against this. Visconti centralisation could look like rule from Milan, and Giangaleazzo was careful not to press attempts at uniformity further than his subjects would accept; consequently many local rights and privileges were left intact.[4] The case of

1. For example, the rule of Milan over Pavia: G. Romano, "Delle relazioni tra Pavia e Milano nella formazione della signoria viscontea," *Archivio storico lombardo* 19 (1892), esp. pp. 566–589. The rule of Florence over Pistoia: D. Herlihy, *Medieval and Renaissance Pistoia* (New Haven and London, 1967), esp. pp. 223–231.
2. P. J. Jones, "Communes and Despots: The City State in Late-Medieval Italy," *Transactions of the Royal Historical Society* 5th ser. 15 (1965), esp. pp. 85–96.
3. G. L. Barni, "La formazione interna dello stato visconteo," *Archivio storico lombardo* n.s. 6 (1941), esp. pp. 16–17, 40–66; Jones, "Communes and Despots," p. 83.
4. D. M. Bueno de Mesquita, "The Place of Despotism in Italian Politics," in *Europe in the Later Middle Ages*, ed. J. Hale, J. R. Highfield and B. Smalley (London, 1965), pp. 327, 330, and *Giangaleazzo Visconti* (Cambridge, 1941), esp. pp. 45–58, 311–319.

Milan, however, is complicated by the fact that it was a *signoria*. The *signore* might give orders that were uniform for the whole of his dominions and send out officials drawn from a common bureaucracy, but he did so by virtue of his position as *signore* of each individual commune. Insofar as there was a strengthening of central authority, it was the authority of the *signore;* the measures taken by the Visconti did not necessarily imply the subordination of one city to another. The rule of one city by another is therefore best studied in cases where the ruling city was a republic. The most obvious examples are Florence and Venice.

There is no study devoted to the relations of Florence and its subject cities as a whole. Lauro Martines noted ten years ago that this was one of the outstanding lacunae in Florentine history, although he himself contributed a valuable preliminary discussion of the constitutional relations of Florence and its subject territories and of the problems arising from conflicting jurisdictions.[5]

Some studies of Florentine relations with individual subject cities do exist, though only in the case of Pisa has the topic attracted any considerable literature. Pietro Silva devoted a long article to the early years of Florentine rule in Pisa. He painted a dark picture. There were significant institutional changes, with all real power passing into Florentine hands. Florentine officials were sometimes oppressive—although the Florentine home government tried to check this—and Pisa had to suffer the presence of large numbers of mercenary soldiers. Early measures were dictated by considerations of security; fortifications were built, and many potentially rebellious Pisans were deported to Florence. Florence imposed heavy taxes on Pisa to cover the costs of its administration and defence and to help the Florentines recoup some of the money they had spent acquiring the city. The wars from 1423 to 1433 led to renewed oppressive measures, increased financial demands, and the presence of larger forces of mercenaries. However, in the years of peace after about 1415 Florence showed signs of recognising the need to assist Pisa, by alleviating financial burdens, trying to encourage trade, and offering concessions to immigrants in order to repopulate the city. But Silva argued that even if these measures had been sustained, they would not have sufficed to counteract the effects of the emigration of many wealthy Pisans, the decline of trade, industry, and agriculture, and the general impoverishment of the city and its inhabitants.[6]

5. L. Martines, *Lawyers and Statesmen in Renaissance Florence* (Princeton, New Jersey, 1968), pp. 220–245: a chapter entitled "Aspects of Territorial Government."
6. P. Silva, "Pisa sotto Firenze dal 1406 al 1433," *Studi storici* di A. Crivellucci 18 (1909–1910), pp. 135–183, 284–323, 529–579.

In an invaluable modern study Michael Mallett reviewed modern revisionary work on fifteenth-century Pisa and tried to provide a balanced picture of Florentine rule as a whole, while also choosing a number of particular topics for special study. He discounted old accusations that Florence deliberately tried to weaken and impoverish Pisa; Pisa was already in a state of decline before 1406 and the Florentines had an interest in its well-being. He emphasised Florentine efforts to make Pisa an important centre of international trade by offering concessions to foreign merchants. While this helped the Pisans only indirectly, and Pisa does seem to have suffered an economic depression in the 1420s and 1430s, Mallett concluded that the traditional view that the Pisans were overtaxed and impoverished has been overstated. Pisan guilds were certainly subjected to their counterparts in Florence, but this was the normal practice in Florentine subject cities. The Pisan woollen industry, which had been in difficulty long before 1406, suffered a further decline under Florentine rule, but other Pisan industries, such as the tanning and leather industry and soap manufacture, were encouraged. It even seems possible that certain industries were allotted to subject cities at the expense of parallel industries in Florence.

The Pisan *contado* was of great importance to Florence, and accusations that the Florentines neglected the land or deliberately allowed it to become derelict are unlikely to be true. Mallett found that some absentee landlords, whether Florentine or Pisan, neglected drainage ditches and allowed arable land to revert to pasture, but the Florentine government tried to hold this movement in check and organise the repair of dykes, ditches, and roads. The acquisition of land in the Pisan *contado* by members of some of the most influential Florentine families, which was an important feature of the second half of the fifteenth century, meant that these men had an interest in Pisan prosperity. Mallett concluded that while Florentine rule was sometimes unjust and oppressive and Pisa suffered a decline in population and wealth during the Florentine period, there were also positive features, such as the attempts to encourage trade, promote immigration, and assist the *contado*.[7]

In a chapter entitled "Problems of Territorial Government" Gene Brucker also discussed Florentine policy towards Pisa in the early years after its conquest. He showed that the Florentines were aware of the need to treat Pisa justly and leniently and avoid measures that would weaken its economy. However, security needs sometimes dictated

7. M. E. Mallett, "Pisa and Florence in the Fifteenth Century: Aspects of the Period of the First Florentine Domination," in *Florentine Studies,* ed. N. Rubinstein (London, 1968), pp. 403–441. Mallett also provides evaluations of other works, notably M. L. Mori, *La dominazione fiorentina a Pisa dal 1451 al 1469* (Pisa, 1936), which I have not seen.

harsher measures, such as the deportation of potential troublemakers—a measure occasionally taken in other Florentine subject cities. Brucker argued that there was a greater preoccupation with problems of territorial government in Florence in the early fifteenth century, and a heightened awareness of the connection between corrupt administration and oppressive taxation on the one hand and outbreaks of unrest or rebellion on the other. He documented the difficulty of ensuring the appointment of honest officials and cited the frequency of complaints against vicars, rectors, and castellans, although not all of these complaints were necessarily justified. There may have been a greater awareness of the problems they faced, but relatively few prominent officials were ever dismissed or punished, and nothing effective seems to have been done to improve the administration of Florentine territory.[8]

Although it is by no means the main theme of his book, David Herlihy discussed briefly the processes of establishing Florentine domination over neighbouring Pistoia, a domination that was achieved only very gradually. He stressed Florentine policy of securing the appointment of its own citizens to the traditional great offices of Pistoia. He demonstrated that the appearance of Florentines in these posts followed closely the ebb and flow of political events in the thirteenth and fourteenth centuries and serves as an index of Florentine control. This policy of controlling appointment to traditional offices allowed for Florentine domination with relatively little institutional change. Herlihy emphasised considerations of security as the motivation for particular Florentine interventions in Pistoiese affairs. The victory of a hostile party in Pistoia provoked the decisive Florentine seizure of the city in 1351. Pistoiese loss of control over the strategically important mountain region led to the demand that a Florentine be elected to the office of captain of the mountains in 1373. Internal factional disputes over offices in Pistoia several times led to the despatch of Florentine commissioners to prepare the electoral bags. Nevertheless from 1351 until 1398 Pistoia was held comparatively loosely. It continued to choose its own *podestà* and retained control over the administration of its own finances, though required to make subventions to Florence, which might be substantial. By the early fifteenth century Pistoia was more closely integrated into the Florentine state, but traditional councils and offices remained, and the Pistoiese regarded service in these posts as by no means valueless.[9]

8. G. Brucker, *The Civic World of Early Renaissance Florence* (Princeton, New Jersey, 1977), pp. 208–225. Much of what he has to say applies to both subject cities and subject territory.

9. Herlihy, *Medieval and Renaissance Pistoia*, pp. 202–204, 223–234, 210–211, 219–231. Similar themes are treated, though more superficially, by E. Altieri Magliozzi, "Istituzioni

Apart from these discussions of Florentine rule in specific subject cities there are also valuable incidental comments by modern scholars in works that are primarily concerned with other aspects of Florentine government and administration. In the course of a discussion of the Florentine financial crisis of the mid-fourteenth century Marvin Becker argued that Florence's search for additional revenue led to increased pressure on its subject cities; Pistoia's defence contribution increased by fifty percent and that of San Gimignano doubled between 1353 and 1368. Such financial demands increased in the late fourteenth and early fifteenth centuries. Handsome sums were drawn from Pisa and other subject cities and, in at least some cases, a surplus remained after the costs of local defence and administration had been met. These mounting demands also led to a loss of financial independence; some local gabelles were collected by Florentine officials and paid directly into the Florentine *camera*. Becker also raised briefly the possibility that Florentine financial policy had a deleterious effect on the economic development of her subject towns.[10]

The economic effects of the establishment of Florentine rule over subject cities were also discussed briefly by Enrico Fiumi. The woollen industries of Prato and San Gimignano were affected by measures taken to protect the Florentine industry. Prato and San Gimignano, like other Tuscan city-states, had had laws prohibiting the acquisition of real property by outsiders. Under Florentine rule they were unable to maintain these prohibitions, insofar as Florentines were concerned, and Florentines acquired property there on some scale. Fiumi also recorded an increase in taxation in San Gimignano, noting that this was not peculiar to San Gimignano, but was part of a general increase in financial pressure on Florentine territory and in Florence itself.[11]

In an interesting recent article Julius Kirshner examined the con-

---

comunali a Pistoia prima e dopo l'inizio della dominazione fiorentina," in *Egemonia fiorentina e autonomie locali nella Toscana nord-occidentale del primo Rinascimento: Vita, arte e cultura*, Atti del Settimo Convegno Internazionale di Studio tenuto a Pistoia nei giorni 18–25 settembre 1975 (Bologna, 1978), esp. pp. 199–205.

10. M. B. Becker, *Florence in Transition, 2: Studies in the Rise of the Territorial State* (Baltimore, 1968), esp. pp. 187–188, 243–244, and "Economic Change and the Emerging Florentine Territorial State," *Studies in the Renaissance* 13 (1966), esp. pp. 34–35, 37.

11. E. Fiumi, *Storia economica e sociale di San Gimignano* (Florence, 1961), esp. pp. 185, 188–191, 214–216; *Demografia, movimento urbanistico e classi sociali in Prato dall'età comunale ai tempi moderni* (Florence, 1968), esp. pp. 126–128, 135–136, 168–169; "Fioritura e decadenza dell'economia fiorentina III," *Archivio storico italiano* 117 (1959), pp. 497–498.

cept of citizenship. This is relevant to the problem of the relations between Florence and its subject cities, because in some cases the act of surrender included clauses that offered inhabitants of the subject city rights of citizenship on favourable terms. For example, guildsmen of the subject city might be allowed to matriculate in the corresponding Florentine guild without payment of fees. Much more important, however, was the question of the eligibility of men from subject cities, especially notaries, to hold public office. This proved a contentious issue, and much of Kirshner's article is concerned with later legislation and legal opinions that tended to restrict officeholding by men from subject territories.[12]

Venice's relations with its subject cities and the formation of the Venetian territorial state have attracted a number of studies. In a long and immensely detailed article A. Pino-Branca considered the position of Padua during the first century of Venetian rule. He argued that the continuity of Paduan institutions and the autonomy enjoyed by Padua were only apparent; in practice Venice assumed direction of all aspects of Paduan civic life, sending out Venetian aristocrats to hold the most important offices, so that Padua became a "città soggetta." Although Venice aimed at equal distribution of financial burdens, and old forms of taxation were maintained, its own increasing financial needs led it to impose heavy taxation with new forms of levy and frequent requests for loans. Venice also assumed the direction of Paduan finances; Venice, not Padua, authorised the renewal of the Paduan *estimo,* decided how the proceeds of Paduan taxation should be used, and tried to improve the technical efficiency of the taxation and accounting systems. In matters of provisioning, trade, and industry, too, Venice controlled the general lines of policy closely and intervened constantly. Usually these interventions were intended to benefit Padua, but their effect was to limit severely the autonomy of the local authorities.

Venice was also concerned to promote its own interests and those of its citizens in Padua and Paduan territory. Venetian products were exempt from import prohibitions designed to protect Paduan industries, and when the export of essential supplies from Paduan territory was forbidden, goods destined for Venice were not affected. The Venetian

---

12. J. Kirshner, "Paolo di Castro on *Cives ex Privilegio:* A Controversy over the Legal Qualifications for Public Office in Early Fifteenth Century Florence," in *Renaissance Studies in Honor of Hans Baron* ed. A. Molho and J. A. Tedeschi (Dekalb, Illinois, 1971), pp. 229-264. On the tax liability of residents of subject cities: W. M. Bowsky, "A New Consilium of Cino of Pistoia (1324): Citizenship, Residence and Taxation," *Speculum* 42 (1967), pp. 431-441, and "Medieval Citizenship: The Individual and the State in the Commune of Siena, 1287-1355," *Studies in Medieval and Renaissance History* 4 (Lincoln, Nebraska, 1967), pp. 195-243.

government also sometimes granted privileges to individual Venetian citizens. An especial problem was the position of Venetians owning property in Paduan territory. Though Pino-Branca found it impossible to estimate the proportion of Paduan land owned by Venetians, the Venetian acquisition of Padua certainly encouraged Venetian investment there. The Paduans demanded that Venetian-owned property be included in the Paduan *estimo* and made liable for dues in Padua, or at least that Padua be compensated for the value of such property if the owners paid dues for it in Venice.[13]

Some of the problems considered by Pino-Branca had already been discussed by A. Bonardi in a study of rebels against Venetian rule in the crisis after the battle of Agnadello. Bonardi stressed that the question of Venetian-owned property in Paduan territory was important for both Venetians and Paduans once Venetian rule had come to an end. He distinguished, in the general attitude of Padua towards Venetian rule, between the aristocracy and upper bourgeoisie on the one hand and the lower classes in the city and peasants in the countryside on the other. The upper classes had lost power and influence by the concentration of authority in Venetian hands. They hoped that by surrendering to Emperor Maximilian (as opposed to the French king) they would be granted the many exemptions, privileges, and immunities enjoyed by the free cities of Germany. The lower classes, however, could hope for no benefits from such local autonomy; they remained conspicuously faithful to Venice, which had brought them peace and justice and had taken measures to assist agriculture.[14]

Pino-Branca occasionally compared specific aspects of Venetian rule in Padua and in Verona, Vicenza, and Treviso and frequently drew more general parallels with other Venetian subject cities, so that his conclusions have wider application than to Padua alone. He concluded that while Venice tried to promote the welfare of its subject territories as a whole, preventing one city or one section of society from benefiting at the expense of another, its policy was one of centralisation, and local autonomy was more apparent than real. In a brief article devoted to the administration of the Venetian *terraferma* as a whole, Carlo Guido Mor, on the other hand, stressed that separate pacts had been made with each city at the time of its submission, thus preserving local laws, local

13. A. Pino-Branca, "Il comune di Padova sotto la dominante nel secolo XV°," *Atti del Reale Istituto Veneto di Scienze, Lettere ed Arti* 93 (1933-34), pp. 325-390, 879-940, 1249-1323; 96 (1936-37), pp. 739-774; 97 (1937-38), pp. 71-100.
14. A. Bonardi, "I padovani ribelli alla repubblica di Venezia," *Miscellanea di storia veneta* ser. 2, 8 (1902), esp. pp. 317-337, 349-370.

customs, and local autonomy. He held a much more favourable view of Venetian government than did Pino-Branca, claiming that Venice respected these pacts not only in the letter but also in the spirit, with what he calls "onesta osservanza." He stressed continuity; where important officials had previously been nominated by the *signore* of a city, Venice simply took over these rights, maintaining traditional names for officials, such as *podestà*, rector, or captain. The only change was that these posts were now filled exclusively from the Venetian aristocracy, something that can have mattered little to the vast majority of the inhabitants of a subject city. The services of an experienced class of Venetian administrators, combined with the decline of local aristocracies and local parties, reduced causes of disorder and enabled Venice to bring to the *terraferma* peace and stability solid enough to survive the crisis of the war of the League of Cambrai.[15]

Some of these problems were also discussed by Angelo Ventura in his *Nobiltà e popolo nella società veneta del '400 e '500*. Unlike Mor, he argued that Venice did not regard itself as bound by the pacts of submission, though in normal circumstances it preferred to observe them. He stressed Venetian centralisation; although there was some local autonomy, and local aristocrats had a role to play in the government of their city, it was a limited role and their position was subordinate to that of Venetian aristocrats. They were therefore much more hostile to Venetian rule than were the lower classes. Ventura distinguished, however, between Venetian treatment of Padua and its treatment of Verona and some of its other subject cities. In Padua there was more feeling for the previous dynasty and Venetian rule was less secure; Padua therefore received harsher treatment than did other Venetian subject cities.[16]

The studies cited above raise many important questions about the rule of one city by another. To what degree were administrative ar-

---

15. C. G. Mor, "Problemi organizzativi e politica veneziana nei riguardi dei nuovi acquisti di terraferma," in *Umanesimo europeo e umanesimo veneziano* ed. V. Branca (Venice, 1963), pp. 1-10.
16. A. Ventura, *Nobiltà e popolo nella società veneta del '400 e '500* (Bari, 1964), esp. pp. 39-52, 92-96, 167-186. Some of these problems have recently been reconsidered by B. J. Kohl, "Government and Society in Renaissance Padua," *Journal of Medieval and Renaissance Studies* 2 (1972), pp. 205-221. He stresses continuity when Padua came under Venetian rule; most of the offices to which the da Carrara *signori* made appointments in the Trecento went to Venetian aristocrats in the Quattrocento, while lesser communal councils continued to be open to Paduan citizens. There was enough local autonomy to keep alive a dream of power among the Paduan aristocracy, but not enough to satisfy their ambitions. Like Bonardi and Ventura, Kohl distinguishes between the aristocracy and the lower classes in their attitude to Venetian rule.

rangements governed by considerations of security? Did outside rule bring great institutional changes and close control by the ruling city, or was there continuity and a measure of local autonomy? To what extent was the subject city free to arrange its own internal affairs, elect its own officials and councils, and control its own finances? Was local autonomy real or only apparent? A subject city was expected to pay for its own defence and administration and might also be required to make contributions to the ruling city for wider needs, but were these heavy and frequent enough to be regarded as oppressive? Was the subject city free to arrange its own economic affairs? If the ruling city controlled the economic life of the subject city, did it try to promote the subject city's interests, or did it pursue its own economic interests and grant favours to its own citizens? The studies so far discussed have given such a wide variety of answers, even when considering the same place and the same period, that it is clear that the last word has not been said, even for the prominent examples of Venice and Florence.

Venice and Florence were both centres of large, complex territories. They governed many subject towns, some quite large, others small enough to be considered villages. Consequently, the distinction between subject towns and subject territory is sometimes unclear. Furthermore, the Venetian and Florentine states were both formed and developed over an extended period of time, and some of the changes undergone by their subject cities may be attributable to the passage of time and changing circumstances rather than to rule from outside. Finally, Venice and Florence both played an active, positive role in the general Italian politics of the time, which meant that they had to provide for needs and face problems that did not arise for lesser states. There seem to be no modern studies of the rule of one city by another at a more modest level, although the problem was by no means confined to Venice or Florence.[17]

There therefore seems to be a place for a study of the rule of one city by another where the ruling city was of lesser importance than Venice or Florence. The period of Pisan rule in Lucca is suitable to serve as such a case study. Pisa's domination was on a smaller scale territorially than that of Venice or Florence. It involved the rule over a single city and its territory, covering a fairly limited geographical area. Pisan territory included some other urban communities, but Lucca was the only centre

---

17. There are a few brief remarks about Paduan rule over Vicenza in J. K. Hyde, *Padua in the Age of Dante* (Manchester, England, 1966), esp. pp. 109, 221-227, 255-256, and about Sienese rule over Montepulciano in S. Favale, "Siena nel quadro della politica viscontea nell'Italia centrale," *Bollettino senese di storia patria* 43, n.s. 7 (1936), esp. pp. 315-320.

large enough to be called a subject city.

Pisan rule forms a short, well-defined period, lasting just over twenty-five years. The comparative brevity of its duration reduces the danger of ascribing to Pisan rule changes in Lucca that may rather have resulted from the passage of time. The brevity of Pisan rule also makes possible effective comparisons with the years before Lucca fell to Pisa and more particularly with the succeeding period, when Lucca was again an independent, self-governing republic. One can thus more easily distinguish problems or policies common to the fourteenth century from those that were the result of the particular circumstances of Pisan rule.

The period of Pisan rule is, however, long enough to enable one to follow changes and developments. Modifications and changes were made in the methods of government in the light of experience. Pisa's primary difficulty was that Lucca would never accept outside rule willingly, let alone with any degree of enthusiasm. Lucca was still large and powerful enough to be dangerous if pushed too far, especially if it were to enlist the aid of Pisa's enemies. Such a subject city was a difficult one to hold. Pisa needed to develop a system of government firm enough to ensure its domination, yet not so harsh as to provoke the Lucchese to resistance.

It is possible to get a reasonably clear picture of Pisan rule in Lucca, because the period is generally well documented, especially from Lucchese sources. Therefore an appropriate prelude to the study itself is a description of the resources of the Lucchese and Pisan Archives. Research in the Archivio di Stato in Lucca is greatly facilitated by the existence of an excellent printed inventory, the *Inventario del R. Archivio di Stato in Lucca*.[18] This six-volume work describes the evolution of those institutions with surviving records; it also lists, sometimes in detail, the content of the records. The Archivio di Stato also possesses a seventeen-volume manuscript inventory that gives greater detail on some of its holdings, especially the years and months covered by each number in the various series.

For the period 1342–1369 nos. 17, 24, and 31 in the series Capitoli contain treaties and leagues in which Lucca was involved, and no. 31 also contains a copy of the diploma in which Charles IV made the Pisan Anziani imperial vicars of Lucca in 1355. Capitoli no. 19 is an important source, since it contains the fourteen compositions negotiated be-

---

18. Hereafter cited as *Inventario*. The original four volumes edited by S. Bongi (Lucca, 1872, 1876, 1880, 1888) have been supplemented by two further volumes of Archivi Gentilizi, vol. 5 ed. E. Lazzareschi (Pescia, 1946), and vol. 6 ed. D. Corsi (Lucca, 1961).

tween Pisa and Lucca from 1345 to 1362 and a number of other agreements that regulated their relations. Capitoli no. 55 lists those who took
an oath of loyalty to the Pisan doge, Giovanni dell'Agnello, in 1366.[19]

For Lucchese internal political affairs the Statute of 1342, compiled
under Pisan rule, survives as no. 5 in the series Statuti del Comune di
Lucca. For purposes of comparison the Statutes of 1308, 1331, and 1372
are nos. 1, 3, and 7 in the same series.[20] But the most important source
for Lucchese internal government is the series Anziani Avanti la
Libertà, which includes the acts of the Anziani and the records of council
meetings. These are by no means complete, however, and much of the
content of certain volumes is routine in nature—licences, safeconducts,
and the like. The series begins in 1330; nos. 17–46 cover the period of
Pisan rule, although little survives for the years 1362–1368.[21] Numbers
47–51 are files of original letters received by Lucca, 1348–1365, and an
additional file (no. 52) contains undated letters from the period of Pisan
rule. Numbers 54 and 55 are registers of outgoing letters, 1342–
1348.[22] These letters have been calendared completely, though not
always entirely accurately, in L. Fumi, ed., Regesto del R. Archivio di Stato
in Lucca, vol. 2, part 1 (Lucca, 1903). Numbers 57 and 58 in the series
Anziani Avanti la Libertà are files of proclamations on civil and criminal
matters and other similar material.[23] In the series Libri di Corredo alle
Carte della Signoria, nos. 4–59 list officeholders for the period 1327–
1510; nos. 12–33 cover the years 1342–1365.[24]

The series Curia de' Rettori nos. 1–30 runs from 1328 to 1367 and
contains the records of the various outside rulers of Lucca and the courts
held under their authority. Numbers 12–30 cover the various phases of
Pisan rule in Lucca, 1342–1367, but much of this series is concerned
with lawsuits, safeconducts, and proclamations rather than with political
affairs.[25]

It is indicative of the continuity of Lucchese institutions, despite
various changes of régime, that many of the Lucchese sources for the
period of Pisan rule are parts of series that begin before 1342 and in
many cases continue after 1369. This is especially true in financial and

19. *Inventario*, 1:59–60, 62, 65–66, 80.
20. *Inventario*, 1:31–35.
21. *Inventario*, 1:121–130. There are some retrospective references to Pisan rule in the
early volumes of the series Consiglio Generale, which record council meetings after
1369.
22. *Inventario*, 1:131–132.
23. *Inventario*, 1:132.
24. *Inventario*, 1:199.
25. This series is fully described in *Inventario*, 1:103–121.

11

judicial matters. The two basic series for the study of Lucchese finances are Camarlingo Generale, Introito-Esito, which records the receipts and expenditure of each *camarlingo generale,* and Ragionieri della Camera e del Comune. The series Camarlingo Generale, Introito-Esito (nos. 3–86), survives for the period 1330–1378, with a few fragments for years up to 1419. Numbers 22–79 cover the period of Pisan rule,[26] but complete figures do not survive for all these years. The Ragionieri accounts are probably more reliable, as well as being easier to use. The *ragionieri* were employed by the commune to audit the accounts of anyone who handled public money. Their accounts are therefore likely to include such moneys in full. They cover the accounts of the treasurers of special funds and loans as well as accounts of the *camarlinghi generali,* enabling one to obtain a reliable picture of Lucchese finances as a whole. Numbers 3–10 cover Pisan rule, out of the series 1–19 for 1331–1381.[27] The series Camarlingo Generale, Mandatorie, records authorisations for the disbursement of public money, as opposed to actual payments. The series survives in a long run, nos. 88–374 for the years 1333–1801, but there is very little for the years of Pisan rule; only nos. 94–98 cover the period 1342–1361.[28] A number of loans and *imposite* raised during the years 1344–1362 are recorded in the series Imprestiti nos. 2–8, but these records are unlikely to include all such loans.[29] Number 4 in the series Imposte Diverse e Straordinarie is a register of Lucchese payments to Pisa, 1348–1362, and nos. 2–3 and 5–14 in the same series record a number of extraordinary levies, 1344–1362, though most of them are of minor importance.[30]

There are also a number of records for individual *proventus.* Series Proventus no. 1 for 15 November 1335–April 1336 describes the various Lucchese gabelles, their yield, and also the main heads of communal expenditure. Numbers 2–12 in the same series, Proventi Incanti, 1337–1360, record the annual auctions of the gabelles, including the names of unsuccessful bidders and details of the bidding and of efforts and inducements by the commune to raise the prices offered. Numbers 13–30, Proventi Contratti, 1323–1433, contain the actual contracts of sale; nos. 22–29 cover the years 1343–1360.[31]

26. *Inventario,* 2:7.
27. Described in detail in *Inventario,* 2:179–190. There are some minor fragments for Pisan rule in nos. 17–19.
28. *Inventario,* 2:7. No. 87, however, records some household expenses of the Anziani, 1344–1352.
29. *Inventario,* 2:192–197.
30. *Inventario,* 2:89–94.
31. *Inventario,* 2:22–32. There are also some fragmentary accounts for the Pisan period in nos. 38–40.

For the years of Pisan rule very little material survives to document the *gabella maggiore,* the most important single branch of the revenues. There is no Statute of the Gabella Maggiore earlier than 1372 (no. 1 in the series Gabella Maggiore), and the series of *gabella maggiore* accounts, nos. 10–50 in the series Gabella Maggiore, Introito della Gabella, 1329–1433, contains very little before 1369.[32] There are some figures for the *dovana salis;* in the series Offizio Sopra il Sale, nos. 2–5, Dovana del Sale, Entrata e Uscita, 1339–1359, preserve accounts for a number of years of Pisan rule, and no. 6 records some arrears for 1343–1345.[33] In the series Gabella Sopra i Contratti e Testamenti nos. 2–18 preserve records of the *proventus dotium, testamentorum, venditionum et alienationum* for 1341–1369, and nos. 321–323 contain fragments for the *proventus pensionum et livellorum,* 1341–1350.[34] There is relatively little before 1369 for the other *proventus*: of the series Provento del Macello nos. 1–42 (1341–1465), only no. 1 (1341–1386) contains any material for the Pisan period; of the series Provento del Vino Venale nos. 1–5 (1342–1417), nos. 1–2 cover the years 1342–1379, and there is also a file (no. 6) containing some material for 1343–1356. There is nothing at all before 1369 for the *proventus farine* and only fragments for some of the minor proventus: Provento dei Molini no. 1, Provento dei Cittadini Silvestri no. 1, Provento de' Borghi e Sobborghi nos. 1–3, and Provento degli Usurai e Ospitatori no. 1.[35]

There are a few scattered accounts for the Pisan period for the vicariates of Barga, Camaiore, Massa, Pietrasanta, Vadriana, Villa Basilica, and S. Gennaro in the series Gabelle del Contado e delle Vicarie, the full run of which is nos. 1–93.[36] The series Estimo records measurements and valuations made in the various administrative divisions of the *contado* and in individual communes. These are arranged by locality rather than chronologically, but of the whole series of 231 volumes nos. 1–106 cover the period from 1284 to the end of the fourteenth century. Only a few of these volumes contain any material for the period of Pisan rule: nos. 21, 22, 25, 26, 30, 39, 68, 71, 75–86, 88, and

---

32. *Inventario,* 2:36, 39–40. No. 12 contains a fragment for May 1348; no. 13 preserves figures for January–March 1351 and a fragment for 1362. No. 51 (Apertura delle Casse Generali e della Cassa del Vino, 1344–1352) is also too fragmentary to be of much value. There are some scattered records of gabelles charged at individual gates (nos. 56, 62) and of tolls between Pisa and Pistoia (no. 66: for part of 1346 and a fragment for Feb. 1347).

33. *Inventario,* 2:121.

34. Described in detail in *Inventario,* 2:42–49, 52–53.

35. *Inventario,* 2:56–58, 60–65.

36. *Inventario,* 2:77–81, gives more details.

98. Most of this material is for the years 1346–1347 and for the vicariate of Camaiore, but no. 39 contains what appears to be a fragment of the general *estimo* authorised in 1366 (dated 1368).[37]

The Archivio di Stato in Lucca has very full records of the various courts and judicial authorities for the period of Pisan rule, and indeed for the fourteenth and fifteenth centuries generally. There are voluminous records for both the civil and criminal courts of the *podestà*. In the series Potestà di Lucca, Curia Civile, nos. 1–2117 run from 1324 to 1530; nos. 115–474 cover the period 1342–1369. In the series Potestà di Lucca, Curia de' Maleficii, Bastardello (i.e. accusations, summonses, and preliminary hearings in criminal cases), nos. 2118–4407 run from 1354 to 1763; nos. 2118–2125 cover the years 1354–1359, after which there is a lacuna until 1385. Numbers 4707–7101 in the series Potestà di Lucca, Inquisizioni, run from 1332 to 1801; nos. 4767–4911 cover the years 1342–1369.[38] Some of the acts of the various captains of the *custodia* and *conservatori* of Lucca during Pisan rule are preserved in the series Capitano del Popolo e della Città nos. 1–4 (1356–1366). The acts of the captain of the *contado* for some of the years of Pisan rule are to be found in the series Capitano o Bargello del Contado nos. 1 (Nov. 1342–Jan. 1343) and 2–11 (1356–1363).[39] Sentences were recorded separately and are preserved in the series Sentenze e Bandi nos. 1–513 for the years 1331–1804; nos. 11–42 cover the years 1342–1369.[40] The records of the major syndic and judge of appeals are preserved in the series Maggior Sindaco e Giudice degli Appelli nos. 1–401 for the years 1327–1402; nos. 75–198 cover the years 1342–1369.[41]

The following are details of the full run of the records of the lesser courts with the numbers and dates of the volumes covering Pisan rule: Curia di S. Cristoforo nos. 1–172 (1260–1356); nos. 127–172 cover 1342–1356. Curia delle Querimonie nos. 1–12 (1333–1347); nos. 3–12 cover 1344–1347. These two courts were then united and the series continues as Curia di S. Cristoforo e delle Querimonie nos. 173–248 (1357–1378); nos. 173–222 cover 1357–1369. Curia de' Foretani nos. 1–117 (1312–1399); nos. 30–92 cover 1342–1369. Curia de' Treguani nos. 1–98 (1328–1478); nos. 37–91 cover 1342–1369. Curia Nuova di Giustizia nos. 1–82 (1328–1349); nos. 54–82 cover 1342–1349—the

37. *Inventario*, 2:127–157, deals with the *estimo* in some detail.
38. *Inventario*, 2:327.
39. *Inventario*, 2:340, 386–388.
40. *Inventario*, 2:400.
41. *Inventario*, 2:391–393. Much of the content of these volumes appears to consist of cases heard as judge of appeals rather than examinations of retiring officials as major syndic.

series is then continued as Curia Nuova di Giustizia e dell' Esecutore
nos. 83–154 (1351–1396); nos. 83–126 cover 1351–1369. Curia de'
Visconti e de' Gastaldoni nos. 1–81 (1331–1372); nos. 29–77 cover
1342–1369. Curia del Fondaco nos. 4–163 (1337–1402); nos. 10–54
cover 1342– 1364.[42]

The Archivio di Stato in Lucca also possesses large numbers of
notarial *protocolli*, preserved in the series Archivio de' Notari. The
resources of the series Archivio de' Notari are described by E. Lazzareschi in *L'Archivio de' notari della repubblica lucchese* (Siena, 1916), which
includes a list of some forty-four notaries active at various dates during
the period 1342–1369 (pp. 20–21).

Lucchese sources can be supplemented from those in the Archivio di
Stato in Pisa. The series Comune A 29 and 37 (Protocolli di Capitoli) include documents important to Pisan-Lucchese relations, such as the
grant of an imperial vicariate over Lucca by Charles IV in 1355, the
twenty-year renewal of the league between Pisa and Lucca and the re-
election of the Pisan Anziani as captains, governors, and defenders of
Lucca in 1357, and the peace concluded by Pisa and Lucca with
Florence in 1364. Comune A 53–65 (Cancelleria del Comune),
1345–1361, contain the records of various Pisan councils, including
much material concerning Pisan rule in Lucca. Comune A 107–143
(Cancelleria degli Anziani: Provvisioni degli Anziani e Consigli del
Popolo), 1343–1369, are less valuable for Lucchese affairs, but Comune
A 122 records mandates for the payment of *stipendiarii* serving in the
Augusta in 1355. There are relatively few volumes of Pisan letters for
this period, but the following registers of letters from the Pisan Anziani
survive and include some Lucchese material: Comune A 205
(1340–1342); Comune A 206 (1361–1362); Comune A 207, 208 (1368).
In addition to these public records there are also some valuable private
documents preserved in the Archivio di Stato in Pisa, notably an account of the payments made to the Pisan *camarlingo* for 1366–1367 by ser
Piero Raù, who held the office of treasurer of the gabelles and *proventus* of
Lucca for those years (Deposito Raù, Pergamena 19 Jan. 1369 [Pisan
style]).

The surviving archival material is full enough to make a study of the
period of Pisan rule in Lucca possible. The primary aim of this study is
to determine the nature of the rule of one city by another in a particular
case. I hope to show what Pisan rule in Lucca meant for both the Pisans
and the Lucchese. From the Pisan point of view, what solutions did the
Pisans find to the problems of ruling a relatively large neighbouring city

42. *Inventario*, 2:293–302, 393–396.

that accepted their rule only reluctantly, and what benefits and burdens did their rule in Lucca bring them? From the Lucchese point of view, what did it mean to be ruled by a neighbour and old enemy: what burdens and restrictions were placed on them, what degree of autonomy did they enjoy, and what measure of civic life were they able to maintain?

I

The Organisation of
Pisan Rule in Lucca

THE CIRCUMSTANCES of the establishment of Pisan authority might be thought to have placed the Pisans in a position to dictate whatever terms they liked. Lucca's misfortunes did not begin with the surrender to Pisa in July 1342. Since the death in 1328 of Castruccio Castracani, who had built up a Tuscan state for himself based on Lucca, the city had not enjoyed independence, but had passed from one outside lord to another—six different rulers between 1328 and 1341. The Lucchese had been reduced to circumstances in which they had virtually no say in their own fate, and the city had several times been sold to the highest bidder.[1] The latest of these outside rulers, Mastino della Scala, lord of Verona, found himself unable to hold Lucca after the loss of Reggio threatened his communications, and he therefore looked round for a purchaser. He agreed to sell the city to Florence, but the Pisans, who had put in an unsuccessful bid, saw Florentine acquisition of Lucca as too great a threat to their own security to go unchallenged. They resorted to force and for eleven months kept Lucca under siege, while the Florentines tried to raise the siege and take effective possession of the city. The conflict was thus between Florence and Pisa, not between Pisa and Lucca; the issue was whether Florence or Pisa should obtain possession of Lucca, not whether Lucca should remain free or fall to Pisa.

When Lucca eventually surrendered to Pisa the terms were extraordinarily generous for a city that had long since ceased to control its own destiny, had been bought and sold several times in the previous fifteen years, and had finally been taken by siege. According to the terms agreed upon on 4 July 1342, there was to be a fifteen-year league between the two cities. Pisa was to have the custody of Lucca, its walls and defences, the citadel known as the Augusta (which had been built by Castruccio Castracani), and also Pontetetto and the tower of Montuoli. Lucca was to bear the cost, but the number of guards and their rates of pay were laid down, and Lucca was to have no further financial obligations for these garrisons. For the duration of the war with Florence Pisa was also to have the custody, at Lucchese expense, of certain other fortresses in the Lucchese *contado*, including Cerruglio, Porcari, Collodi,

1. *Inventario*, 1:91–103.

and S. Gennaro, but these were to be restored to Lucca once peace was made. Lucca was to be ruled "ad comune" by Anziani, *podestà,* and other officials, whom the Lucchese should elect themselves, provided that they were not enemies of Pisa. The Pisans undertook not to interfere directly or indirectly in Lucchese government or financial affairs. Pisa promised not to alienate Lucca or the Augusta or to assign them to anyone else, and when the fifteen-year period was over Lucca and its territory were to be restored to independence.[2]

Had these terms been observed they would have rendered rule by another city as bearable as it was possible for it to be. Indeed such a system could hardly be described as Pisan rule of Lucca at all. However, it must be doubted whether the terms were really workable. They might have been satisfactory for the rule of a very large and powerful city over a much smaller and weaker neighbour. But Pisa was probably not strong enough to rule a city as large as Lucca in this way, without even the right to put its own garrisons in most of the fortresses of the *contado.* Held on so light a rein Lucca would soon have tried to free itself, and Pisa could never have felt secure even in the limited authority granted by the agreement. In fact the terms began to be eroded almost at once. A clause in the agreement itself authorised the Anziani of Pisa and Lucca to issue any decrees necessary in the future for the benefit of the two communes,[3] and the original terms were to be altered beyond recognition by many subsequent agreements and decrees. As early as September 1342 the Lucchese Anziani authorised Pisan intervention in

2. Notarized copy of the league of 4 July 1342, dated 20 Jan. 1344, in Capitoli 19, fols. 2r-8r, esp. caps. ii, ix, xi, xii, xviii, xxiii. Published by N. Cianelli in *Memorie e documenti per servire all'istoria del principato Lucchese,* 1 (Lucca, 1813), pp. 321-335. [All manuscripts cited are from the Archivio di Stato in Lucca unless otherwise stated.]

3. "Quod super predictis omnibus et singulis et quolibet eorum et dependentibus et connexis et super aliis quibuscumque pro tempore emergentibus per antianos comunis pisani et antianos comunis lucani qui sunt et pro tempore erunt pro dictis comunibus possint provideri et declarari, ordinari et fieri quecumque eis videbuntur utilia pro dictis comunibus et pro quiete et pace et bono et pacifico statu eorum eorumque civium et districtualium una vice et pluribus et quotiens eis ut dictum est videbitur et placuerit vel per sapientes utriusque comunis ab eis elegendis": Capitoli 19, fol. 8r, cap. xxiv. The terms of the agreement of 4 July 1342 were comparable with the agreement of 1351 between Florence and Pistoia. Under this Pistoia did enjoy considerable autonomy until 1398, but even in this case, though Florence was comparatively powerful and Pistoia relatively weak, considerations of security led to repeated Florentine interventions in Pistoiese internal affairs: D. Herlihy, *Medieval and Renaissance Pistoia* (New Haven and London, 1967), pp. 223-234, 228. Also N. Rubinstein, "Florence and the Despots: Some Aspects of Florentine Diplomacy in the Fourteenth Century," *Transactions of the Royal Historical Society* 5th ser. 2 (1952), p. 35.

the vital matters of the election of the Anziani, their chancellor and council, and other Lucchese officials for the coming year.[4]

In 1342 Pisa was under the nominal authority of the twelve-year-old Ranieri della Gherardesca, count of Donoratico, and he was appointed to a similar position in Lucca. He was elected captain-general of Lucca in July, and on 5 October 1342 he was given the title of protector, governor, and defender of Lucca for five years, with the right to appoint deputies. This put Pisan authority in Lucca on a different basis, since he was given authority over the defences of the city and *contado* and over the general administration of Lucca.[5] On his death in 1347 Lucca elected the Pisan Anziani as captains and defenders of Lucca with similar powers.[6] In 1355 Pisan authority was rendered independent of any grant from the Lucchese, when the Pisan Anziani obtained an imperial vicariate over Lucca from Charles IV. However the Pisans were careful to obtain the renewal for another twenty years of both the league between Pisa and Lucca and the election of the Pisan Anziani as captains and

---

4. The Lucchese Anziani gave messer Dino della Rocca, Count Ranieri's vicar, the same powers as they themselves had over the extraction of the Anziani for October and November, the sorting of the new *tasca*, and the election of officials for the year beginning 1 January 1343. He could also elect the chancellor of the Anziani for whatever period he thought fit and order the council of the Anziani. There is also a reference to the *tasche* of the Anziani having been compiled "per oratores et pacificatores pisani comunis tunc existentes in civitate lucana": Anziani Avanti la Libertà [hereafter cited as Anz. Av. Lib.]18, fols. 26r–26v, 21 Sept. 1342.

5. He is said to have been elected "generalis capitaneus guerre" by the General Council of Lucca in July 1342, though no such election is recorded: Anz. Av. Lib. 18, fol. 38r, 5 Oct. 1342. The General Council with additional *invitati* authorised the Anziani to elect him protector, governor, and defender of Lucca on whatever terms they thought fit, and to elect messer Tinuccio della Rocca as his deputy. The vote was 293 in favour to 5 against: Anz. Av. Lib. 18, fols. 36r–37v, 4 Oct. 1342. The Anziani then elected him for a period of at least five years on the same terms as his election as captain general, but his election as protector, governor, and defender was additional to his election as captain general and was not to derogate from it: Anz. Av. Lib. 18, fols. 38r–38v, 5 Oct. 1342. This was ratified and he accepted and took the oath of office: fol. 42r, 17 Oct. 1342. His term of office was renewed for another five years: Anz. Av Lib. 26, fols. 40v–41r, 28 March 1347; also fols. 41r–41v, 25 March, 15 April 1347.

6. This was done in the presence of the rector by the Anziani and 90 *invitati,* acting on authority granted to them by the General Council and *invitati.* The election was for five years ending 3 Oct. 1352. They were to have full powers concerning the "bono statu seu custodia" of Lucca: Anz. Av. Lib. 26, fols. 67r–68r, 7 July 1347. This was renewed by the Council of Fifty and *invitati* on 13 September 1352, when the Pisan Anziani were specifically stated to have "merum et mixtum imperium et gladii potestatem," though with a saving clause for the rights of the Lucchese Anziani: Anz. Av. Lib. 34, fols. 60r–61r, 13 Sept. 1352, printed by Cianelli in *Memorie e documenti,* 1:375–376.

defenders of Lucca.[7] Relations between Lucca and Pisa were also regulated by a series of compositions between the two cities. There were fourteen such agreements between 1345 and 1362; most of them were for a year only, and they became increasingly detailed and elaborate.[8] Much of the history of the relations between Pisa and Lucca can be read in these compositions.

Thus it is idle to discuss Pisan rule over Lucca in terms of the agreement of 4 July 1342, pointing out the various ways in which it was contravened. That agreement was superseded by the elections of Ranieri della Gherardesca and the Pisan Anziani as captains and defenders of Lucca and by other subsequent agreements to which Lucca consented and subscribed, though it may have had little option.[9] As a result of these changes in the basis of Pisan rule in Lucca and of many modifications in practice as problems arose, a system of government emerged which, if it bore little resemblance to that envisaged in the agreement of 4 July 1342, was far from the "assoluto governo dei suoi vicini" exercised "con ogni crudeltà e immoderatezza," of which Lucchese historians write.[10]

The system under which Pisa was to rule Lucca can be seen taking shape fairly shortly after 1342. Though Pisa administered some of the vicariates of the Lucchese *contado* directly, especially those recovered after 1342,[11] Lucca was always governed separately. There was no attempt at centralisation or the assimilation of Lucca. Pisa and Lucca were

---

7. Boehmer, *Regesta Imperii,* 7:157. Rough copy in Capitoli 31, pp. 273–275 (modern pagination; not foliated). Renewal of the league Archivio di Stato in Pisa [hereafter cited as A.S.P.] Comune A 29, fols. 117r–118r; election, fols. 118r–119r, both dated 19 May 1357.

8. These compositions are preserved in Capitoli 19.

9. The Lucchese are certainly found writing in terms that can hardly have expressed their real views. For example, in informing messer Ranieri of his election they wrote "dominationem vestram cum instantia deprecamur quatenus illam nostri gratia et amore velitis et placeat acceptare et dictam civitatem Lucanam pro contentatione nostri et nostrorum civium personaliter visitare. Nam ex hoc cives Lucani exhortationem magnam suscipient et inde non modicum letabuntur": Anz. Av. Lib. 26, fols, 41r–41v, 29 March 1347. When on his death they elected the Pisan Anziani, they claimed to do this "considerantes . . . quod ipsa civitas Lucana cum suo comitatu fortia et districtu sine capitaneo et defensore bene ac tute subsistere non valerat, considerantes etiam affectionem quam comune et populus pisanus et ipsius populi et comunis antianatus officium sive collegium habuerint et habent ad dictum comune lucanum et commodum et utilitatem quam et quod dicta Lucana civitas eiusque comitatus et districtus ex hiis verisimiliter consequentur": Anz. Av. Lib. 26, fols. 67r–67v, 7 July 1347.

10. S. Bongi in *Inventario,* 1:104 and 2:91.

11. The vicariates of Pietrasanta, Massa Lunense and some of the lands in the Garfagnana; also Cerruglio. See below, Chapter V, pp. 91–92.

never regarded as one state; they remained separate and Lucca retained its own administration. Pisa appointed, more or less directly, the officials responsible for the garrisoning of Lucca and the maintenance of order in the city and the *contado*. The traditional machinery of internal government was retained, but Pisa exercised an indirect control over the election of the *podestà*, Anziani, chancellor, and certain other officials. This gave it a sufficiently secure position to enable it to allow Lucca a large measure of autonomy in day-to-day affairs.

The most important of the officials that Pisa sent directly were the rectors and vicars, who combined the functions of castellans of the Augusta with the general supervision of Lucchese internal government. They also had a court with jurisdiction in certain cases.[12] From 1342 until 1347 Count Ranieri had sent vicars, vice-vicars, rectors, and castellans,[13] and from 1347 onwards the Pisan Anziani sent three Pisan citizens, usually a judge and two notaries, to act as their vicars and rectors in Lucca. In addition to their formal duties they acted as liaison between the Pisan Anziani and Lucca, sending back information to Pisa or passing on instructions to the Lucchese. For example, they warned Pisa of disaffection in Lucca in 1355 and sent on reports of threats to parts of the *contado* from exiles or other enemies.[14] The Pisans often used them to urge the Lucchese Anziani to make payments on time or to obtain information on a petition,[15] and in 1362 they were ordered to raise forces in Lucca for Pisan service.[16]

12. *Inventario*, 1:107. The series Curia de'Rettori, nos. 14–28, preserves the acts of their court. At least one of the rectors had always to remain in the Augusta: Anz. Av. Lib. 39, fols. 29v–30r, 10 April 1358; Anz. Av. Lib. 41, fol. 48v, 11 May 1361; Anz. Av. Lib. 42, fol. 52v, 27 June 1362.

13. *Inventario*, 1:103–106.

14. A.S.P. Comune A 60, fol. 29r, 5 June 1355; Comune A 62, fols. 47v–48r, 15 Nov. 1357; Comune A 64, fols. 9r, 10r–10v, 13 July 1359; Comune A 65, fols. 38v, 15 March, 45v, 17 March 1361. Also Comune A 206, fols. 42r, 9 March, 49r, 17 March 1361, concerning Florentines crossing Lucchese territory to Barga.

15. Anz. Av. Lib. 39, fols. 52r–52v, 16 May 1358; A.S.P. Comune A 206, fols. 12r, 24 Jan., 63r, 9 April, 88v, 9 May, 94r, 18 May, 106v, 2 June, 143r–143v, 4 Aug., 144v, 7 Aug., 184v, 20 Oct., 187r, 21 Oct. 1361. The Pisan Anziani sent a petition to the rectors, who were to consult with the Lucchese Anziani about it: *Regesto del R. Archivio di Stato in Lucca*, 2, part 1, ed. L. Fumi, hereafter cited as *Regesto* (Lucca, 1903), no. 767 (7 July 1356). The original is in Anz. Av. Lib. 50. The rectors were ordered to deal with a petition themselves: Comune A 206, fol. 153v, 27 Aug. 1361.

16. Anz. Av. Lib. 42, fols. 21v–22r, 31 March 1362. They were also instructed to compose a quarrel between the *podestà* and the *conservatore* (A.S.P. Comune A 206, fol. 86v, 7 March 1361), to assist in the execution of a sentence of the Curia S. Cristoforo (fol. 46r, 13 March 1361), to settle a dispute over an election in the hospital of S. Maria Filiporte (fol. 17r, 31 Jan. 1361), and to ensure that only citizens friendly to Pisa were elected to Lucchese vicariates (Comune A 60, fol. 48v, 20 June 1355).

The Pisans also elected an official as captain of the *custodia* of Lucca, whose duties were concerned with the custody and good order of the city. It became customary for this office to be held concurrently with that of *conservatore*, who was responsible for dealing with plotters and conspirators, those suspected of speaking in favour of the enemies of Pisa or Lucca, spreading rumours, carrying arms, or receiving rebels.[17] It was already said to be usual for the two offices to be held together in April 1352.[18] The link between them enabled the Pisans to control rather neatly the choice of this important official, because they elected the captain of *custodia*, whose election came first, and then informed the Lucchese Anziani of their choice, requesting that he should also be elected *conservatore*, as usual. Thus, though Lucca retained the formal right to elect the *conservatore*, it had no real influence over the choice of candidate.[19]

For much of the period of Pisan rule there was also an official called variously captain of the *contado*, *ufficiale sopra gli sbanditi*, or *bargello*, who was responsible for the maintenance of order and the capture of *banniti* in the *contado*. At first these duties were assigned to the captain of the *custodia* of Lucca and were performed by a deputy responsible to him,[20]

17. His full title was "conservator boni et pacifici status Lucane civitatis." For his duties: Anz. Av. Lib. 34, fols. 52v–54v, 22 Aug. 1352. He was also as "exactor" sometimes employed to enforce payment of dues: Anz. Av. Lib. 42, fols. 69r–69v, 3 Oct., 70v–71v, 12 Oct., 69r, 27 Oct. 1362, 132v–133r, 19 June 1363, Anz. Av. Lib. 43, fol. 37v, 16 July 1363.

18. Anz. Av. Lib. 34, fols. 23r, 12 April, 52v, 22 Aug., 79v, 31 Dec. 1352; Anz. Av. Lib. 35, fol. 61v, 28 June 1353. The offices had been held jointly earlier: *Regesto* nos. 374 (11 April 1348), 472 (23 Sept. 1350), 509 (10 April 1352); Anz. Av. Lib. 18, fol. 61v, 23 Nov. 1342.

19. Pisan elections of captain of *custodia*: A.S.P. Comune A 56, fols. 49r–49v, 27 Aug. 1349; Comune A 57, fol. 21r, 15 March 1350. Requests from Pisa that the captain of *custodia* also be elected *conservatore*: Anz. Av. Lib. 34, fols. 23r, 12 April, 52v, 22 Aug., 79v, 31 Dec. 1352; Anz. Av. Lib. 35, fols. 61v, 28 June, 68v, 15 July 1353; Anz. Av. Lib. 37, fols. 4r–4v, 9 Jan., 56v, 18 July 1354; Anz. Av. Lib. 39, fols. 45r, 30 April, 91v, 28 Sept. 1358; Anz. Av. Lib. 42, fol. 34v, 2 May 1362; *Regesto* nos. 545, 573, 579, 661, 690, 740, 788, 809, 818, 872. Lucca twice extended the term of office of a *conservatore* in obedience to letters from Pisa: Anz. Av. Lib. 26, fol. 46r, 16 Oct. and 27 Nov. 1347. Series Capitano del Popolo, nos. 1–4, contains the acts of some of these officials. One *conservatore*, Bartolomeo d'Arezzo, was described by Giovanni Sercambi as "homo crudelissimo": *Le chroniche di Giovanni Sercambi* (Rome, 1892), 1:119.

20. In Anz. Av. Lib. 18, fols. 14r–15r, 2 Sept. 1342, ser Scherlatto Maffei de Rasinopoli was authorised to proceed against *banniti, maladrini,* and those assisting them in the *contado*, though he was captain of *custodia* of Lucca. The series Capitano del Contado no. 1 contains condemnations by his deputy, ser Pino Bandini de Bibbiena, 4 Nov. 1342–25 Jan. 1343. See also *Inventario*, 1:388. Ser Guido da Pratovetere had similar duties: Anz. Av. Lib. 33, fol. 7r, 11 June 1352; *Regesto* no. 517. Also perhaps the *podestà*; *Regesto* no. 516.

but in 1352 the Pisan Anziani decided to revive the office of *ufficiale sopra gli sbanditi*. They enquired what *familia* and salary he had had and how and by whom it had been paid.[21] The Lucchese had the right to elect this official,[22] but again Pisa was able to control the choice of candidate, in this case simply by writing to say whom they had selected and requesting the Lucchese Anziani to elect him.[23] Pisa's first choice for the office, ser Arimberio de'Finetti of Città di Castello, abused his position. On complaints from Lucca that he was releasing captured *banniti* and extorting money from Lucchese *contadini*, the Pisan Anziani allowed him to be replaced.[24] But Lucchese attempts to secure the dismissal of a later holder of the office were unsuccessful. Despite Lucchese complaints against ser Nuto d'Arezzo and the fact that he had been dismissed with the knowledge of Pisan officials in Lucca, the Pisan Anziani insisted not only that he be reinstated, but that he be confirmed in office for another six months.[25] The Lucchese clearly felt strongly about the matter; it took at least three increasingly peremptory letters from the Pisan Anziani before the Lucchese finally re-elected him.[26] The incident demonstrates

21. *Regesto* no. 512 (22 May 1352). Also nos. 516, 517. Anz. Av. Lib. 33, fol. 7r, 11 June 1352. His duties included capturing *banniti* and vagabonds, and men suspected of plotting against Lucca or Pisa, or carrying arms. Sometimes other duties, especially those of a military character, were committed to him: *Regesto* nos. 762, 769, 801; also A.S.P. Comune A 60, fol. 48r, 20 June 1355.

22. *Regesto* no. 517, 9 June 1352.

23. *Regesto* nos. 517, 526, 536, 594, 669, 686, 752, 783, 851, 856, 859. For the Lucchese electing the candidate named by the Pisan Anziani: Anz. Av. Lib. 33, fol. 7r, 11 June 1352; Anz. Av. Lib. 34, fols. 63v–64r, 31 Oct. 1352; Anz. Av. Lib. 35, fols. 37v, 10 May, 87v–88r, 9 Nov. 1353; Anz. Av. Lib. 37, fol. 33r, 18 April 1354. The series Capitano del Contado, nos. 2–11, contains the acts of some of these officials 1356–62.

24. He is said to have been "ab ipso officio digne remotus": Anz. Av. Lib. 34, fols. 63v–64r, 31 Oct. 1352; *Regesto* nos. 526, 527–529, 536.

25. *Regesto* nos. 707, 711–713, 725; A.S.P. Comune A 60, fol. 48r, 20 June 1355. Lucca was obliged to dismiss the candidate it had already elected to replace him and Pisa later insisted that he be compensated: *Regesto* no. 734.

26. The Pisan Anziani wrote on 30 October 1355, "quia sentimus electionem discreti viri ser Nuti de Aritio officialis bannitorum vestri comunis factam non esse miramur et merito nec credebamus expedire totiens vobis scribi debere de hoc": original letter in Anz. Av. Lib. 49, corresponding to no. 728 in *Regesto*. Also nos. 725–726. Pisa's insistence and Lucca's reluctance may be connected with the fact that he held office in 1355, the year of the abortive rising in Lucca against Pisan rule. There was further trouble over this office later, when Lucca objected to the proposed election of Pietro de'Marti of Pisa in January 1358 because the term of office of ser Giovanni de Rassignano, the current holder of the office did not expire until December of that year. Although the grounds they gave for their objection were that anticipated elections led to disputes, the person concerned may have been unacceptable. Pisa had already supported his claim to £125 for losses sustained in the rising of May 1355, despite a general amnesty: *Regesto* nos. 714, 851, 856, 859.

that the Pisans might signify their wishes in the form of courteously worded requests, but they expected to be obeyed. If their instructions were not quickly carried out, less courteous letters soon followed. This is, however, the only recorded example of Pisa insisting on an official who was clearly unacceptable to the Lucchese.

There was little *formal* change in the internal administration of Lucca, and traditional institutions and offices were retained. A new Statute was compiled shortly after the establishment of Pisan rule, and the decree authorising it asserted that a new Statute was necessary because of the confusion brought about by the many changes of régime in the preceding period.[27] This might be thought to imply that there were to be major modifications in the machinery of government, but the Statute of 1342 in fact retains the traditional arrangements for the election of such officials as the *podestà,* the Anziani, the chancellor, and the councillors. Pisan rule was to be less a matter of bringing about institutional changes than of controlling the selection of the holders of traditional offices. However, Pisan control of the selection of such officials might itself involve violations of statutory procedure.

Pisa was gradually able to control the choice of the *podestà.* Under the terms of the peace with Florence of 9 October 1342 the right to nominate the Lucchese *podestà* went to the duke of Athens, as lord of Florence, but this right lapsed when he was driven out the next year.[28] It is not clear how the *podestà* was chosen for the next four years,[29] but by the end of 1348 the system to be followed for the rest of the period of Pisan rule was well established. The Lucchese retained the formal right of election, but the Pisan Anziani nominated a single candidate, invariably a Pisan citizen, for them to elect.[30] If at first the Pisans "paternaliter

27. Series Statuti del Comune di Lucca no. 5, Statuto del 1342. The compilation of a new Statute was authorised by messer Dino della Rocca, vicar of Count Ranieri, and the General Council of Lucca, who empowered the Lucchese Anziani to elect *statutarii* for this. The vote was 198 in favour to 5 against: Anz. Av. Lib. 18, fols. 20v–21r, 10 Sept. 1342. Election of *statutarii* by the vicar and the Anziani: fol. 21v, 10 Sept. 1342. The Statute was completed by January 1343: Anz. Av. Lib. 20, fol. 2r, 11 Jan. 1343.
28. Capitoli 19, fols. 15v–16r. He was to nominate the *podestà* for the remaining fourteen and a half years of Pisan custody of Lucca, and did nominate for the next two semesters: *Regesto* no. 174 (6 May 1343); Anz. Av. Lib. 18, fols. 43v–44r, 22 Oct. 1343.
29. The *podestà* for the second semester of 1345, the whole of 1346, and the first semester of 1347 was a Florentine ghibelline exile living in Lucca, messer Ciupo degli Scolari. From the second semester of 1347 onwards the *podestà* was always a Pisan: *Inventario* 2:314–315; *Regesto* no. 229 (5 Sept. 1345); Anz. Av. Lib. 26, fol. 75r, 29 July 1347; Anz. Av. Lib. 28, fol. 20r, 19 Feb. 1348.
30. By 1348 the compositions between Lucca and Pisa contained a clause that in the election of the *podestà* "servetur modus consuetus": Capitoli 19, fols. 50v, 53r, 57r, 61r.

suaderunt"[31] the Lucchese to accept their nominee, and if the nomination was always in the form of a request, the system seems to have become more rigid as time went on. By 1358 the Pisan Anziani were requesting the election of a man they themselves had already elected.[32] Eventually they adopted the practice of electing a number of candidates at once, keeping their names in a "tasca" to be drawn out when the time came to fill the office.[33] This method of electing the *podestà* was a serious contravention of the provisions of the Statute of 1342, which laid down that no *podestà* should come from the same city as his predecessor,[34] but the control of this key office was essential for any power trying to rule another city.

Pisan rule brought no outward change in the various colleges and councils by which Lucca had been governed.[35] The college of ten Anziani (two for each of the five "porte" into which the city was divided) continued, as did the General Council and the two smaller councils of Fifty and Twenty. There is evidence that constitutional niceties were observed. For instance, the election of the *podestà*, formality though this now was, always took place in the General Council, as laid down in the

---

Lucchese election of a candidate named by Pisa: Anz. Av. Lib. 28, fol. 37v, 2 Sept. 1348; Anz. Av. Lib. 34, fols. 30r, 23 May, 63r–63v, 30 Oct. 1352; Anz. Av. Lib. 35, fols. 34r–34v, 18 April, 97v, 16 Dec. 1353; Anz. Av. Lib. 37, fols. 37r–37v, 21 April, 77r, 10 Nov. 1354; Anz. Av. Lib. 39, fols. 53v–54r, 21 May, 101r–101v, 23 Nov. 1358; Anz. Av. Lib. 41, fols. 52v–53r, 26 May 1361; Anz. Av. Lib. 42, p. 328 (modern pagination; no foliation), 29 Dec. 1363. Also *Regesto* nos. 446, 456, 458, 474, 476, 534, 562–563, 595, 597–598, 691, 727, 761, 763, 765, 843, 874–875, 930. On 22 Oct. 1349 the Lucchese wrote asking the Pisans for the name of the candidate, "quatenus de ipso nostro potestate placeat providere ut iuxta vestram provisionem exinde cum nostro generali consilio ut est moris electionem facere valeamus": Anz. Av. Lib. 47; no. 446 in *Regesto*. Also no. 618.

31. Anz. Av. Lib. 28, fol. 37v, 2 Sept. 1348.

32. Anz. Av. Lib. 39, fols. 53v–54r, 21 May, 101r–101v, 23 Nov. 1358; A.S.P. Comune A 206, fol. 98v, 21 May 1361. The renewal of the league between Pisa and Lucca on 19 May 1357 included a clause that the election of the *podestà* should be conducted in the way that had become customary: A.S.P. Comune A 29, fol. 117v.

33. *Regesto* nos. 562 (17 April 1353), 595 (20 Oct. 1353), 930 (3 June 1363); Anz. Av. Lib. 41, fols. 128r–128v, 27 Nov. 1361; Anz. Av. Lib. 42, p. 328 (no foliation), 29 Dec. 1363; A.S.P. Comune A 206, fol. 195r, 17 Nov. 1361.

34. Statuti del Comune di Lucca no. 5, Statuto del 1342, Lib. III, cap. i. It was only the method of selecting the *podestà* that was changed. His powers, the rules about his *familia*, underwent no significant modifications: Statuto del 1342, Lib. I, cap. i, Lib. III, caps. i and ii.

35. Cf. P. Silva, "Pisa sotto Firenze dal 1406 al 1433," *Studi storici* di A. Crivellucci, 18 (1909–1910), pp. 146–147, for much greater changes in internal government when Pisa came under Florentine rule.

Statute.[36] But, if the statutory machinery was to be allowed to continue to function, Pisa needed to exercise some degree of control over it. This applied above all to the key office of the Anziani. Pisa had already begun to interfere in the election of the Anziani in September 1342.[37] The Statute of 1342 laid down an elaborate procedure of indirect election, but apparently this was not long observed.[38] Pisa seems to have kept a close grip on this vital matter. The system of electing the Anziani for a year or more in advance and extracting the names from a *tasca* every two months apparently continued, and the conditions about eligibility were probably observed,[39] but Pisa took care that only men on whom it could rely were elected. The Pisan Anziani are found writing to their chancellor in Lucca for information about men suitable to be elected Anziani, which suggests that they had control of the selection of candidates.[40] As the *tasche* were

36. Statuto del 1342, III, cap. i; Anz. Av. Lib. 34, fols. 30r, 23 May, 63r–63v, 30 Oct. 1352. Other examples of the observance of the requirement of authorisation by a particular council: Anz. Av. Lib. 34, fols. 9v–10r, 27 Feb., 12r, 28 Feb. 1352; Anz. Av. Lib. 35, fols. 12r–12v, 30 Jan., 23r–23v, 20 March, 47r–50v, 5 June 1353; Anz. Av. Lib. 37, fols. 78r–78v, 30 Nov. 1354; Anz. Av. Lib. 39, fols. 37r–37v, 17 April, 46r–46v, 3 May, 102r–102v, 30 Nov. 1358. Prohibition on the Anziani taking action contrary to the Statute: Anz. Av. Lib. 39, fols. 20r–20v, 20 March, 34v–35v, 16 April 1358.

37. Anz. Av. Lib. 18, fols. 26r–26v, 19 Sept. 1342. The Lucchese Anziani granted messer Dino della Rocca "omnem auctoritatem et bayliam quam habet lucanum comune et collegium Antianorum lucani comunis in extrahendo Antianos pro mensibus Octobris et Novembris proxime futuris de Taschis seu Bussolo compilatis per oratores et pacificatores pisani comunis tunc existentes in civitate Lucana ante Kalendas Octobris per spatium decem dierum prout sibi videbitur et placuerit. . . . Item dominus vicarius possit assortire et ordinare gitas dictorum Antianorum hodie electorum pro decem mensibus per nos et consilium nostrum et consules mercatorum et alios sapientes ad predicta convocatos incipiendis in Kalendis Februarii proxime futuris duraturis duobus mensibus pro rata."

38. Statuto del 1342, II, caps. ii and iii.

39. Statuto del 1342, II, caps. ii and iii. It was necessary to be a Lucchese citizen of legitimate birth, aged at least thirty and possessing real property worth £1,000 in the Lucchese state. There was also a "vacation" of at least a year before the office could be held a second time, and certain close relatives could not sit in the same college. Lists of Anziani in *Regesto*, 2, part 1, pp. xix–xxix, and part 2, pp. xi–xxxv, show that many holding the office during Pisan rule belonged to the same families that held office before 1342 or after 1369.

40. Anz. Av. Lib. 48, 23 Nov. 1352 (no. 607 in *Regesto*, where dated 1353): "De sufficientibus viris lucanis votis pisani comunis in casibus occurrentibus consonis ex quibus Antianatus lucani officium pro futuris duobus mensibus reformari possit de quo nobis Antiani noviter scripxerunt et tu volumus ut sapienter et solicite te informas et de ipsis sufficienter informatus Pisas coram nobis accedas." The terms in which the Pisan Anziani write make it clear that at this point at least the Lucchese Anziani were either being selected separately every two months or that Pisa was not leaving the drawing out of the names entirely to chance.

apparently kept in Pisa, the election may well have been conducted there too. The sources do not make it clear whether the election was done by Lucca or Pisa, or a combination of both. However, a provision of the Pisan Anziani of 3 July 1362, referring to the reviewing and refilling of the *tasca* of the Lucchese Anziani with good men as seemed best to the Pisan Anziani, suggests that Pisa was playing a large part in the actual process of election, as well as controlling the choice of candidates.[41] Certainly the extraction of the Lucchese Anziani was normally done in Pisa; there are many letters from the Pisan Anziani giving the Lucchese Anziani the names of their successors.[42] It was apparently the Pisan Anziani who filled any vacancies due to absence, refusal to serve, or any other cause.[43] They also made the decisions in exceptional cases: in 1351 they elected the Anziani for just the next two months when there was too little time to remake the *tasca*,[44] and in 1355 they confirmed in office for

41. "Item quod tasca Antianorum lucani comunis revideatur et revideri debeat et reformetur et reformari debeat de bonis viris de quibus videbitur Antianis pisani populi": Capitoli 19, fol. 121r. Even the procedure laid down in the Statute of 1342 provided for the vicar to perform the important task of sorting the successful candidates into groups of ten, "predictus dominus vicarius solus cum dictis guardiano [fratrum minorum] et priore [Sancti Augustini] debeant sociare dictos nominatos de quibus fuerint obtentum decem simul videlicet duos per quamlibet portam et burgum prout eis melius visum fuerit." The vicar could also count the votes for each candidate, alone if he wished, or with the guardian and prior: Statuto del 1342, II, cap. ii. Lucchese sources contain almost nothing about the election of the Anziani, and are full enough for this silence to be significant.

42. *Regesto* nos. 471, 504, 511, 520, 524, 537, 547, 558, 566, 612, 642, 652, 662, 665, 684, 773, 789, 804, 814, 822, 834, 850, 869, 880, 882, 886, 896, 899, 911, 953, 959, 983. An examination of the originals of these letters reveals little of the exact process of election. Until about 1356 the usual formula was to give the names of the Anziani "quos duximus eligendos Antianos et pro Antianis lucani comunis." Later just the names were given, but the Pisan Anziani occasionally use the word "elegimus." There are some references to extraction from the *tasca*, "de taschis ipsorum Antianorum penes nos existentibus": A.S.P. Comune A 206, fols. 185v–186r, 21 Oct. 1361, and similar expressions, fols. 32v, 76r, 117v, 152r, 201v; also *Regesto* nos. 869, 886, 899. In April 1349 the extraction of the Anziani for the next sixteen months was to be done in Lucca, but the *tasche* containing the names were sent from Pisa. The Pisans had apparently selected the Lucchese Anziani and sorted them into colleges, fixing the period for which they were to sit, and also selecting the ten *spiccinati* as replacements for any who might be absent when their names were drawn out.

43. *Regesto* nos. 702, 729–30, 764, 887, 912, 913, 961; A.S.P. Comune A 206, fols. 33v, 23 March, 121r, 24 June, 156r, 30 Aug., 157v, 2 Sept. 1361. They would naturally have done so, if the *tasche* were kept in Pisa.

44. *Regesto* no. 499, 23 Nov. 1351. They excused a man who needed to be absent from Lucca and appointed a substitute: no. 576, 5 July 1353. They decided that a man who had changed his residence since his election should sit for his original *porta:* A.S.P. Comune A 206, fol. 186v, 21 Oct. 1361.

a further month the Anziani who had already served their two-month term at a time of internal unrest in Lucca.[45]

Closely connected with the Anzianate, and possibly even more valuable for Pisa to control, was the office of chancellor of the Anziani. He lived with the Anziani in the palace; he was present at their meetings, wrote their acts, and saw all petitions and incoming and outgoing letters.[46] He could obviously keep a useful watch on the Anziani and be an important source of information to Pisa. His value was increased by the fact that he held office for much longer periods than did the Anziani themselves. It was common for the chancellor to be reappointed; the same man might hold office for several years. As with the Anziani, Pisan intervention in the office of chancellor began very soon after Lucca fell to Pisa; the Pisan vicar was authorised to fill the office in September 1342.[47] After that the election seems to have been done by the Lucchese. In the first years of Pisan rule the office was held by a Lucchese citizen, as the Statute required, but later a Pisan was normally appointed, usually with a Lucchese as his scribe.[48] As with the *podestà*, a *tasca* of chancellors was kept and the names extracted as the office fell vacant.[49]

There is much evidence that the Pisan chancellor of Lucca performed functions beyond the normal scope of the office. He was sometimes used as ambassador between Pisa and Lucca.[50] He was employed in the delicate matter of proceedings against one of the Lucchese Anziani for

---

45. *Regesto* no. 692 (which should be dated 1 June 1355), A.S.P. Comune A 60, fol. 17r, 1 June 1355. Extensions of the office of the Anziani were not uncommon in Pisa in times of crisis; there were eight such extensions in the 1350s and 1360s: E. Cristiani, *Nobiltà e popolo nel comune di Pisa* (Naples, 1962), p. 210 and n. 132. It had occasionally been done in Lucca before 1342: *Regesto*, pp. xiii–xix. The Pisan Anziani also apparently elected directly as the next Lucchese Anziani ten citizens whose names were brought back in writing from Lucca by Pisan ambassadors who had recently been there: A.S.P. Comune A 60, fol. 48v, 20 June 1355.
46. Statuto del 1342, Lib. II, cap. iii. Petitions were only to be read and dealt with in his presence.
47. Anz. Av. Lib. 18, fols. 26r–26v, 19 Sept. 1342.
48. Statuto del 1342, Lib. II, cap. iii. *Regesto*, 2, part 1, unnumbered page following p. xxix, contains an incomplete list of Lucchese chancellors, 1333–1361.
49. *Regesto* nos. 884, 927, 942; Anz. Av. Lib. 39, fol. 94v, 8 Oct. 1358: the Pisan Anziani wrote asking the Lucchese to elect a man "de taschis cancellariorum vestrorum per nos nuper extractus per ipsum officium assumendo." Similarly A.S.P. Comune A 206, fols. 31v, 19 Feb 1361, and also 156r, 31 Aug. 1361, where the Lucchese were asked "de ipso electionem facere seu nostram electionem more solito confermare."
50. A.S.P. Comune A 55, fol. 29r, 10 Nov. 1345. Also *Regesto* no. 658, 19 June 1354.

disloyalty to Pisa.[51] He provided information on Lucchese affairs,[52] and he acted as the agent of the Pisan Anziani in seeing that their instructions were obeyed.[53] The appointment of a Pisan to this office, so closely connected with the innermost counsels of Lucca, must have been an invaluable method of exercising discreet supervision without overt intervention in Lucchese affairs.

The Statute of 1342 also provided for a General Council of two hundred and fifty members, fifty for each of the five *porte* of the city, and for two smaller councils of Fifty and Twenty. Pisa does not seem to have intervened directly in their election. The councils of Fifty and Twenty were elected by the Lucchese Anziani in the presence of one or two of the Pisan rectors.[54] As Pisa had taken care to ensure the selection of reliable Anziani, probably nothing further was necessary to ensure the election of acceptable councillors. At least one of the Pisan rectors was almost invariably present at council meetings, and this must have discouraged the discussion of anything likely to be ill-received in Pisa.[55] These councils,

51. A.S.P. Comune A 206, fol. 50r, 17 March 1361. The Anziano was Bartolomeo Ronghi. The exact nature of his offence is not clear, but there are references to his arrest and confession and to proceedings against him and others by the *conservatore*: A.S.P. Comune A 206, fols. 50v, 19 March, 52v, 23 March 1361.

52. *Regesto* nos. 512, 544, 546, 607, 647, 901; A.S.P. Comune A 57, fol. 23r, 22 March 1350. He was asked Lucchese intentions about certain ordinances that Lucca had sent for confirmation.

53. *Regesto* nos. 438, 548, 572, 585, 586, 631, 667, 672; Anz. Av. Lib. 36, fols. 82r–83v, 8 Nov. 1353. *Regesto* no. 625: he was reproved because the Lucchese Anziani wanted to pay a sum due half in florins and half in silver *grossi*.

54. Each council held office for six months beginning 4 May and 4 November. The council of twenty "bonorum virorum" consisted of four citizens from each of the five *porte* of the city, and they with the addition of another six citizens per *porta* made up the Council of Fifty. The elections of these councils, including the names of the councillors, are recorded very frequently: Anz. Av. Lib. 34, fols. 24r–25r, 18 April, 61r–61v, 20 Oct. 1352; Anz. Av. Lib. 35, fols. 34v–35v, 18 April, 86r–86v, 19 Oct. 1353; Anz. Av. Lib. 37, fols. 71r–71v, 20 Oct. 1354; Anz. Av. Lib. 39, fols. 44r–44v, 17 April, 97r–97v, 19 Oct. 1358; Anz. Av. Lib. 41, fols. 31r–31v, 12 April, 115r–115v, 12 Oct. 1361; Anz. Av. Lib. 42, fols. 71v–72r, 19 Oct. 1362, 122v–123r, 25 April, pp. 307–308 (modern pagination; no foliation at this point), 19 Oct. 1363.

55. The names of one or two Pisan rectors present are almost invariably given. Exceptions are so rare that it may be that the names have been accidentally omitted rather than that no Pisan rector was present, though on 23 June 1358 a council where no Pisan rector is recorded as attending was said to be held with the licence of the rectors: Anz. Av. Lib. 39, fols. 66v–67r. Other councils where no Pisan rector is named as present: Anz. Av. Lib. 35, fols. 35v–36r, 20 April 1353; Anz. Av. Lib. 42, p. 307, 19 Oct. 1363. A comparison of the councillors stated to be present and the voting figures suggests that the Pisan rectors also had a vote. On at least one occasion it was one of the Pisan rectors who made the proposal that was put to the vote (Anz. Av. Lib. 41, fol. 87r, 16 Aug. 1361), though this was normally done by a Lucchese councillor.

especially the Council of Fifty, are recorded as having met regularly and frequently, and it was there that the basic business of the Lucchese commune was conducted.[56] There is less evidence for the method of electing the General Council, but the procedure laid down in the Statute of 1342 was probably followed.[57] The names of the members of the General Council for certain years have been preserved, sometimes with indications of the meetings at which they had been present.[58] The business transacted in the General Council was important from a legal point of view, but was often formal in character; certain sentences had to be read there, sales of *proventus* were formally approved there, and important elections were conducted there, such as those of the *podestà* and of Lucchese ambassadors.[59] The General Council seems to have retained this role under Pisan rule, meeting relatively infrequently for the conduct of the most solemn, but often formal, business.

The Pisans hoped to round off their position by securing the appointment of a Pisan as bishop of Lucca. They began to press for this in October 1348, several months before the death of Bishop Guglielmo Dulcini.[60] The Lucchese were obliged to second their efforts, writing to the pope and a number of cardinals.[61] The Pisans had still not given up

---

56. Meetings of the Council of Fifty, usually listing the councillors and *invitati* present, are recorded very frequently. There are fewer mentions of the Council of Twenty, but the following meetings are recorded for 1352: Anz. Av. Lib. 33, fols. 4r, 15 Feb., 7r, 11 June, 11v, 31 July; Anz. Av. Lib. 34, fols. 8v, 28 Jan., 11v, 27 Feb., 12r, 28 Feb., 14v, 6 March, 23r, 12 April, 31r, 31 May, 43v, 22 July, 47v, 23 July, 52v, 22 Aug., 59r, 5 Sept., 62r, 23 Oct., 63v, 31 Oct., 68r, 9 Nov., 78v, 29 Dec., 79v, 31 Dec. 1352. There is no reason to believe that the council did not meet regularly in other years also.

57. Statuto del 1342, Lib. II, cap. v.

58. The names of the General Council for 1351, which met at least four times: Anz. Av. Lib. 32, fols. 82r–87v. The General Council for 1353, which met at least eight times: Anz. Av. Lib. 36, fols. 84r–88v; and that for 1355, which met at least four times: Anz. Av. Lib. 38, fols. 52r–57r.

59. Statuto del 1342, Lib. I, cap. cviii, Lib. II, cap. vii; also Anz. Av. Lib. 34, fols. 49v–50r, 6 Aug. 1352. The election of the *podestà* and other important business is regularly recorded as having been conducted in the General Council. There are also numerous references to the election of ordinary officials in the General Council in November each year, and occasional references to the Lucchese Anziani acting on a mandate from the General Council, even where no such council meetings are themselves recorded.

60. *Regesto* no. 406b, 19 Oct. 1348. The bishop died on 8 April 1349: *Regesto* no. 424.

61. *Regesto* nos. 406b, 407, 411–414, 424–425, 431, 438, 442, 445.

hope in September and October 1349, when they sent another embassy, "cum dictum negotium multum oportet comuni pisano."[62] The effort was not successful, and eventually the Pisans had to rest content without this final strengthening of their position in Lucca.[63]

62. A.S.P. Comune A 56, fols. 62r–62v, 19 Sept. 1349, fols. 74v–76r: instructions for embassy to the pope, 9 Oct. 1349. The Pisan candidate, fra Niccolò of S. Martino, was said to be universally desired as bishop of Lucca. The Lucchese again had to join in these efforts: Regesto no. 445. Lucchese living outside Lucca and therefore much less subject to Pisan influence may have worked against these attempts, as Fumi suggests in the introduction to the Regesto, p. x. For other efforts against Pisa by Lucchese living outside their city, G. Tommasi, "Sommario della storia di Lucca," Archivio storico italiano 10 (1847; reprinted anastaticamente, 1969), p. 219.

63. Regesto no. 452, 21 Feb. 1350: Berengario Blasini, treasurer of the Patrimony, announced his election as bishop of Lucca. For similar attempts by Padua to obtain the appointment of a favourable bishop in the subject city of Vicenza, see J. K. Hyde, Padua in the Age of Dante (Manchester, England, 1966), pp. 225–226, and for Venice choosing bishops for its subject cities, A. Bonardi, "I padovani ribelli alla repubblica di Venezia," Miscellanea di storia veneta ser. 2, 8 (1902), p. 334.

II

The Administration of Lucca under Pisan Rule

EVEN without a Pisan as bishop, Pisan control over Lucca was secure. Garrisoning the city, the Augusta, and the fortresses of the *contado,* appointing rectors to oversee Lucchese affairs, controlling the peace-keeping offices of *podestà, conservatore,* and captain of the *contado,* and ensuring reliable Anziani, chancellors, and, indirectly, councils, Pisa felt secure enough to allow the Lucchese a large measure of autonomy in matters of ordinary administration. Internal affairs that did not affect finance or the security of the state—though admittedly these are large qualifications—were left to the Lucchese. The Pisans might intervene spasmodically, and some individual Pisan officials might interfere in matters that were outside their office, but the general policy was to leave internal affairs to the Lucchese.

This is the more striking, given the fact that the Pisans were often invited to intervene. The establishment of Pisan rule over Lucca encouraged men to address petitions directly to Pisa over the heads of the Lucchese Anziani. There was an obvious temptation for those who felt they had been unfavourably affected by a Lucchese decision to appeal to Pisa. The vicariate of Camaiore provides a good example of this. Lucca had agreed on the petition of the communes of the vicariate to have a new *estimo* compiled. After twenty months' work the new *estimo* was almost completed when the Lucchese heard that a Pisan notary had been instructed to tour the vicariate and ask in each commune if the local inhabitants were satisfied with the result. Lucca wrote to the Pisan Anziani explaining that it was the rich communes and individuals, who did not want to pay their proper share of dues, who had made false complaints to Pisa.[1] In other cases a petition seems to have been addressed to Pisa in the first instance. In 1352 Cerruglio petitioned for the continuation of a concession on the price at which it had to receive salt.[2] The communes of the vicariates of Valdriana and Villa Basilica petitioned for a reduction

---

1. Letter of the Lucchese Anziani to Pisa, 20 Feb. 1348: original in Anz. Av. Lib. 47; no. 350 in *Regesto.* For the *estimo* itself: Anz. Av. Lib. 24, fols. 20r–23v, 24 March 1346. Also *Regesto* no. 289.
2. Anz. Av. Lib. 34, fols. 55v–56r, 28 Aug. 1352. Pisa remitted this to Lucca for action.

in the large number of officials whose salaries they had to pay.[3] An individual petitioned against an assessment on his son in an *imposita*.[4] Occasionally the Pisan Anziani were prepared to take action themselves, though never without making an enquiry. They ordered their rectors in Lucca to investigate a complaint by the men of the vicariate of Valdilima about increased claims by tax farmers[5] and conducted their own enquiry into a dispute about the obligation of the vicariate of Valdriana to contribute to the salary of the vicar of Cerruglio.[6] They granted the men of Pontito, in the vicariate of Valdriana, a special immunity with freedom from all dues except gabelles, the salt tax, and their share of the vicar's salary. Lucca was not consulted and only learned about it later.[7] In one or two other cases Pisa instructed Lucca to take a specific course of action in response to a petition, rather than leaving it to the Lucchese to decide how it should be dealt with. Lucca had granted the men of Aramo three years' freedom from legal proceedings for debt, and they had taken advantage of this to rob the house of one of their creditors. Having no other redress the creditor petitioned the Pisan Anziani, who took up his case and ordered Lucca to see that his property was restored and the guilty punished.[8]

But these cases are all rather unusual. There are relatively few examples of Pisa's taking action itself or issuing specific instructions to the Lucchese. The more usual practice was for Pisa to refer such petitions to Lucca with only very general instructions. The Lucchese were to settle

---

3. A.S.P. Comune A 206, fol. 5r, 15 Jan. 1361. Lucca was consulted about this and the decision left to it: Anz. Av. Lib. 41, fols. 25r–27r, 18 March 1361.

4. A.S.P. Comune A 206, fol. 74r, 21 April 1361. It was decreed that he should be regarded as a *forensis:* fol. 78r, 27 April 1361.

5. A.S.P. Comune A 206, fol. 106v, 2 June 1361.

6. A.S.P. Comune A 206, fols. 153r–153v, 26 Aug., 186v, 21 Oct., 193v, 11 Nov. 1361. They found that it was not customary and gave orders to Pisan and Lucchese officials that the men were not to be troubled for this. A similar case earlier: *Regesto* no. 826, 3 Sept. 1357.

7. Anz. Av. Lib. 36, fol. 58r, 5 Sept. 1353: Lucca freed them from a fine of £25 imposed by the official of the *fundaco* in 1349, as the offence was covered by this immunity. In one or two other cases the Pisan Anziani seem to have contemplated action without reference to Lucca (A.S.P. Comune A 206, fol. 189r, 27 Oct. 1361), but this involved a man accused of a crime and the *podestà* and rectors were instructed to deal with it.

8. Anz. Av. Lib. 31, fols. 17r–19r, 18 Dec. 1349; *Regesto* nos. 448–449. In 1361 the Pisan Anziani ordered Lucca to deal with a petition of the Cardinal of S. Lorenzo in Damaso, who held the Lucchese monastery of S. Giorgio in commenda, in such a way as to satisfy him, which probably did not leave Lucca much freedom of action: A.S.P. Comune A 206, fol. 146v, 11 Aug. 1361. Also *Regesto* no. 615, 10 Dec. 1353.

the matter, provide as they thought best, and see that justice was done.[9] In September 1348 a petition from the communes of the Six Miles was remitted to Lucca with the fairly general instruction that provision should be made so that the inhabitants were not reduced to beggary.[10] When Aramo petitioned for some relief from its debts in 1345, the Pisan Anziani undertook only to write to the Lucchese Anziani, asking them to make provision.[11] Even the bishop of Lucca, petitioning the Pisans that the men of the communes of the *Iura Episcopi,* over which he had jurisdiction, be freed from certain customary payments made to Lucca each year, was told that he should arrange this with the Lucchese.[12]

Pisa obviously could have taken advantage of such petitions to increase its authority in Lucchese internal government, had it wished to do so. There are no indications of such a policy. Pisa seems to have been reluctant to intervene in Lucchese internal affairs, even when it received direct petitions. The normal procedure was to refer such petitions to the Lucchese with only very general instructions, if any at all, about the action they should take. This happened very frequently. In many cases, though no petition or letter survives, Lucchese decrees contain statements that the case originated in a petition addressed to the Pisan Anziani but sent back to Lucca for action.

There were aspects of Lucchese life in which there was more Pisan intervention. Pisan consent seems to have been required for the issue of new ordinances, though the Pisan attitude is probably typified by a decree of 1350 that anything contrary to Pisa or the good custody of Lucca should be struck out of proposed new ordinances and the rest accepted.[13]

9. "Placeat vobis super ea providere et inde facere quod vobis videbitur convenire": Anz. Av. Lib. 54, fol. 82v (foliation at bottom of page), 14 Dec. 1344 (and not as given in *Regesto* no. 196). "Faciatis id quod juri et honori pisani comunis et vestrum videritis convenire," letter of Pisan Anziani, 4 June 1353: original in Anz. Av. Lib. 48; no. 568 in *Regesto*. "Provideatis prout melius videritis convenire": A.S.P. Comune A 206, fol. 5r, 15 Jan. 1361.

10. "Provideatis super ipsis in petitione comprehensis quod crederitis convenire ad substentationem comitativorum predictorum ne ex onerum gravaminibus mendicare cogantur," letter of 18 Sept. 1348: Anz. Av. Lib. 47; no. 390 in *Regesto*. Similar expressions in Anz. Av. Lib. 57, pp. 179–180, 20 Sept. 1348. The Anziani were to act together with the Pisan rectors.

11. A.S.P. Comune A 55, fols. 26r–26v, 20 Oct. 1345. The men of the commune had later dispersed, and were given grace by Pisa to return to their homes. Lucca then granted them relief from arrears of the salt tax from 1348 onwards: Anz. Av. Lib. 35, fols. 96r–96v, 8 Dec. 1353.

12. A.S.P. Comune A 55, fol. 27v, 24 Oct. 1345.

13. "Et petatur et sciatur a dicto Vanne [the Lucchese chancellor, who was a Pisan citizen] de intentione comunis lucani super qualibet parte dictorum ordinamentorum et que viderint venire contra comune pisanum vel bonam custodiam lucane civitatis

Pisan consent also seems to have been required for the pardon of *banniti* or the reduction of their fines. *Banniti* had not necessarily committed a very serious crime, and it was customary to grant pardons at certain feasts such as Christmas, Easter, and S. Croce to poor men whose inability to pay the fines imposed upon them had led to their imprisonment, and also to decree periodically a scale of reduced fines to enable men to be free of their banns more easily.[14] Such decrees could, however, affect Pisa, because they might involve the reduction or remission of fines due to Pisa or the cancellation of banns of Pisan officials, which could not be done without Pisan authorisation. In some cases public order might be affected.

Pisan intervention was not always unwelcome; Lucca sometimes actively sought Pisan assistance. In 1348 the Lucchese Anziani asked Pisan aid to prevent the men of Menabbio, where two-thirds of the houses had been destroyed in a fire, from abandoning their commune.[15] In 1349 they asked for Pisan aid in preventing the officials and men of Pietrasanta, once Lucchese but now administered by Pisa, from exacting dues from the property of Lucchese citizens there, since it had been agreed that the Lucchese were not liable for such dues.[16] Pisan assistance was even more valuable against the men of the communes over which the bishop of Lucca had jurisdiction, when they tried to evade their customary obligations to Lucca.[17]

---

excludatur exinde, alia vero consentiant'': A.S.P. Comune A 57, fol. 23r, 22 March 1350. Pisa confirming Lucchese ordinances: *Regesto* nos. 180–181, 455, 841; sending amended statutes of Lucchese vicariates, no. 650; ordering the observance of an ordinance they enclosed, no. 670.

14. Pisa confirming the amnesties that were routinely granted to prisoners at certain feasts: Anz. Av. Lib. 54, fols. 83r, 22 Dec. 1344, 116r, 24 Dec. 1345; *Regesto* nos. 197, 256; Anz. Av. Lib. 55, fols. 123v–124r, 14 Sept. 1348; A.S.P. Comune A 206, fols. 143r–143v, 4 Aug., 144v, 7 Aug. 1361. Also *Regesto* no. 369. Other ''secas'' and readmissions of *banniti: Regesto* nos. 420 (23 Jan. 1349), 580 (20 July 1353), 780 (26 Sept. 1356); A.S.P. Comune A 206, fols. 146r, 12 Aug., 147r, 11 Aug. 1361. The Pisan Anziani authorised those of Lucca to fix a ''seca'' for *banniti* who had made peace with their victims, but it was not to apply in cases of treason, forgery, highway robbery, arson, or crimes committed for money: Capitoli 19, fols. 120v–121r, 3 July 1362. Lucchese ambassadors raised the question of readmitting *banniti:* A.S.P. Comune A 56, fol. 64r, 28 Sept. 1349. Pisa also took an active interest in the exaction of the salaries of certain of its officials, including the captain of the *contado*, fines imposed by them, which went to Pisa, and money destined for defence or the repair of fortresses: *Regesto* nos. 715, 722–724, 733, 803, 826, 830.

15. Anz. Av. Lib. 55, fol. 111v, 16 March 1348; no. 359 in *Regesto.*

16. Original letter of 30 Sept. 1349 in Anz. Av. Lib. 47 (not as given in *Regesto* no. 443). Also *Regesto* no. 441.

17. The Pisan Anziani wrote 26 Aug. 1357 to the *conservatore* and captain of the *contado*, ''volumus et vobis presentis tenore mandamus quatenus ad petitionem Antianorum

Pisan intervention must have been much less welcome in the appointment to offices in Lucca. There were many minor offices in the courts, the financial administration, and the *contado* that were of no importance as far as Pisan control of Lucca was concerned, but nevertheless Pisa is found asking that a particular individual be appointed.[18]

There was also intervention in appointments to more important offices, especially that of vicar. In some cases Pisa seems to have been selling such offices. In 1347 the Lucchese Anziani wrote to the Anziani of Pisa, praising the achievements of Ciuccio Castracani degli Antelminelli as vicar of Gallicano, where he had managed to keep both the guelfs and the ghibellines quiet, something that none of his predecessors had ever managed to do. The Lucchese Anziani and the Pisan rectors in Lucca had therefore confirmed him in office for a further year, and they asked that Pisa accept this, even if money were offered for the office. They added that the salary and profits of Gallicano were only half those of the other Lucchese vicariates.[19] The Pisan Anziani agreed to this request without denying that they might in some cases accept money for appointments to offices.[20] Another indication that there were irregular ap-

---

lucani comunis contra quoscumque in consequenda iura lucani comunis et maxime contra illos qui dicuntur de iura domini lucani episcopi et illos qui dicuntur de terris lucani capitoli vestrum et officialium vestrorum prestetis libere brachium et favorem ut ipsum comune lucanum contra predictos suum debitum consequatur'': original letter in Anz. Av. Lib. 50; no. 820 in *Regesto*. Also nos. 469, 481–485.

18. *Regesto* nos. 793, 828, 837, 846, 888, 902. On one occasion Lucca is found electing the candidate named by Pisa with the consent of the official who had already been appointed to the post: Anz. Av. Lib. 48, 26 May 1352; no. 513 in *Regesto*. Pisa sometimes went beyond merely asking for an appointment; on 8 Nov. 1361, hearing that the Lucchese had not elected a particular notary as requested, the Pisan Anziani wrote ''miramur credentes vos causam justam excusationis habere non posse'' and instructed that he be elected ''ne contra vos turbationis materiam habeamus cum pro utili comunium vestri et nostri electio ipsa sit facta'': A.S.P. Comune A 206, fol. 173v. They also ordered the Lucchese to confirm the *camarlingo generale* in office for a further period: letter of 18 March 1357, Anz. Av. Lib. 50; no. 808 in *Regesto*. Also nos. 811, 812, 844.

19. ''Quare paternitatem vestram rogamus actenti quatenus si ab alio concive nostro vel forense de dicto officio pecuniam vobis porrigerentur velitis in predictis responderè prout honori vestro et nostro et saluti dicte vicarie vobis videbitur convenire. Nam dicta vicaria in utilitate et salario est pro dimidia aliarum vicariarum lucani comunis'': Anz. Av. Lib. 55, fol. 63r, 23 Sept. 1347; no. 338 in *Regesto*.

20. They replied that they were ''parati exinde respondere omnibus qui postulationem de eo facerent prout honori vestro et nostro et confirmationi dicte electionis viderimus convenire'': Anz. Av. Lib. 55, fol. 63r, 24 Sept. 1347; no. 339 in *Regesto*. There is a reference to another purchase of an office in January 1347, though not from Pisa directly. Messer Ranieri and the Lucchese Anziani, having heard of the death of messer Francesco Acceggia degli Antelminelli, who ''officium de Camaiore a

pointments was the case of Giovanni di Lemmo di Poggio in 1357, though there is no reason to believe that money was involved. His family and *consortes* had asked that he be given a Lucchese vicariate for each of the next ten years. Pisa agreed that he should have a vicariate for the next five years, leaving Lucca with only the formal role of carrying out the elections.[21] Interference in appointments to vicariates was, in fact, particularly frequent, though the candidates were almost invariably Lucchese. The vicariate (the governorship of one of the local divisions of the Lucchese *contado*) was a particularly important office, control of which was valuable in maintaining the Pisan hold on the Lucchese state.[22]

Apart from this intervention by the Pisan authorities there were also requests from influential individuals in Pisa, especially members of the Gambacorta family, for the election of particular candidates.[23] Pisan officials in Lucca also sometimes asked for appointments, and even tried to compel the Lucchese to make them.[24] All this undoubtedly constituted interference in Lucca's internal government, contrary to the terms of the agreement between Lucca and Pisa, but the number of recorded examples is not very great.[25]

Nuccino Boctaccii emerat," gave it to his son for the first semester of 1347: Anz. Av Lib. 55, fol. 52r, 2 Jan. 1347.

21. Anz. Av. Lib. 57, 24 Sept. 1357 (p. 325 in the modern pagination; no foliation). They also asked Pisa to have him knighted.

22. *Regesto* nos. 835, 836, 839, 906, 907, 909. The need to control appointments was not the reason given. In 1356 Pisa went so far as to replace the vicars of Valdriana and Valdilima chosen by Lucca, but this was for the first semester of the year, shortly after the rising in Lucca and at a time when parts of the Lucchese *contado* were still threatened by exiles: *Regesto* no. 738, 1 Jan. 1356. On 20 June 1355 Pisa had provided that the Pisan rectors and Lucchese Anziani were to appoint vicars who were "amici et devoti pisani comunis et presentis status . . . et aliter dicti rectores ipsas electiones fieri non permictant": A.S.P. Comune A 60, fol. 48v. In 1361 Pisa asked for the election of Guido Pasciuti of Lucca as vicar of either Valdriana or Valdilima for a year, but he had an imperial privilege for the office: A.S.P. Comune A 206, fol. 167r, 22 Sept. 1361. There is also an undated reference (the year to which it refers is uncertain) to messer Niccolò Buglie de' Gualandi as vicar of Valdilima and Valdriana for Pisa: Anz. Av. Lib. 58, pp. 633-634 in the modern pagination. All this applies in the vicariates still under Lucca. In the vicariates that had once been Lucchese, but which Pisa was now ruling directly Pisa naturally appointed the vicars, who would normally be Pisans.

23. *Regesto* nos. 531-532, 574-575, 587, 611.

24. Capitoli 19, fol. 5v, cap. xi, of the agreement of 1342.

25. Anz. Av. Lib. 40, fols. 10r-10v, 12 Oct., 11r-11v, 13 Oct. 1360; nos. 903 and 904 in the *Regesto*. Also nos. 793, 902, 908. In at least some cases there was some special reason for the request, such as a desire to compensate the candidate for losses or

There were probably many other examples of Pisan intervention that have gone unrecorded, but in general the ordinary methods of election were followed. Many officials were to be elected each November for the following year. This was done in the General Council, either by direct election or "ad brevia," a system whereby each councillor received a slip of paper, many of them blanks, but some of them inscribed with the name of an office to which the recipient then nominated a candidate. There are many references to elections that proceeded in the ordinary way.[26] Comparatively minor irregularities, such as holding the elections a little earlier or a little later than laid down in the Statute, required a special ordinance.[27]

Many offices required particular qualifications; some were reserved for judges or notaries, some for Lucchese citizens, and some for *forenses*. Records of the names of office-holders are by no means complete, but such indications as there are suggest that these qualifications were respected. Citizens of Lucca continued to be appointed to offices designated for Lucchese. Pisans appear in offices to which *forenses* had to be appointed, but there is no sign of them in those for which Lucchese citizenship was required, with a few very limited and particular excep-

---

reward him for services, though these would usually be services to Pisa rather than to Lucca. The patriarch of Aquileia and Gualtieri de Hochschlitz, the lieutenants that Emperor Charles IV left in Pisa in 1355–1356, intervened far more frequently in appointments to Lucchese offices (*Regesto,* nos. 678, 693, 775–776, 778–779, 781, 786), and the patriarch of Aquileia also asked for grants of Lucchese citizenship and other favours (nos. 679–680, 699, 703, 753, 777).

26. Statuto del 1342, Lib. III, caps. iv–vii, x. References to ordinary elections: Anz. Av. Lib. 26, fols. 124r–124v, 27 Nov. 1347; Anz. Av. Lib. 27, fols. 31r, 5 Nov., 31v–32r, 15 Nov., 33v, 22 Nov., 34v, 27 Nov. 1347; Anz. Av. Lib. 35, fols. 92v–93r, 30 Nov. 1353; Anz. Av. Lib. 39, fols. 102r–102v, 30 Nov. 1358. In April 1358 after complaints of irregularities the regulations were re-affirmed in greater detail: Anz. Av. Lib. 39, pp. 3–26 (modern pagination; no foliation), 29 April 1358. The Pisan rectors were present at the elections, and the Pisan Anziani seem to have confirmed them in some cases (*Regesto* nos. 339, 840, 845), and refused to confirm them in another (no. 842). In 1348 Pisa had apparently removed some officials elected in Lucca, but the number involved and the reasons for the removal are not stated: *Regesto* nos. 362, 29 March 1348, 365, 31 March 1348 (originals in Anz. Av. Lib. 47).

27. Anz. Av. Lib. 24, fols. 126r–126v, 29 Nov. 1346; *Regesto* no. 849, 12 Dec. 1357. Other minor irregularities: Anz. Av. Lib. 26, fols. 119r, 24 Nov., 124r–124v, 27 Nov. 1347, 143v–144r, 3 Jan. 1348. The Pisan rectors suspended elections "ad brevia" for four offices for the coming year, as the Pisan Anziani meant to confer them as they wished: Curia de'Rettori 26, p. 229 (modern pagination; no foliation), 25 Nov. 1360. But only four offices were involved, and they were not of major importance.

tions.[28] Even where the Pisan Anziani or individual Pisan citizens asked for appointments the candidate normally seems to have been properly qualified. In at least one case the Pisan Anziani agreed that another candidate be appointed to an office when it was pointed out that the appointment they had requested was contrary to Lucchese ordinances.[29] Pisan insistence on the strict observation of the statutes was occasionally an embarrassment to the Lucchese. In one case the Lucchese asked Pisa for permission to elect Giovanni Onesti vicar of Valdilima, despite a statutory provision to the contrary. Pisa agreed, but revoked the consent when it was discovered that, since only knights were eligible for the office, Onesti was not technically qualified.[30]

Tax farming and most of the offices in the financial administration continued to be in the hands of the Lucchese. The agreement of 14 August 1342 (which assigned Lucchese *proventus* to Pisa) and the first composition between Lucca and Pisa on 14 October 1345 had provided that all officials for the Lucchese *proventus* should be Lucchese, except that Pisa should have the right to elect the *camarlingo generale,* the *camarlingo* of the *gabella maggiore,* and certain other gabelle officials.[31] The *ragionieri* accounts show that these offices were held by Pisans until at

---

28. Statuto del 1342, Lib. III, caps. iv–vi; Anz. Av. Lib. 39, pp. 3–26, 29 April 1358. Examples of Pisans in minor Lucchese offices: Anz. Av. Lib. 26, fol. 123v, 26 Nov. 1347; Anz. Av. Lib. 57, p. 175, 5 Sept. 1348, p. 181, 22 Nov. 1348 (this is a file, but the items have been given a modern pagination). There are occasional appointments contrary to strict statutory requirements. The re-appointment of the existing major syndic was authorised by the Lucchese General Council, as no other suitable person could be found (Anz. Av. Lib. 35, fol. 62v, 3 July 1353); another official was confirmed in office (Anz. Av. Lib. 37, fols. 78r–78v, 30 Nov. 1354). The Lucchese Anziani asked to be allowed to make an appointment despite the "vacation" regulations, in view of the candidate's special expertise and the lack of any other suitably qualified person: letter of 19 May 1352, Anz. Av. Lib. 48; no. 510 in *Regesto.* Also nos. 638, 671. One major exception to the continuance of regular elections is, of course, the appointment of a Pisan citizen as chancellor of Lucca. The composition of 1357 laid down that the statutes were to be observed in the election of officials, except in the cases of the *podestà,* the chancellor, and the vicar of Gallicano, where "servetur modo et ordo proxime consuetus": Capitoli 19, fol. 78v, and repeated in later compositions, fols. 83v, 91r, 98v–99r, 108r, and, in 1362, fol. 117r. The Pisan Anziani were not to elect, confirm, or dispense from any other offices belonging to Lucca: Capitoli 19, fols. 85r–86r (1358).

29. *Regesto* no. 894. In another case they admitted they had been deceived and restored to Lucca the freedom to make the election: *Regesto* no. 823. Also nos. 825, 827.

30. Anz. Av. Lib. 37, fols. 27v–28r, 7 April, 28r–28v, 10 April 1354. Pisa on other occasions asked for the appointment as vicars of men who do not seem to have been knights (*Regesto* nos. 738, 909), or for appointments for a year instead of the statutory six months (nos. 906, 907, 909).

31. Capitoli 19, fols. 12v, 46r.

least 1345 and probably later, but by 1349, when the continuous series of the records begins again, all the officials of the Lucchese financial administration were Lucchese.[32] While Lucchese revenues were administered directly by Pisa, the Pisans also seem to have appointed one or two of their fellow citizens to individual Lucchese *proventus.* The Lucchese Anziani complained bitterly of the conduct of ser Bacciomeo Salvi of Pisa in the *proventus dotium, testamentorum, venditionum et alienationum.* They stated that he had forced Lucchese citizens to make payments for which they were not liable and had not handed over to Pisa all the money he had exacted in Lucca.[33] But the appearance of Pisans as officials of the Lucchese *proventus* or as buyers of them when they were farmed was extremely rare. The system of auctioning the various *proventus,* which had been disrupted during the siege of Lucca, was resumed in the autumn of 1342 on the same basis and under exactly the same conditions as previously. This continued until at least the early 1360s. The bidders, both successful and unsuccessful, for these *proventus* were almost invariably Lucchese, and indeed there was continuity of personnel; those who appear as tax farmers after 1342 were in many cases the same men who had engaged in this business before that date. The fact that the *proventus* remained in Lucchese hands meant, of course, that the profits of tax farming would go to Lucchese businessmen and also that individual Lucchese paying their gabelles and dues would be dealing with their fellow citizens and not with Pisans. The only *proventus* that were sometimes sold to non-Lucchese, though not necessarily to Pisans, were the *proventus barattarie,* the right to run a gambling den, and the *proventus meretricium,* the right to run a city brothel. The *proventus barattarie* was sold to a Pisan for the year 1348, though it was shortly afterwards re-sold to a Lucchese.[34] In 1361 the buyer was a Florentine and in 1362 a Pisan, though both resided in Lucca.[35] The *proventus meretricium* was bought by

32. Pisans as *camarlingo generale* 20 Aug. 1342–19 Feb. 1343, Ragionieri della Camera e del Comune [hereafter cited as Ragionieri] 3, fols. 51r–55r, 20 Feb.–19 Aug. 1343, fols. 33r–36v, 20 Aug. 1343–19 Feb. 1344; Ragionieri 4, 6r–7v, 20 Feb.–19 Aug. 1344, fols. 45r–48v, 20 Feb.–19 Aug. 1345, fols. 26r–28r (various foliations). Pisans as *camarlingo* of the *gabella maggiore,* 23 Aug. 1342–19 Feb. 1343, Ragionieri 3, fols. 19r–24r; 20 Aug. 1343–19 Feb. 1344, Ragionieri 4, fols. 3v–4r; 20 Feb.–19 Aug. 1344, fols. 36r–39v; 20 Feb.–19 Aug. 1345, fols. 10r–13v (various foliations). This probably came to an end with the composition, beginning 1 Oct. 1348, under which Lucca was to collect its own revenues. The Pisan Anziani named a Pisan, Filippo Clerici, as official of the *gabella maggiore* on 23 Nov. 1357: *Regesto* no. 844.

33. Letter of 8 June 1349 in Anz. Av. Lib. 47; no. 433 in *Regesto.* The sale of this *proventus* for the year beginning 1 Oct. 1348 is not recorded in the series Proventi Incanti or Proventi Contratti, as it is for the previous year and for 1351.

34. Proventi Contratti 24, fols. 49r–49v, 31 Dec. 1347., 6 Feb. 1348.

35. Proventi Contratti 29, fols. 110v–111v, 112r–112v.

a Pisan for the year beginning 16 October 1356, and for the year beginning 2 August 1358 by a Pratese who later transferred it to a Pisan.[36] In 1360 the buyer was again a Pratese.[37] However, all these non-Lucchese are said to have resided in Lucca, and the *proventus barattarie* and the *proventus meretricium* seem to have been regarded rather differently from the other *proventus*. They were sometimes sold to non-Lucchese even after 1369. The only other examples of *proventus* sold to non-Lucchese are the *proventus medie uncie panis* in the city, which was sold to a Pistoiese resident in Lucca for the year beginning 9 October 1356,[38] and the *proventus Cerrulii,* the local gabelle at Cerruglio, which was sold to a Pisan citizen, again resident in Lucca, for the year beginning 23 February 1357.[39] These very rare examples of sales to non-Lucchese must be set against regular and numerous sales to Lucchese. Obviously Pisa made no attempt to participate in the farming of Lucchese *proventus,* since Pisans do not appear even among the bidders at the auctions. This important aspect of Lucchese administration therefore remained in the hands of the Lucchese.

In general Pisa tried to ensure the continuance of an orderly and regular administration in Lucca. It tried to secure the observation of Lucchese statutes, to prevent irregularities and abuses by its officials, and to treat individuals fairly. When disputes arose or petitions were made, the primary Pisan reaction was to discover what the law was or what had previously been done in similar cases and then to decide the issue on that basis. The Pisan Anziani were probably not being entirely hypocritical when they wrote of the need to maintain justice "que est omnium mater et regina virtutum."[40] Petty acts of tyranny and injustice towards individuals would have alienated the Lucchese unnecessarily and weakened the Pisan hold on the city. The Pisans were careful to maintain the rights, especially the property rights, of individuals. The compositions between Lucca and Pisa stipulated that Pisa was to pay rent for any houses occupied by its officials.[41] If a man wanted to recover possession of a house, Pisa ordered its officials to

36. Proventi Contratti 28, unfoliated section at the end; Proventi Incanti 11, fols. 52r–53v.
37. Proventi Contratti 29, fols. 134r–134v, year beginning 10 Sept. 1360.
38. Proventi Contratti 28, fols. 34r–37r.
39. Proventi Contratti 28, unfoliated section at the end.
40. Anz. Av. Lib. 19, fols. 38r–38v, 28 Nov. 1342. Pisa searching for precedents: *Regesto* no. 647.
41. Capitoli 19, fol. 6v, cap. xix of the agreement of 1342. Included in the compositions 1345–1361, fols. 46v, 50v, 53v, 58r, 62r, 65v–66r, 74r, 78v, 84r, 91r, 99r, 108r. Also *Regesto* no. 263, 17 Jan. 1346 (Anz. Av. Lib. 55, fol. 7r).

vacate it immediately.[42] Pisa was also quick to compensate the owners of houses inside the Augusta that had been rented for the *familia* of the *conservatore* or for mercenary soldiers and damaged or burned down through their negligence.[43] Even when it was planned to rent the many apparently empty houses in the Augusta, the Pisan Anziani ordered the rectors to make careful enquiry about their ownership first, "manutenendo quemlibet in suo iure, si dominos reperitis earum."[44]

There were also efforts to check Pisan officials, to prevent disputes between them, and to prevent them from encroaching on matters which were not their concern. The Pisan rectors had a court, which was a continuation of the practice of earlier foreign rulers of Lucca. Though Bongi speaks of the arbitrary nature of this court, it is clear that it had precise and well-defined functions and that the various ordinary courts in Lucca continued unchanged. The rectors' court was to deal with both civil and criminal cases involving *forenses* and especially with cases involving mercenary soldiers.[45] The records of the rectors' court during the period of Pisan rule are by no means complete, but those surviving show some cases where at least one of the parties seems to have been Lucchese. It is not clear why these cases came into the rectors' court, though the frequent complaints that Lucchese citizens and subjects were registering as

---

42. A.S.P. Comune A 206, fol. 17r, 31 Jan. 1361. Another example: fol. 138r, 26 July 1361. Reprimands to Pisan officials for delays in vacating the house: fols. 145v, 8 Aug. and 160v, 8 Sept. 1361. Also *Regesto* nos. 259, 264, 13 and 17 Jan. 1346.

43. Anz. Av. Lib. 40, fols. 10r–10v, 12 Oct., 11r–11v, 13 Oct. 1360; nos. 903, 904 in *Regesto.*

44. A.S.P. Comune A 206, fol. 171r, 29 Sept. 1361. This did not prevent complaints from the owners of such property. Niccolò and Antonio Asquini complained that their grandfather had had three houses within the walls of the Augusta, "quas ipse Guccius cohactus per pisanos sicut fuerunt multi alii lucani cives ad vendendum ipsas domos comuni pisano vendidit ipsi comuni pro libris ducentis octuaginta monete pisane predictas domos que valebant tunc ultra florenos mille": Consiglio Generale, Riformagioni 3, fol. 85r, 30 Dec. 1371.

45. Bongi, *Inventario,* 1:91. That this court was arbitrary was technically true. Under the agreement of 4 July 1342 the jurisdiction of Pisan officials had been rather more limited: Capitoli 19, fols. 7r–7v, cap. xxi. In November 1342 it was provided that offences were to be dealt with according to the Lucchese Statute, but the court was given discretion to impose heavier or lighter penalties: Anz. Av. Lib. 19, fol. 38r, 28 Nov. 1342. The rectors' court was given jurisdiction over offences against the Lucchese sumptuary laws by *forensis* women and over licences for *forenses* to carry arms: A.S.P. Comune A 57, fols. 14r–14v, 20 Feb. 1350. The rectors seem to have been especially concerned with *forenses* generally, for example taking up the complaints of *forenses* who had been included in the *imposita grani* in Lucca: A.S.P. Comune A 206, fol. 49r, 17 March 1361. For the court of the earlier outside rulers of Lucca, see Curia de' Rettori nos. 1–11 and *Inventario,* 1:91–103.

forenses in order to evade tax burdens and other obligations provide one possible explanation.[46] In some cases the rectors' court may have been encroaching on the jurisdiction of the ordinary courts, but the limitations of its authority were generally recognised and its competence was occasionally challenged. On several occasions one of the parties maintained that the rectors' court could not deal with a case because it had already been settled in another court.[47] In another case the defendant argued that the matter was beyond the competence of the rectors' court.[48] There are also many examples to show that the rectors themselves recognised that their authority was limited to cases concerning *forenses* and left jurisdiction over Lucchese to the *podestà*. In 1353 the rectors ordered the *podestà* not to proceed against two men, a Veronese and a Lombard, on the grounds that, as *forenses,* they were accountable to the jurisdiction of the rectors.[49] However, the rectors accepted as justified the complaint of a man who had been fined by both the *podestà*'s and the rectors' courts, though he was not a *forensis,* and Lucchese citizens and *contadini* came under the jurisdiction of the *podestà*.[50] A particularly clear example is the case of seven men accused of the murder of Bartolomeo, son of Francesco Mordecastelli, in 1366. Three of the

46. Complaints about this: A.S.P. Comune A 62, fol. 45v, 10 Nov. 1357; Anz. Av. Lib. 40, fol. 76r, 24 Aug. 1360; A.S.P. Comune A 206, fols. 194r, 195r, 11 Nov. 1361, where it is said to be "in dampnum non modicum lucani comunis et sine utilitate aliqua pisani comunis." Also fol. 49r, 17 March 1361.

47. Curia de' Rettori 14, fols. 7r-7v (various foliations), 10 Jan. 1347, concerning a case in the court of S. Cristoforo; 45r-45v, 9 April 1347, concerning a case pending in the *podestà*'s court.

48. Curia de' Rettori 15, p. 151 (modern pagination; no foliation), 16 March 1349. The plaintiff maintained that the rectors' court was competent. It was even possible to argue that precedents from the time of Count Ranieri could not be applied to the period when the court derived its authority from the Pisan Anziani. *Forenses* could, of course, challenge the authority of the *podestà*'s court; a woman from Calci, in the Pisan *contado,* claimed on 28 August 1355 that since she was a *forensis,* the *podestà* was not a competent judge, and that her case belonged to the rectors: Potestà di Lucca, Inquisizioni, no. 4846, fols. 18r-19v.

49. Curia de' Rettori 18, pp. 165-166 (modern pagination; no foliation), 22 Oct. 1353. Anz. Av. Lib. 41, fols. 90v-91r, 30 Aug. 1361: the rectors take up the case of two *forenses* included in a Lucchese *imposita*. The treatment of *forenses* became rather a vexed question. In 1360 the Pisan Anziani instructed the rectors to examine the claims of men to be *forenses*. Lucca was not to be defrauded, but *forenses* were to be treated as such: Anz. Av. Lib. 40, fol. 76r, 24 Aug. 1360. The complaint of an individual and a Pisan declaration that he was to be treated as a *forensis:* A.S.P. Comune A 206, fols. 74r, 21 April, 78r, 27 April 1361.

50. Anz. Av. Lib. 35, fol. 8r, 21 Jan. 1353. The petition was accepted in principle, but since only the Pisan Anziani could quash sentences of the rectors' court, the other fine was reduced to a third.

accused, two from Buti in the Pisan *contado* and one from the *contado* of Pistoia, were tried in the rectors' court. The other four were Lucchese *contadini* and were left to the *podestà*.[51]

Nevertheless there probably were abuses by the rectors and other Pisan officials in Lucca. Even though most officials were only sent for a period of a few months, the temptations and possibilities for abuse are obvious. There is evidence that some officials were at the least over-zealous and tended to interfere in Lucchese affairs or encroach on the spheres of other Pisan officials. The compositions between Pisa and Lucca contained an increasing number of general and particular prohibitions of abuse and malpractice by Pisan officials. The composition of 1345 contained a general clause stating that Pisan officials should observe the Lucchese statutes,[52] and in 1350 an additional clause was introduced forbidding them to impede the collection of Lucchese *proventus* or to grant any immunities that would reduce their yield.[53] Later other prohibitions were introduced. The rectors were not to interfere in lawsuits between Lucchese citizens or *contadini* or in cases that involved Lucca,[54] nor were they to claim jurisdiction over men accused of defrauding the gabelles.[55] No rector or any other Pisan official was to act as advocate or counsel in any civil or criminal case in Lucca,[56] and procedures and penalties were laid down to deal with anyone in Lucca found trying to bribe the *podestà* or any Pisan official.[57] The *conservatore* was not to interfere in any matter outside his sphere of office,[58] and more specifically he was not to interfere in offences committed in Lucca before curfew or in the *contado* at any time.[59] Limitations were placed on the granting by

---

51. Curia de' Rettori 29, p. 567 (modern pagination; no foliation). The murder was committed on 23 July 1366 and the case began on 2 August the same year.
52. Capitoli 19, fol. 46v.
53. Capitoli 19, fol. 54r (1350). Repeated in later compositions, fols. 58r, 62r, 66r, 69v. Privileges and immunities from dues granted by Pisan officials in Lucca were cancelled: fols. 69v–70r (1355); also fols. 74v, 79r, 84r, 91r, 99r, 108r.
54. Capitoli 19, fol. 75r (1356), repeated fol. 79r. They were not to do this even on commission from the Pisan Anziani: fol. 84v (1358); also fols. 91v–92r, 99v–100r, 108v, and Anz. Av. Lib. 57, p. 5, 15 March 1358.
55. Capitoli 19, fols. 63v, 27 July 1353: regulations for the Pisan rectors. Also fol. 75r (1355).
56. Anz. Av. Lib. 36, fols. 82r–83r, 8 Nov. 1353.
57. Capitoli 19, fols. 102v–103r (1360), repeated, fols. 110r–110v (1361), 117v–118r (1362).
58. Capitoli 19, fol. 74r (1356), and repeated later, fols. 78r–78v, 83r–83v, 90v, 98r, 107v, 116v.
59. Capitoli 19, fols. 111r–111v (1361) and 118v–119r (1362). His jurisdiction was over offences committed in Lucca after the curfew bell and before the day bell.

Pisan officials of safeconducts to Lucchese *banniti.*[60] Pisan officials were also forbidden to grant security to debtors contrary to Lucchese statutes and without the consent of their creditors.[61] The rectors and the *conservatore* were not to force the Lucchese Anziani or council to elect anyone to any office without an express commission from the Pisan Anziani on pain of a fine of £100 *pis.,* nor were they to ask for such an election on pain of a fine of £50 *pis.*[62] Even the Pisan Anziani were forbidden to use the pretext of their imperial vicariate or their captaincy of Lucca to elect to any offices which should be filled by the Anziani and council of Lucca.[63] The Lucchese chancellor was not to impede or interfere in petitions to the Lucchese Anziani, though they had to be opened and read in his presence,[64] and the Lucchese Anziani were to be free to petition the Pisan Anziani with the knowledge of the rectors.[65]

If all these indicate abuses committed by Pisan officials in Lucca, they also show attempts by the Pisan home government to check them. Pisan officials, like those of Lucca, were ordinarily liable to an examination of their conduct on the expiry of their term of office. For Pisan officials this was carried out by the major syndic of Pisa, to whom the Lucchese had the opportunity of making their complaints, anonymously if they so wished.[66] In addition to this routine procedure the Pisans made special efforts to control their officials. They issued general ordinances that the statutes and customs of Lucca were to be observed and more specific decrees prohibiting particular malpractices, in some cases with heavy fines. They also gave orders to individual officials in particular cases. Only one register of letters survives for this period in the Pisan Archives, but it provides a number of examples of reprimands to Pisan officials and instructions not to interfere in Lucchese affairs. In the single year 1361 the Pisan Anziani had to deal with a dispute between the *podestà* and the *conservatore* over the limits of their respective jurisdic-

---

60. Capitoli 19, fols. 54r–54v (1350), and repeated later, fols. 58v–59r, 62v, 66r–66v, 70r, 75r, 79v, 85r, 92r–92v, 100r–100v, 108v–109r. The Pisan Anziani and other Pisan officials were not to order the freeing of any *banniti* during the compositions of 1358 (fol. 85r), 1359 (fol. 92v), and 1360 (fol. 100v).

61. Capitoli 19, fol. 85r (1358), and repeated later, fols. 92v, 100v, 109r, 117r.

62. Capitoli 19, fols. 85v–86r (1358), and repeated later, fols. 93r, 101v, 109r–109v, 119r–119v.

63. Capitoli 19, fols. 109r–109v (1361) and 117r (1362). Prohibitions with certain named exceptions: fols. 93r, 100v–101v.

64. Capitoli 19, fol. 112v, decree of the Pisan Anziani of 5 June 1361, repeated fol. 119v (1362).

65. A.S.P. Comune A 65, fol. 9v, 22 Jan. 1361; Comune A 206, fol. 13r, 25 Jan. 1361.

66. Anz. Av. Lib. 25, fols. 19v, 12 June, 47v, 24 Nov., 1 and 2 Dec. 1346; Anz. Av. Lib. 30, p. 17 (modern pagination; no foliation), 24 Jan. 1348. Occasionally when the

tions, and several warnings had to be issued to the *conservatore* about interference in matters outside his office.[67] Pisa had to deal with Lucchese complaints that its merchants' letters were being opened in a way not previously customary and that Pisan officials were interfering in the salt gabelle.[68] There were also complaints that the Anziani were being impeded from leaving the palace at night to visit their own homes. The *conservatore* was instructed not to molest them in this way: "pro honore officii antianatus et ipsorum antianorum quos tamquam nostros confratres cupimus benigne tractari."[69] In one case a Lucchese citizen had been wrongfully tortured.[70] Finally, Pisa had to issue more general orders that statutory procedures should be observed.[71]

There are no signs of any attempt to encourage Pisan immigration or to establish in Lucca a group of Pisans with special interests. There was indeed a provision in the new statute of 1342 to encourage marriages between Lucchese and Pisans. The Anziani were to elect a commission of five men twice a year to arrange such marriages, and financial in-

---

Lucchese complained of a particular official, the Pisan Anziani allowed him to be dismissed: *Regesto* nos. 526–529. For corrupt practices of Paduan officials in the subject city of Vicenza, J. K. Hyde, *Padua in the Age of Dante* (Manchester, England, 1966), pp. 109, 224.

67. A.S.P. Comune A 206, fols. 86v, 7 May, 101r, 26 May, 105r, 1 June 1361 (concerning interference in "in civilibus"), fol. 176v, 9 Oct. 1361 (a second warning in another matter). Also Anz. Av. Lib. 41, fols. 19r–19v, 26 Feb. 1361. There were a number of petitions from men who had been fined by both the *podestà* and the *conservatore* for the same offence (Anz. Av. Lib. 41, fols. 49v–50r, 19 May, 57v, 18 June 1361), but such confusions arising from unclearly defined or overlapping jurisidictions were not uncommon in medieval communes. There were also petitions from people fined by both the *podestà* and the captain of the *contado:* Anz. Av. Lib. 41, fols. 19v–20r, 27 Feb. 1361; Anz. Av. Lib. 42, fol. 141r, 16 Aug. 1363. On 3 July 1362 the Pisan Anziani agreed to appoint a commission to examine condemnations made by ser Guido da Sanminiato, ex-*conservatore*, beyond his sphere of office: Capitoli 19, fol. 120v.

68. A.S.P. Comune A 206, fols. 13v–14r, 25 Jan. 1361. Another, more insistent, letter from the Pisan Anziani to the official concerned: fol. 15v, 28 Jan. 1361. Also complaints that the Pisan rectors were impeding an *imposita grani* in Lucca and the raising of money in the *contado* to pay for it: A.S.P. Comune A 206, fols. 93r, 15 May, 94r, 18 May 1361.

69. A.S.P. Comune A 206, fol. 194v, 11 Nov. 1361.

70. A.S.P. Comune A 206, fol. 60v, 5 April 1361.

71. A man who had been arrested was to be handed over to the proper authorities: A.S.P. Comune A 206, fol. 59v, 3 April 1361. The *podestà* and the *conservatore* were both to drop proceedings, as the case had already been dealt with by the previous *podestà:* fol. 108v, 4 June 1361. The *conservatore* was warned that certain fines belonged to Lucca: fol. 194v, 11 Nov. 1361. The captain of the *contado* was asked to justify his actions in the case of a man who had petitioned: fol. 63r, 9 April 1361. *Regesto* no. 717, 19 Sept. 1355, for an earlier attempt by the Pisan Anziani to restrain an official.

ducements were offered: no gabelle was payable on the dowry contract, and the Lucchese Anziani were to give Lucchese taking Pisan brides a gift of up to £25. However there is no record that such a commission was ever elected, and nothing more is heard of the promotion of marriages between Pisans and Lucchese.[72]

There were legal barriers to the establishment of a group of Pisans with interests in Lucca, for Lucchese statutes prohibited the acquisition of land and houses by *forenses,* and this applied equally to Pisans. Lucchese citizenship was always quite distinct from Pisan citizenship. There were no provisions that the citizens of one should be regarded as citizens of the other, nor were there special arrangements permitting Pisans to hold offices reserved for Lucchese or to acquire property in Lucca.[73] The prohibition against the acquisition of land by non-Lucchese was especially important. It would be necessary to undertake a close examination of Lucchese records, especially the copious series of notarial records, before one could state with confidence that there were no significant contraventions, but extensive soundings suggest that the prohibition was observed. I have found no example of a sale of land to a non-Lucchese before 1364, when this prohibition was relaxed by

72. Statuto del 1342, Lib. II, cap. v. In contrast when Pisa came under Florentine rule marriages were at first prohibited, but this prohibition was soon abandoned: M. E. Mallett, "Pisa and Florence in the Fifteenth Century: Aspects of the Period of the First Florentine Domination," in *Florentine Studies,* ed. N. Rubinstein (London, 1968), p. 432. A similar prohibition, but with exemptions, in Vicenza under Paduan rule: Hyde, *Padua in the Age of Dante,* pp. 224-225.

73. Statuto del 1342, Lib. V, cap. xlv, Anz. Av. Lib. 14, fols. 12v-13r, 5 April 1339, also provided that no one was to sell property to anyone not subject to Lucca. Anz. Av. Lib. 14, fols. 88r-88v, 8 Dec. 1339: a licence was granted to a woman, possibly herself Lucchese, but the widow of Bono da Pistoia, to sell property to three men of Calci, in the Pisan *contado,* who lived in Lucca and undertook to pay the same dues as she did. Other cities also had prohibitions on the acquisition of lands by non-subjects: E. Fiumi, *Storia economica e sociale di San Gimignano* (Florence, 1961), p. 214; P. Riesenberg, "Citizenship at Law in Late Medieval Italy," *Viator* 5 (1974), pp. 338-340. But it was rare for subject cities to be able to maintain these against the ruling city. For various kinds of special arrangements for citizens of subject cities: J. Kirshner, "Paolo di Castro on *Cives ex privilegio:* A Controversy over the Legal Qualifications for Public Office in Early Fifteenth-Century Florence," in *Renaissance Studies in Honor of Hans Baron,* ed. A. Molho and J. A. Tedeschi (Dekalb, Illinois, 1971), esp. pp. 229-230, 234-236, 256-258; W. M. Bowsky, "Medieval Citizenship: The Individual and the State in the Commune of Siena, 1287-1355," *Studies in Medieval and Renaissance History* 4 (Lincoln, Nebraska, 1967), esp. pp. 220-223, 233-234; and B. G. Kohl, "Government and Society in Renaissance Padua," *Journal of Medieval and Renaissance Studies* 2 (1972), esp. p. 215. These arrangements did not go unchallenged, however.

Giovanni dell'Agnello, and very few leases.[74] Dispensations from this statute were occasionally granted, but they seem to have been regarded as a very serious matter and were only made in exceptional cases. That the very rare decrees of this sort often devote considerable detail to the special circumstances alleged suggests that such a grant was by no means automatic. It might be justified on the grounds that the beneficiary had long lived and worked in Lucca, or that it enabled the grantee to provide security for a Lucchese wife's dowry. The beneficiaries were not necessarily Pisans, and there is no evidence of an increased number of such dispensations being granted to Pisans after 1342. In any case the total number of such grants is microscopic.[75]

Lucca also seems to have been able to retain control of grants of citizenship without much interference from Pisa in this important aspect of civic life. While it was regarded as desirable to make grants of citizenship to *forenses* who wished to come and live in Lucca with their families, ply a trade, and pay dues and taxes, since new citizens would obviously help to fill the gaps left by those who had emigrated or died in the plague, Lucca imposed strict rules to prevent Lucchese *contadini* from abandoning their communes to become Lucchese citizens, leaving the other inhabitants to pay their dues and shoulder their burdens. Before they could ask for citizenship, *contadini* had to live in Lucca with their families, plying a trade and paying all dues and taxes there for five years, while at the same time paying all dues for any property they had in the *contado*. After five years they could ask that their share of the *estimo* of their commune be cancelled and citizenship granted. Very shortly after Lucca came under Pisan rule there was apparently a request from Pisa that a Lucchese *contadino* be granted citizenship. The Lucchese Anziani wrote to the Pisan chancellor explaining that this grant would be contrary to the statutes, though agreeing that it should be made if the Pisans still insisted.[76] It is not clear whether this grant was made, but the Pisans do not seem to have made any further such requests. In the 1340s

---

74. Potestà di Lucca, Inquisizioni, 4898, fols. 34v–35r, 29 Nov. 1364, and below, Chapter VI, pp. 116–117.

75. Anz. Av. Lib. 24, fols. 24r–24v, 31 March 1346; Anz. Av. Lib. 26, fols. 2v–3r, 3 Jan. 1347 (for the same man, who was from San Miniato); Anz. Av. Lib. 34, fols. 42r–43r, 4 July 1352: in order to provide a dowry for his daughter a man was allowed to sell property to a kinsman who was a Pisan citizen, as he could not find a Lucchese buyer. It should be pointed out that the seller was also a Pisan.

76. Anz. Av. Lib. 54, fol. 10r, 30 Aug. 1342, no. 131 in *Regesto*. Charles IV, through the patriarch of Aquileia, asked for grants of citizenship for Francesco Cioni of Corsanico and ser Manfredo Brondi of Camaiore, who almost certainly did not qualify under Lucchese statutes: Anz. Av. Lib. 49, letters of 27 Feb., 1 March 1355; nos. 679, 680 in *Regesto*.

the strict rules about grants of citizenship were not always observed; some *contadini* were allowed to become citizens while continuing to live in their communes, which gave rise to protests from their fellow *contadini*.[77] Nevertheless it was Lucca that made such grants and settled the resulting disputes. In December 1346 it was laid down that grants contrary to the strict statutory requirements could only be made by the Anziani, the vicar, and fifty *invitati* per *porta*. From about 1348 onwards grants of citizenship seem normally to have been made in the Council of Fifty.[78]

A number of Pisans must have been resident in Lucca temporarily as mercenary soldiers, sergeants guarding the Augusta or the city walls, holders of various offices, and members of the *familia* of officials. *Forenses* resident in Lucca who were not mercenaries, officials, or household servants had to take an oath each year. The records of these oaths are very fragmentary, but they probably give some idea of the relative numbers of *forenses* from different cities. In 1356 there were sixty-three Pisans in Lucca itself, with another forty-three in the *contado* and forty-one in the suburban communes.[79] In 1366 there were about a hundred and fifty in the city, with eighteen in the suburban communes and thirty-one in the *contado*.[80] The oath of 1366 may have been more carefully administered in view of the recent rise to power of Giovanni dell'Agnello as doge. Even if there was indeed the sort of increase in the numbers of Pisans resident in Lucca that these figures suggest, too much significance should not be attached to it. Eighty-eight *forenses* from Florence (including Prato) and seventy from Pistoia were resident in Lucca, as well as large numbers from the Valdarno, Valdinievole, and Garfagnana.

The fact that there was no significant group of Pisans with economic and other interests in Lucca must have been an important factor in the maintenance of a degree of Lucchese autonomy. It was certainly unusual for a subject city to be able to maintain prohibitions on the acquisition of land in its teritory by citizens of the ruling city. Florentines acquired property on a large scale in Pisan territory in the fifteenth century, and so did Venetians in Padua and other subject cities of the *terra-*

---

77. Anz. Av. Lib. 57, p. 7, 27 Sept. 1346, is such a grant made by Lucca.
78. Anz. Av. Lib. 24, fol. 139r, 5 Dec. 1346. For Venetian interference in the regulations concerning Paduan citizenship after 1406: A. Pino-Branca, "Il comune di Padova sotto la dominante nel secolo XV," *Atti del Reale Istituto Veneto* 93 (1933–34), pp. 375–380.
79. Curia de' Rettori 21, pp. 301–329 (modern pagination; no foliation). Rather curiously there were only about 25 Pisans among those taking the oath in the city and seven in the *contado* in 1357: Curia de' Rettori 22, pp. 207–226, 239–244 (no foliation).
80. Capitoli 55, pp. 3–80 (modern pagination; no foliation).

ferma.[81] This could be beneficial in that the new owners would be anxious to promote the economic prosperity of the regions in which they had invested. But it also had its disadvantages. It exposed the subject city to the pressure of powerful outsiders and was likely to lead to increased intervention by the ruling city to promote the interests of its own citizens, as in the question of whether such property should be included in the local *estimo* or taxed in the ruling city.[82] The fate of Florentine property in Pisa and especially of Venetian property in the cities of her mainland dominions became a vexed question when the subject city shook off the authority of the ruling city.[83] The prohibition on non-Lucchese acquiring land in Lucchese territory meant that Lucca was free of pressures of this kind during and after the period of Pisan rule. Motives for intervention were reduced, and Lucca was able to maintain more easily a degree of autonomy in internal affairs. Ultimately, when Pisan rule came to an end, this prohibition probably explains why the transition was so simple and why so little trace of Pisan rule remained.

81. Mallett, "Pisa and Florence in the Fifteenth Century," pp. 427–441; Fiumi, *San Gimignano,* pp. 214–216 and table p. 217; Pino-Branca, "Il comune di Padova sotto la dominante," pp. 925–927, and continuation in *Atti del Reale Istituto Veneto* 96 (1936-37), pp. 750–755; Hyde, *Padua in the Age of Dante,* pp. 224–225, 227.

82. Pino-Branca, *Atti del Reale Istituto Veneto* 93 (1933-34), pp. 924–940, and 96 (1936-37), pp. 739–744; Mallett, "Pisa and Florence in the Fifteenth Century," esp. pp. 439–441; Fiumi, *San Gimignano,* pp. 214–219.

83. A. Bonardi, "I Padovani ribelli alla repubblica di Venezia," *Miscellanea di storia veneta,* ser. 2, 8 (1902), esp. pp. 349–370. Similar problems when Vicenza shook off Paduan rule: Hyde, *Padua in the Age of Dante,* pp. 255–256.

III

The Economy

LUCCA was also allowed a large measure of autonomy in economic affairs. The city did not flourish under Pisan rule, but this was not because
of any policy that sacrificed its interests to those of Pisa or impeded
measures to assist its economy. Lucca was already much declined by
1342. Its economic difficulties went back at least to the early years of the
fourteenth century, when political disturbances within the city and
several changes of régime had led to repeated waves of emigration of
merchants and silk workers, so that Lucca's most important industry
was harmed and that of its rivals assisted.[1] By 1345 Lucchese ambassadors were instructed to ask for a reduction of the amount Lucca was to
pay the Pisans: "exponent et narrent eis gravedines et paupertates et
dissolutiones et malum statum lucane civitatis et diminutionem civitatis
et mercationum defectum."[2]

The Lucchese *contado* had also suffered heavily from invasions and
wars since the death of Castruccio Castracani. There were serious attacks on Lucchese territory in the period October 1330–February 1331,
in 1334, and again in September and November 1336.[3] Large numbers
of petitions from individuals and whole communes complained of
depopulation,[4] impoverishment, and indebtedness.[5] Immunities and

1. The most important of these was on 14 June 1314. For emigration from Lucca: N.
Tegrimi, *Vita Castruccii Antelminelli, Lucensis Ducis, 1301–1328,* R.I.S. 11 (1727), cols.
1320–1321; T. Bini, *I Lucchesi a Venezia* (Lucca, 1843), pp. 174–178; G. Livi, "I
mercanti di seta lucchesi a Bologna nei secoli XIII e XIV," *Archivio storico italiano,* ser.
4, 7 (1881), pp. 35–37.
2. Anz. Av. Lib. 54, fols. 95v–96r, 17 Feb. 1345; no. 206 in *Regesto.*
3. Anz. Av. Lib. 2, fols. 61r–61v, 11 Feb., 67r–67v, 10 March 1331; Anz. Av. Lib. 6, p.
11 (modern pagination; no foliation), 30 April, p. 27, 14 July, p. 29, 19 July, p. 37, 21
Sept. 1334; Anz. Av. Lib. 7, fols. 16r, 2 June, 35v, 31 Aug., 48v, 18 Oct. 1334; Anz.
Av. Lib. 10, fols. 75v, 11 June, 78v, 9 July 1336; Anz. Av. Lib. 12, fols. 4r, 7 Aug., 9r,
1 Sept., 9v, 3 Sept., 17r, 30 Sept., 27v–28v, 5 Oct., 31r, 9 Oct., 37v, 5 Dec., 51r, 29
Dec. 1336.
4. Anz. Av. Lib. 4, fols. 19r–19v, 24 Nov. 1333; Anz. Av. Lib. 5, fol. 11v, 4 Jan. 1334;
Anz. Av. Lib. 7, fols. 2r, 12 April, 7v, 14 May, 64r, 22 Dec. 1334; Anz. Av. Lib. 12,
fol. 33v, 26 Oct. 1336; Anz. Av. Lib. 14, fols. 75r, 75v, 22 Oct. 1339. There are one or
two examples of communes uniting because of depopulation: Anz. Av. Lib. 14, fols.
75v–76r, 22 Oct. 1339; Anz. Av. Lib. 18, fols. 76v–77v, 17 Dec. 1342.
5. Anz. Av. Lib. 5, fol. 11v, 4 Jan., pp. 30–31 (modern pagination; no further foliation),
14 Jan. 1334; Anz. Av. Lib. 7, fols. 29r, 12 Aug., 62r, 12 Dec., 63r, 19 Dec., 64r, 22

tax reductions were granted on a large scale, especially in the Six Miles, and with renewals and extensions some of these immunities were still in force in July 1341.[6]

Difficulties continued after Lucca came under Pisan rule. During the siege of Lucca, which lasted from 1 August 1341 to 6 July 1342, Pisan and Florentine forces did much damage in the area immediately surrounding the city.[7] There were shortages of grain and other commodities in 1342 and 1343, 1346 (especially severe), 1353, and perhaps 1360.[8] The war against Florence and military operations for the recovery of parts of the Lucchese *contado* still resisting Pisan rule continued until 1344,[9] and in 1344–1345 Lucchese territory was attacked by a Milanese force under Luchino Visconti,[10] all doing further damage.

Dec. 1334; Anz. Av. Lib. 10, fols. 19v, 8 June, 36r, 31 July 1336; Anz. Av. Lib. 13, p. 146 (modern pagination; no foliation), 22 Oct., p. 169, 27 Nov. pp. 174–176, 12 Dec. 1338; Anz. Av. Lib. 14, fols. 32r, 26 May, 75r, 22 Oct., 79v, 31 Oct., pp. 176–179 (no further foliation), 14 Dec., pp. 183–184, 24 Dec. 1339.

6. Anz. Av. Lib. 5, p. 56, 12 Feb. 1334, renewing an earlier grant of 31 Oct. 1332; Anz. Av. Lib. 6, pp. 38–39, 21 and 22 Sept. 1334; Anz. Av. Lib. 7, fols. 45v–46r, 7 Oct. 1334; Anz. Av. Lib. 9, fols. 7v, 31 Jan., 13v–14v, 8 Feb. 1335; Anz. Av. Lib. 12, fols. 51r–59r, 29 Nov. 1336, 59v–61v, 7 July, 61v–62r, 16 Aug. 1337. Renewals: Anz. Av. Lib. 13, pp. 103–116, 14 July 1338; again Anz. Av. Lib. 14, fols. 57r–58v, 24 July, 64v–65v, 25 Aug., 78r–78v, 27 Oct. 1339; Anz. Av. Lib. 16, fols. 29r–29v, 11 Jan., 30r–36v, 23 Jan. 1341 (until 1 July 1341).

7. Anz. Av. Lib. 17, fols. 41r–43r, 13 July 1342.

8. Anz. Av. Lib. 18, fols. 23r, 15 Sept., 39r, 11 Oct., 44r, 23 Oct., 63v, 30 Nov. 1342; Anz. Av. Lib. 21, fols. 2r, 2 July, 88v, 31 Dec. 1343; Anz. Av. Lib. 24, fols. 56v, 14 July, 57v, 18 July, 61v–62v, 24 July, 64r, 3 Aug., 16 Aug., 85v, 5 Sept. 1346. Maximum prices were fixed: fol. 101v, 28 Sept., and again at a higher level, fol. 137v, 3 Dec. 1346. Anyone with supplies was to declare them: Anz. Av. Lib. 25, fols. 23v–24r, 12 Oct., 33v, 12 Sept., 34r, 15 Sept. 1346. Measures against hoarders: Anz. Av. Lib. 25, fols. 20r, 17 June, 25v, 29 July 1346. There are many other references to difficulties in 1346 in Anz. Av. Lib. 24 and 25. Also Sercambi, 1:92, and G. Pinto, "Firenze e la carestia del 1346–47," *Archivio storico italiano*, 130 (1972), pp. 3–84. Shortages in 1353: Anz. Av. Lib. 35, fols. 44r–44v, 21 May, 85v–86r, 3 Oct. 1353; Anz. Av. Lib. 36, fols. 58v–61r; many provisions regarding cereals found hidden, 9 Sept.–12 Oct. 1353. In 1360 Lucca arranged to buy corn: Anz. Av. Lib. 40, fols. 4r–5v, 7 Aug., 76r, 2 Aug. 1360; Anz. Av. Lib. 41, fols. 6v–7v, 13 Jan. 1361, but it may have over-estimated the need, as it had difficulty selling it in 1361: Anz. Av. Lib. 41, fols. 15v, 18 Feb., 28v, 20 March, 46v, 4 May, 49r, 19 May 1361. Accounts for the purchase of grain in 1360 are to be found in Ragionieri 10, fols. 53r–66v.

9. Anz. Av. Lib. 17, fol. 39r, 12 July 1342; Anz. Av. Lib. 18, fol. 2v, 5 Aug. 1342; Anz. Av. Lib. 19, fol. 2r, 2 Aug. 1342; Anz. Av. Lib. 21, fols. 41r–41v, 16 Sept., 46r–46v. 25 Sept., 56v, 21 Oct. 1343; Anz. Av. Lib. 22, fols. 20v, 14 April, 21r, 15 April, 31r–33r, 26 May 1344.

10. Anz. Av. Lib. 23, fols. 43v, 27 Aug., 47v, 15 Sept. 1345. The Lombards controlled "a Ponte S. Pietro ultra" in March, April and May 1345, according to Anz. Av. Lib. 24, fols. 65v–66r, 18 Aug. 1346.

In 1348 came the first great plague, followed by a further outbreak in 1362. It is not therefore surprising that complaints about depopulation, impoverishment, and over-taxation continued, and that petitions for relief were regularly made by communes of the *contado*.

But grants of relief and measures to ease the situation also continued. Unions of small neighbouring communes continued to be arranged, in order to spare them expenses for officials and administration.[11] Communes that had contracted debts that they could not repay were granted respites,[12] and general immunities were given to places that had suffered loss and damage in the wars.[13] Individual communes were granted a reduction of their *estimo*,[14] or were allowed to pay dues on a smaller number of hearths,[15] or were granted a period of years of exemption from certain dues.[16] Attempts were made to repopulate deserted places by offering immunities to new settlers or to their former inhabitants if they would return.[17] More general relief measures are found again later. There is a reference to a *balia* with general powers to lighten the burdens on the *contado* in 1360 and 1361.[18] The Pisan doge, Giovanni dell' Agnello, and a commission of Lucchese citizens agreed on general

11. Anz. Av. Lib. 24, fol. 129r, 29 Nov. 1346; Anz. Av. Lib. 26, fols. 70r–70v, 18 July 1347; Anz. Av. Lib. 28, fols. 33v–34r, 24 July 1348. These unions sometimes led to disputes and quarrels and had to be dissolved: Anz. Av. Lib. 31, fol. 108v, 5 Dec. 1346; Anz. Av. Lib. 34, fol. 2r, 19 Jan. 1352.

12. Anz. Av. Lib. 18, fols. 46v, 5 Nov., 49v, 12 Nov., 53v–55v (three different places), 18 Nov. 1342. There were sixteen such grants between 5 November and 31 December 1342: Anz. Av. Lib. 18, fols. 46v–86r and Anz. Av. Lib. 19, fols. 17v–40v, and some of these were extended and new ones granted to other places in the next few years.

13. Anz. Av. Lib. 17, fols. 41r–43r, 13 July 1342; Anz. Av. Lib. 18, fol. 64v, 30 Nov. 1342. A general immunity for the communes of the mountains of Pietrasanta: Anz. Av. Lib. 22, fols. 15r–16r, 26 Feb. 1344.

14. Anz. Av. Lib. 37, fols. 81r–82v, 29 Dec. 1354; Anz. Av. Lib. 39, fols. 72v–73v, 23 July, 74r, 27 July 1358; Anz. Av. Lib. 41, fol. 9v, 29 Jan. 1361; Anz. Av. Lib. 42, fols. 138r–138v, 4 Aug., 148r–148v, 12 Sept. 1363.

15. Anz. Av. Lib. 21, fol. 9r, 28 July 1343.

16. Anz. Av. Lib. 18, fols. 73v–74r, 17 Dec. 1342; Anz. Av. Lib. 21, fol. 8r, 28 July 1343; Anz. Av. Lib. 24, fols. 37v–38r, 19 May 1346. A commune granted a year's extension: Anz. Av. Lib. 24, fols. 49r–49v, 1 July 1346. Other extensions: Anz. Av. Lib. 24, fols. 55v–56r, 11 July, 57r, 14 July 1346; Anz. Av. Lib. 42, fols. 108r–108v, 10 Feb. 1363. New grants: Anz. Av. Lib. 34, fol. 6r, 23 Jan. 1354; Anz. Av. Lib. 39, fols. 17v–18v, 16 March 1358.

17. Anz. Av. Lib. 24, fols. 70v–71r, 25 Aug. 1346; Anz. Av. Lib. 26, fols. 48r–49r, 16 April 1347, 49v–50r, 16 April 1347; Anz. Av. Lib. 39, fols. 99r–99v, 22 Nov. 1358; Anz. Av. Lib. 42, fol. 126v, 3 June 1363.

18. Anz. Av. Lib. 41, fol. 9v, 29 Jan. 1361, where it is said to have been elected 31 Jan. last. Also mentioned Anz. Av. Lib. 41, fol. 83r, 6 Aug. 1361.

relief measures in 1365, mainly for places that had suffered in the war against Florence 1362-1364.[19]

The fact that Lucca was now under Pisan rule in no way impeded relief measures for the communes in Lucchese territory. There is no sign that Pisa took a harsher attitude towards Lucchese subjects than did the governments before 1342 or the Lucchese themselves. It is true that the relief measures did not directly affect or damage Pisan interests. Many of them did not result in a decrease in Lucchese revenues. Even when they did, this would not necessarily cause any loss to Pisa. For much of this period Lucca was responsible for the collection of its own revenues, paying an agreed annual sum to Pisa, which would, of course, be unaffected by any grants of tax relief to Lucchese subjects. Pisa occasionally took the initiative,[20] but in general the Lucchese were left to grant tax concessions and immunities in the Lucchese *contado* and to take whatever measures they considered necessary. Petitions from communes of the Lucchese *contado* direct to Pisa were remitted to Lucca, and the Pisan attitude is well illustrated by the case of S. Martino in Colle. Its inhabitants had dispersed, and they asked for various immunities to enable them to return and rebuild their houses. When Count Ranieri's vicar was consulted, he replied that he was content that they should return and rebuild their houses, but that the financial matters were the concern of the Lucchese and should be dealt with by them.[21]

Perhaps Pisan initiative lay behind the attempt to attract back to Lucca men who had been forced into exile or who had gone voluntarily as a result of the political troubles of Lucca before 1342. The first measures of this kind were taken just before Lucca fell to Pisa, when in response to a petition it was agreed that guelf exiles and rebels who had left Lucca when it came under the rule of Uguccione della Faggiuola and Castruccio Castracani on 14 June 1314 or since should be pardoned and

---

19. Anz. Av. Lib. 44, fols. 10v-12r, 29 Nov. 1366 (Pisan style, i.e. 1365). There were reductions of rents and a respite for debts for places in the Six Miles and suburbs that had suffered in the Florentine war. (These decrees are calendared in *Regesto* no. 973 under 6 Aug. 1365.)

20. Anz. Av. Lib. 35, fols. 96r-96v, 8 Dec. 1353; Anz. Av. Lib. 36, fol. 58r, 5 Sept. 1353. Giovanni dell'Agnello as doge authorised the compilation of a new *estimo:* Anz. Av. Lib. 44, fol. 12r, 15 Dec. 1365. It had been mentioned as urgently required: Anz. Av. Lib. 42, fols. 79v-80r, 28 Nov. 1362. Pisa agreed to an immunity that involved the pardon of a fine due direct to it: Anz. Av. Lib. 24, fols. 31v-33r, 11 April 1346. It also allowed the tax for military purposes on the *contado,* known as the *taglia delle cinquantasettemila lire e la paga dei pedoni,* to lapse: *Inventario,* 2:81-82. This had produced £15,775 5s. 3d. *picc.* November 1335-1 April 1336: *Inventario,* 2:28.

21. Anz. Av. Lib. 26, fols. 48r-49r, 16 April 1347.

allowed to return to Lucca and claim their property.[22] Later these decrees were confirmed and the time limit extended. Such important measures, which involved the readmission of guelfs, must have had the consent of the ghibelline Pisans. They should probably be seen as part of an effort to repopulate the city and revive its economic life; as such they could expect to have Pisan support.[23]

In the same context there were efforts to attract back to Lucca merchants and craftsmen who had been plying their trade elsewhere. In November 1342 those who had been absent from Lucca with their families for at least five years were offered an immunity from all public burdens except the gabelles for a period of seven years, providing that they returned within a certain term.[24] The Pisans seem to have taken an active interest in this grant of privileges, and they even intervened in what was basically a Lucchese internal matter when the Lucchese Anziani asked for a ruling on the validity of some of the grants. The Anziani of Pisa took legal advice as to whether the privileges had been properly granted and whether the beneficiaries had fulfilled the conditions attached to them.[25] The measure in fact met with some success. Twenty-

22. This petition was first discussed and approved (Anz. Av. Lib. 17, fols. 22r–24r) on 19 June 1342, the day before it was agreed to negotiate peace with Pisa (fols. 25r–26r). Details of the terms on which exiles could return and claim their property: Anz. Av. Lib. 17, fols. 31r–33v, 28 June 1342. Decree extending the time limit for this: Anz. Av. Lib. 21, fol. 70v, 30 Nov. 1343, referring to another decree of 12 May 1343.

23. No records survive of the claims and proofs of the property of men who returned, as they do for a similar amnesty offered in 1331 (Series Curia de'Rebelli e dei Banditi no. 3), but there is a petition by men who returned (Anz. Av. Lib. 21, fol. 70v), 30 Nov. 1343. Some of the merchants and craftsmen claiming the immunity offered on 12 Nov. 1342 would seem to come into the categories covered by the decrees of 19 and 28 June 1342.

24. Anz. Av. Lib. 18, fols. 50v–51r, 12 Nov. 1342. These measures were said to be "pro aumentatione dicte civitatis et pro tranquillitate et pace conservanda." The time limit was extended on 30 Oct. 1345. This decree does not survive, but is referred to Anz. Av. Lib. 24, fols. 3v–4v, 21 Jan. 1346. The immunity was then for five years. There was a further extension of the time limit: Anz. Av. Lib. 24, fols. 137r–137v, 2 Dec. 1346.

25. Anz. Av. Lib. 31, fols. 46r–48r, 1 Aug. 1349. They decided that some of the grants were valid and some were not. They were probably mainly considering whether or not the beneficiaries had proved that they had indeed been absent with their families for the required period. One of the grants they declared invalid had earlier been revoked, since it had been discovered that, although the grantee had been absent from Lucca since 1327, his family had lived in Lucca all the time, so that the grant should never have been made: Anz. Av. Lib. 24, fols. 29v–30v, 9 May 1346. The case of a man who did not have a family caused especial difficulty. The immediate cause for the Pisan Anziani taking legal advice may have been disputes about liability for *prestanze*, for it was stated that those whose immunities were declared invalid

three families (a total of thirty-one men, since some families included fathers and sons or several brothers) claimed the immunity between July and December 1343. A further twenty-three families (thirty-seven men) claimed in 1346, and sixteen families (eighteen men) in 1347.[26] There were almost certainly others claiming the immunity in 1344 and 1345, years for which no records survive.[27] Since one of the conditions of these grants was that the beneficiaries should return to Lucca and engage in business there, the city must have benefitted insofar as this condition was enforced. But there was a tendency in 1346 and 1347 to allow Lucchese merchants living outside the city to enjoy the immunity whether they returned or not.[28] The merchants usually expressed an intention of trading in Lucca and keeping factors and goods there. Among the reasons given for granting immunities on these terms was that it would help fill the city with merchants and encourage others to return and that Lucca would benefit from the presence there of their merchandise.[29] The effect of such grants is not entirely clear, but the relaxation of the condition that the beneficiaries must return to Lucca probably reduced the benefit to the Lucchese economy.

A number of other measures suggest that depopulation was a serious problem and that both the Lucchese and the Pisan authorities were anxious to do everything they could to prevent any further emigration. In January 1346 the Lucchese Anziani asked for confirmation of certain reductions in fines for offences that did not affect the security of

---

should pay the *prestanza*. Lucca had asked Pisa for a ruling on this matter on 21 July 1349: Anz. Av. Lib. 31, fols. 46r–46v.

26. These grants are recorded in Anz. Av. Lib. 21, 24, and 26. Livi, "I mercanti di seta lucchesi," esp. pp. 38–47 and Doc. III, giving rather different figures and dates.

27. Men with claims to immunities, who are not among those whose grants are recorded in Anz. Av. Lib. 21, 24 and 26, are listed in Anz. Av. Lib. 31, fols. 47r–48r, 1 Aug. 1349.

28. Jacobo Normannini, who had been granted an immunity on his return from England on 7 Nov. 1343, was given licence to go "ad partes de ultramontibus" for two years on 1 July 1345: Anz. Av. Lib. 21, fols. 63r–64r. He was among those whose immunities were declared invalid: Anz. Av. Lib. 31, fol. 47r, 1 Aug. 1349. Men allowed to enjoy the immunity without necessarily returning: Anz. Av. Lib. 24, fols. 58r–58v, 20 July 1346, 108r–108v, 26 Oct. 1346, 109r–109v, 26 Oct. 1346 (another case), 112v–113r, 28 Oct. 1346, 113v, 30 Oct. 1346; fols. 114r–115r, a grant was made to four brothers who probably did not all return personally, 30 Oct. 1346.

29. "Volentes providere quod civitas lucana mercatoribus et mercantionibus repleatur ex quo dicta civitas augmentatur personis et divitiis": Anz. Av. Lib. 24, fol. 58r, 20 July 1346; similar expressions, fol. 108r, 26 Oct. 1346; a merchant spoke of sending goods "ex quibus non modicum in utilitatem et commodum lucane gabelle et honorem lucane civitatis predicte redundavit et redundat," fol. 113v, 30 Oct. 1346.

Pisa or Lucca, urging that this would produce "maior utilitas et minor fuga vel absentia gentium."[30] After the suppression of the revolt against Pisan rule in May 1355 the Pisans were well aware of the danger that many Lucchese might flee from the city for fear of reprisal. They took immediate action both to reassure the Lucchese and to prevent them from leaving. On 25 May 1355 officials were instructed "quod ortentur Lucenses et dicant eis quod de nicchilo timeant qui volunt bene agere et bene vivere. Et quod non permictant aliquem disgomberare de civitate lucana aliquas res vel massaritias vel familias discedere." This was quickly followed up by the production of a written form of the amnesty that had been granted, so that it might be shown to the Lucchese to reassure them, and by financial concessions, which it was hoped would dissuade merchants and others from leaving the city.[31]

Apart from these important efforts to repopulate the city by attracting back exiles and preventing others from leaving at a time of political crisis, Lucca was left free to take whatever measures were possible to assist its trade and industry. The Lucchese economy seems to have been allowed to remain entirely separate from that of Pisa, and there was remarkably little Pisan intervention in economic affairs. Thus the Court of Merchants in Lucca was free to issue general ordinances, clarifying many points of detail about such industrial matters as the organisation of trading companies and the manufacture of silk cloth, and forbidding various abuses.[32] The Lucchese issued ordinances forbidding the export, to the detriment of local industry, of unfinished silk cloth or the tools and implements and gold and silver thread that were used in silk manufacture.[33] On at least one occasion the Pisans cancelled a licence they had granted for the export of silks and implements on the grounds that this was contrary to their undertakings to Lucca.[34] The Lucchese were also free to take action to prevent the defrauding of the gabelle by the import of woollen cloth cut up instead of whole, so that it paid a

---

30. Anz. Av. Lib. 55, fol. 6r, 16 Jan. 1346.
31. A.S.P. Comune A 60, fol. 9v, also fols. 14v, 29 May, 37v, 11 June 1355, quoted below, Chapter V, p. 96.
32. Anz. Av. Lib. 25, fols. 2v–4v, 5 Jan. 1346; Anz. Av. Lib. 30, pp. 18–23 (modern pagination; no foliation), 24 Jan. 1348.
33. Anz. Av. Lib. 25, fols. 11r–11v, 2 March 1346; Anz. Av. Lib. 39, fols. 84r–84v, 6 Sept., 103r, 5 Dec., 105v–106r, 10 Dec. 1358.
34. A.S.P. Comune A 123, fol. 40v, 10 Nov. 1355. This was said to be done "pro honore pisani comunis et iuris debito ac etiam pro conservatione promissorum et conventorum comuni lucano ex forma compositionis vigentis." The licence had been granted on 12 Oct. 1355, and had probably provoked a protest from Lucca.

lower rate of duty,[35] or by buying and selling goods in villages near Lucca instead of bringing them to the city itself.[36]

It could be argued that these measures would not affect Pisa directly, since Lucca's main industrial activity, silk manufacture, did not compete with the leather industry or manufacture of woollen cloth in which Pisa specialised. This is true enough, but Lucca was also allowed independence in matters that did concern Pisa directly. Lucca was allowed to prohibit exports of foodstuffs to Pisa even in times of shortage. Letters from Pisa, unfortunately undated, ask that certain Pisan vintners, who had bought wine ''ante inhibitionem per vos factam de non extrahendo vinum de vestro districtu,'' be allowed to export it in view of the special circumstances, but the principle that Lucca could prohibit exports even to Pisa was not challenged.[37] There were still tolls between Lucca and Pisa; they applied to goods crossing Lucchese territory on their way to Pisa from Lombardy or the Valdinievole and Valdriana and vice versa, as well as goods going to one city from the other. The tolls were not only maintained, but Lucca was allowed to adjust them to its own financial advantage, reducing them in the hope of increasing the volume of traffic, but maintaining prohibitions on silk, silk goods, and gold and silver thread, which might have damaged the silk industry.[38] Another measure prohibited the transport of cloth from Lucca to Pisa for dyeing. There are only two recorded examples of licences granted to do this despite the prohibition, and in each case the exception was justified on the grounds that no one in Lucca was able to do that particular kind of work.[39]

---

35. Anz. Av. Lib. 35, fols. 55v–56v, 12 June, 17 June 1353.

36. Anz. Av. Lib. 35, fols. 82r–83r, 26 Sept. 1353.

37. Letters in Anz. Av. Lib. 52, dated 13 and 14 July but with no indication of the year or indiction. Similar letters 11–14 March 1353, *Regesto* nos. 553, 554, 556 (originals in Anz. Av. Lib. 48).

38. Anz. Av. Lib. 18, fols. 83r–84r, 31 Dec. 1342; Anz. Av. Lib. 34, fols. 3r–4r, 23 Jan., 4v–5v, 26 Jan., 32v–33v, 15 June 1352; Anz. Av. Lib. 35, fol. 8v, 21 Jan. 1353; Anz. Av. Lib. 37, fols. 45v–46r, 10 May, 60v–61r, 5 Aug. 1354; Anz. Av. Lib. 39, fol. 100r, 22 Nov. 1358; also *Regesto* no. 841, 21 Nov. 1357. No doubt the Pisans wished for lower tolls for their merchants, but there is no reason to believe that the Lucchese were yielding to pressure, cf. N. Caturegli, *La signoria di Giovanni dell'Agnello in Pisa e in Lucca e le sue relazioni con Firenze e Milano* (Pisa, 1921), pp. 129–130. For a comparable situation on local regulations in Florentine territory, see D. Herlihy, *Medieval and Renaissance Pistoia* (New Haven and London, 1967), p. 159.

39. Anz. Av. Lib. 39, fol. 27v, 27 March 1358: a licence was granted because there was no one in Lucca skilled in dyeing in woad; Anz. Av. Lib. 39, fols. 89v–90r, 28 Sept. 1358: because of lack of ''magisteria opportuna.''

There was no attempt to subordinate the Lucchese guilds to their counterparts in Pisa, as happened in Pisa itself under Florentine rule.[40] Lucchese guilds were left entirely independent, and the supervision and regulation of guild affairs was left to the Lucchese Anziani, councils, and officials. Disputes between the *tabernarii* and the *casearii* about the types of meat each guild could sell were dealt with by the Anziani,[41] who also regulated complaints about the fouling of the streets and the stench caused by butchers and shieldmakers.[42] They dealt, too, with disputes between guildsmen and Lucchese officials over the *podestà*'s application of the statutes forbidding butchers to allow blood to run in the streets,[43] for example, or the attempt by an official of the gabelle to change the arrangements for distributing among the various *bancherii* and *campsores* the sum they had to pay jointly each year to the gabelle.[44] Lucca also dealt directly with outside powers in disputes over trading matters that led to the grant of reprisals. The Lucchese Anziani took action when the factors of a number of Lucchese merchants were arrested in England[45] and dealt with the claims and counter-claims of Lucchese and Pistoiese merchants.[46] All these matters were dealt with by the Lucchese in accordance with Lucchese statutes. When modifications were made in the regulations, it was because Lucchese interests were felt to require it. All in all Lucca was left remarkably free to regulate its own economic affairs and do what it could to promote a revival.

It is unlikely, however, that the measures taken by Lucca produced much effect. Lucca was by no means alone in experiencing the problems of depopulation, impoverishment, and indebtedness in the *contado*. Neighbouring cities sought similar remedies of tax relief and respites for debts and, like Lucca, tried to attract new settlers. Lucca could hold out no inducements that its neighbours were not also offering, and indeed

---

40. M. E, Mallett, "Pisa and Florence in the Fifteenth Century: Aspects of the Period of the First Florentine Domination," in *Florentine Studies,* ed. N. Rubinstein (London, 1968), pp. 420–421. This was the normal position for guilds in Florentine subject cities.

41. Anz. Av. Lib. 19, fols. 24r–25r, 11 Dec. 1342; Anz. Av. Lib. 18, fols. 71r–72r, 11 Dec., 81r–82r, 21 Dec., 82r–82v, 24 Dec. 1342.

42. Anz. Av. Lib. 26, fols. 3v–4r, 7 Jan., 39r, 22 March 1347; Anz. Av. Lib. 34, fols. 65v–66v, 9 Nov. 1352.

43. Anz. Av. Lib. 39, fols. 6v–7r, 23 Jan. 1358; Anz. Av. Lib. 42, fols. 48v–49v, 13 June 1362.

44. Anz. Av. Lib. 35, fols. 84v–85r, 20 Sept. 1358.

45. Anz. Av. Lib. 26, fols. 7r–8r, 17 Jan. 1347.

46. Anz. Av. Lib. 26, fols. 32v–33v, 21 March 1347. Reprisals generally: Anz. Av. Lib. 26, fols. 15r–15v, 29 Jan. 1347; Anz. Av. Lib. 30, p. 27, 30 Jan. 1348. There are very many references to reprisals in the *Regesto*. Pisa was probably glad to be able to disclaim any responsibility for the actions and claims of Lucchese merchants.

some offered more generous immunities and tax relief to settlers.[47] In any case the malaise in the countryside was too deep to be seriously affected by such palliatives. Nor did Pisan rule bring a period of peace and stability, which might have encouraged economic recovery. Lucca had already suffered more seriously than most of its neighbours from warfare, disorders, and invasions before 1342. Pisan rule brought only a relative improvement, for fighting continued until 1345. There was an abortive rising followed by attacks from Lucchese exiles in 1355–1356, and Pisan rule involved Lucca in the war with Florence in 1362–1364, which brought further destruction in its territory. In the city, too, the problems were deeply rooted, and although some merchants and craftsmen responded to the offer of immunities and returned to Lucca, the effects must have been marginal. No more than eighty-six men are actually recorded as having taken up the immunity, and by no means all of those were engaged in trade or manufacture. Despite the inducements offered, others probably did not find it attractive to return to their native city while it was under Pisan rule. Certainly Sercambi relates that once Lucca recovered its freedom in 1369 many exiles returned without any inducement.[48] As a minor commune in a state of decline and under the rule of a neighbour, Lucca can have exercised little attraction for immigrants from outside the state.

The ineffectiveness of the efforts to aid the Lucchese economy is probably best demonstrated by the fact that similar problems continued after 1369. There are still references to the depopulation and impoverishment of the *contado,* the reduced population of the city, the decline of the silk industry, and other economic difficulties. But if the problems were the same, so were the measures taken to deal with them. The free republic of Lucca could find no better remedies for its economic problems after 1369 than those found while under Pisan rule. It is clear, therefore, that Pisan rule had not prevented Lucca from taking what measures were possible to assist its economy. If the measures taken under Pisan rule produced little effect, it was because the basic problems were too deeply rooted—and too widely shared—to be responsive to any measures that communal governments had at their disposal. Certainly there is little evidence that the measures were any more successful after 1369 than they had been before.

47. E. Carpentier, *Une ville devant la peste: Orvieto et la Peste Noire de 1348* (Paris, 1962), pp. 148, 237; W. M. Bowsky, "The Impact of the Black Death on Sienese Government and Society," *Speculum* 39 (1964), pp. 24–26, 31–33. Pisa offered more favourable immunities than Lucca at a slightly later date: P. Silva, "Il governo di Pietro Gambacorta in Pisa e le sue relazioni col resto della Toscana e coi Visconti," *Annali della R. Scuola Normale Superiore di Pisa* 23 (1912), pp. 141–142.
48. Sercambi, 1:171.

IV

Finance

PERHAPS THE most likely cause of strong resentment against Pisan rule was the financial arrangements. The Pisans naturally expected the costs of the defence and administration of Lucca to be recovered from Lucchese revenues. Only in exceptional circumstances, and then very reluctantly, would the Pisans be prepared to contribute from their own resources.[1] From the Lucchese point of view this meant that large sums of money could be seen passing into Pisan hands.[2] In order to see whether the charges of financial oppression made by contemporaries and later historians are justified, however, it is necessary to examine the sums paid in the light of the expenditure they were to cover, and to compare this where possible with the revenues and expediture of Lucca in periods when it was independent and with those of other cities.

In fact the sums that Lucca had to pay to Pisa seem to have been carefully calculated with regard to the expenditure they were to cover. In August 1342 all Lucchese revenues were assigned to Pisa for the duration of the war with Florence. Pisa was authorised to spend 55,000 florins per year during the war, and Lucca was not to be obliged to make any payments beyond this amount. Pisa was also to hand over to Lucca 9,000 florins annually for the salaries of certain Lucchese officials and the expenses of the Anziani. If the revenues amounted to more than these 64,000 florins and certain additional sums required to pay specified debts, the surplus was to go to Lucca. If they amounted to less, Pisa was to make up the difference and recover it once the war was over.[3] The first composition between Lucca and Pisa after peace had been made shows a similar careful attempt to balance revenues and expenditure, though the peacetime figures were lower. Under an agreement for three years beginning on 1 October 1345, most of the Lucchese

---

1. A.S.P. Comune A 60, fol. 32v, 7 June 1355, fol. 37v, 11 June 1355. This was in the exceptional period after the rising against Pisa during the expedition of Charles IV.

2. S. Bongi calculated that 813,875 florins were handed over by Lucca under the compositions 1342–1361, excluding any extraordinary payments and the sums that Pisa received from the direct administration of Lucchese revenues after 1362: *Inventario*, 2:91.

3. Notarized copy of agreement between Pisa and Lucca of 14 August 1342, dated 28 Jan. 1344: Capitoli 19, fols. 11v–12r. It was therefore envisaged that Lucchese revenues would produce 79,000 florins; see *Memorie e documenti*, 1:336.

revenues were again assigned to Pisa, and Pisa was to pay most of the expenses, 5,000 florins a year being reserved to Lucca to cover certain listed salaries and other charges. The revenues assigned to Pisa were apparently expected to bring in about 40,000 florins a year. If they yielded more, the surplus was to be used towards the 2,3331/3 florins that Lucca had to pay as her third share of an annual sum due to Florence under the treaty of 15 November 1343; otherwise Lucca would have to pay this from some other source.[4]

In these first years Lucchese revenues were administered by Pisa, but from 1348 to 1362 a system was adopted under which the Lucchese collected their own revenues and paid Pisa an annual sum specified in the compositions. One might expect that Lucca would prefer a system giving it control of its own revenues, but it seems to have been Pisa that wanted the new system and Lucca that was reluctant to agree. In 1345 Pisa had wanted an agreement under which Lucca collected its own revenues and paid its own expenses,[5] but the Lucchese could not be induced to accept this, and the existing system had to be retained for a further three years.[6] Pisa's desire for a change in the system was probably connected with revenue difficulties. Though figures for the 1340s are scanty, the revenues for the year 20 August 1343–19 August 1344 were only £141,720 4s. 1d. *picc.*, the equivalent of about 40,491 florins. This represented a marked decline on the figure of £186,162 14s. 5d. *picc.*, or about 53,188 florins, for the year 20 August 1342–19 August 1343. The decline in the year 1343-1344 occurred predominantly in the second semester, when the yield of a number of the most important *proventus* was substantially reduced.[7] There are no figures for the semester

4. The *proventus* not assigned to Pisa included the *dovana salis*, which Pisa had handed over to a group of Lucchese citizens for the repayment of a loan of 8,000 florins beginning 1 May 1346. The *proventus farine*, which had been assigned to another group of Lucchese citizens for the repayment of a loan of 6,500 florins, was not to be included until the sum of about 1,400 florins which was still outstanding had been repaid. A number of other *proventus* were also excluded, but these were ones which produced only trivial sums or which had been suspended or dropped: composition between Pisa and Lucca of 14 October, Capitoli 19, fols. 45r-48v. Also A.S.P. Comune A 55, fols. 18r-18v, 7 Sept. 1345. For the payments to Florence: Capitoli 19, fols. 26r-26v.

5. A.S.P. Comune A 54, fol. 27v, 11 Aug. 1345, fols. 34v-35r, 23 Aug. 1345.

6. A.S.P. Comune A 54, fols. 34v-35r, 23 Aug. 1345; Comune A 55, fols. 17v, 23 Aug., 18r-18v, 7 Sept. 1345.

7. The yield was £84,243 17s. 10d. for the semester 20 Aug. 1343–19 Feb. 1344, and £57,476 6s. 7d. for the semester 20 Feb.–19 Aug. 1344: Ragionieri della Camera e del Comune [hereafter cited as Ragionieri] 4, fols. 6r-7v, 45r-48v. The corresponding figures for the previous year were £90,282 8s. 7d. for 20 Aug. 1342–19 Feb. 1343, and £95,880 5s. 10d. for 20 Feb.–19 Aug. 1343: Ragionieri 3, fols. 51r-55r, 33r-36v. (These volumes contain various different sets of foliation and also unfoliated sections.

20 August 1344–19 February 1345, but those for 20 February–19 August 1345, when the total yield was £53,245 3s. 4d. *picc.*, were again down compared with 1342-1343.[8] There seem already to have been reductions in the amounts tax farmers were prepared to offer for the various Lucchese gabelles in the mid 1340s,[9] and Pisa's renewed insistence that Lucca should collect its own revenues in the new composition of 1348 was almost certainly connected with the sharp fall in the prices the *proventus* fetched in the auctions after the Black Death. This situation would already have been apparent when the negotiations for a new composition began early in September 1348.[10]

Perhaps another factor in Pisa's desire for a change in the financial arrangements was the changing value of Lucchese *piccioli* in relation to the florin. The exchange rate, which had normally been about £3 10s. 1d. *picc.* to the florin in 1343 and 1344, had risen to £3 16s. 8d. *picc.* by 1349 and later was to rise still further. Florins stood at an average of £4 0s. 0d. *picc.* in 1350, £4 4s. 0d. in 1351-1352, and £4 6s. 0d. in 1354-1355, with Lucchese *camarlinghi* sometimes obliged to buy florins at £4 7s. 0d. *picc.* or more. Lucchese *piccioli* later recovered slightly and stood at £4 4s. 0d. to the florin in 1356-1359. The compositions were stipulated in florins, which offered Pisa relative stability and protection against the decline in the value of Lucchese currency. The compositions sometimes allowed for payment of a proportion of the sums due in

---

Folio numbers are given wherever they exist.) There is no obvious explanation for the reduced figure for the second semester of 1343-34; there were significant reductions in the yield of some of the main gabelles, notably the *proventus farine, proventus macelli, dovana salis, proventus cassarum generalium et vini ad portas,* and a number of other less important ones. It could mark the end of special war levels of taxation, though there is nothing in the sources to indicate this, and war taxation did not normally involve any increase in the customary gabelles. For a comparable drop in the yield of gabelles in Florence, though at a slightly earlier date: M. B. Becker, *Florence in Transition* (Baltimore, 1968), 2:166-167.

8. Ragionieri 4, fols. 26r-28r. There are no further figures for a continuous period until December 1349.

9. In November 1345 Lucca informed the Pisans "quod proventus medie uncie panis civitatis, proventus vini venalis dicte civitatis, et proventus farine dicte civitatis diminuuntur in venditione ultra modum consuetum quos vendere non est deliberatum absque vestra conscientia." The Pisans decided "quod vendantur maiori et meliori pretio quo possunt ita tamen quod nulla inde venditio fieri possit sine consensu Rectorum vel unius eorum": A.S.P. Comune A 55, fol. 29v, 10 Nov. 1345. The auctions of the Lucchese gabelles for the period 1336-1360 are recorded in the series Proventi Incanti 2-12 and Proventi Contratti 17-29. There are also some scattered figures for 1322-1336 in Proventi Contratti 13-16.

10. *Regesto* nos. 387 (16 Sept. 1348) and 393 (26 Sept. 1348). Also nos. 395, 397, 399, 401, 403-406, 408-409, 1004.

coinage other than florins, but only at rates negotiated in relation to the florin.[11] It seems fair to conclude that the change in the financial relations of Pisa and Lucca which began in 1348 worked out to the advantage of Pisa. Lucca had the trouble and anxiety of collecting the revenues in difficult circumstances, while Pisa was assured of a trouble-free annual sum from Lucca, fixed in a stable currency, with the amount and the dates of payment known in advance.

The new system was to operate for fourteen years. The sum Lucca had to pay was subject to regular renegotiation, but it varied only slightly from year to year, and there was no definite upward trend. Lucca paid 35,000 florins a year for the two years beginning on 1 October 1348,[12] and 36,000 florins a year from 1 October 1350 to 1 April 1355.[13] This was reduced to 33,000 florins in an agreement made after the abortive rebellion of 1355, a reduction that was continued in the next composition.[14] The sum was raised again to 36,000 florins in 1357,[15] and to 40,000 in 1358.[16] In 1359 it was only 34,341 florins, but Lucca also granted Pisa the *proventus vini venalis*.[17] In 1360 and 1361 Lucca was again paying 40,000 florins.[18] In addition to its payments to Pisa Lucca had to find the 2,333⅓ florins a year due to Florence and to spend an agreed sum that varied between 800 and 1,000 florins each year on the repair of fortresses. It also had to pay directly the salaries and other charges that had been estimated to total 5,000 florins in the composition of 1345.[19] Lucca must, therefore, have needed something over 8,000 florins a year beyond what it had to pay to Pisa to cover these expenses.

11. Lucca had to pay at least half of the sums due in florins, and there were limitations on the other coinages it could use and in what proportions. The sum paid was always to be the equivalent of the amount due in florins at the date the payment was made: Capitoli 19, fols. 49v, 52v, 56v, 60v, 64v, 67v, 72v, 76v, 81r–81v. After 1359 Lucca appears to have had to pay in florins: fols. 87v, 95v, 106r. Decrees concerning payments in florins and other coinage and the rates: Anz. Av. Lib. 35, fols. 56v–57r, 12 June, 57r, 2 July, 85r–85v, 27 Sept. 1353; Anz. Av. Lib. 38, fol. 75r, 26 Oct., 19 Nov. 1355. Also *Regesto* nos. 486 (28 March 1351) and 625 (10 Jan. 1354).
12. Capitoli 19, fol. 49v. This composition of 28 October 1348 is printed in *Memorie e documenti*, 1:364–369.
13. Capitoli 19, fols. 52v, 56v, 60v, 64v.
14. Fols. 67v, 72v.
15. Fol. 76v.
16. Fol. 81r.
17. Fol. 87v. This *proventus* was valued at 5,659 florins, and it was stipulated that if it yielded more the sum of 34,341 florins should be reduced accordingly, and if it yielded less Lucca was to make up the difference: fol. 88r.
18. Fols. 95v, 106r.
19. Fols. 46v–47r.

The records of the *ragionieri,* or public auditors, for this period show that in most years the revenues passing through the hands of the *camarlingo generale* fell short of the sum required to meet the payments to Pisa plus the various charges for which Lucca was directly responsible. In the year December 1349–November 1350 the *camarlingo* received just over 43,000 florins at a time when 35,000 florins had to be paid to Pisa, but at least 3,733 florins of these receipts came from an extraordinary levy, an *imposita.*[20] In the year December 1350–November 1351 the *camarlingo* received only 39,469 florins, though the payment to Pisa had risen to 36,000 florins in October 1350.[21] In the year December 1351–November 1352 41,628 florins were received,[22] and in December 1352–November 1353 42,645 florins.[23] Only in December 1353–November 1354, when receipts were 53,449 florins,[24] can these revenues have covered the 36,000 florins due to Pisa and the 8,000 florins required for Lucchese expenses. In the troubled year of December 1354–November 1355 receipts

20. Ragionieri 5, fols. 52r–54v, 67r–68v, 86r–87v, 14r–16v, 50r–50v, and ⌐n unfoliated. Receipts were £153,381 19s. 1d. *picc.,* the equivalent of 39,99? ⌐s at the current rate of £3 16s. 8d. *picc.* per florin, plus 3,733 florins rece ⌐n florins from the *imposita.* The *camarlingo* had a surplus of £2,512 2s.)⌐⌐., which he handed over to his successor. The *imposita* was perhaps the one referred to as collected in 1350: Anz. Av. Lib. 35, fol. 11r, 26 Jan. 1353.
21. Ragionieri 6, fols. 21r–23v, 52r–54r, 66r–68v and then unfoliated. A total of £195,524 8s. 10d. *picc.* was received by the six officials who held the office in this period, but sums totalling £37,647 2s. were transferred to the accounts of successors and therefore appear in two accounts. With these subtracted the total receipts are £157,877 6s. 10d., the equivalent of 39,469 florins at £4 to the florin, which was the average rate for that year.
22. Ragionieri 6, fols. 14r–17r, 38r–41r, 82r–85v, 15r–17v, 32r–34r, 43r–45r. £222,174 5s. *picc.* received, less £47,334 6s. 6d. transferred to successors as surpluses, leaves £174,839 18s. 6d., or 41,628 florins at the average rate that year of £4 4s. to the florin.
23. Ragionieri 7, fols. 16r–19r, 46r–49r, 61r–65r, 16r–18r, 35r–37r, 48r–48v. £229,155 8s. 8d. *picc.* received, less £50,045 9s. 3d. transferred to successors as surpluses, leaves £179,109 19s. 5d., or 42,645 florins at £4 4s. to the florin.
24. Ragionieri 7, fols. 22r–24v, 48r–50r, 3r–7r, 26r–30r, 55r–58v, 93r–95v. £251,960 5s. 2d. *picc.* received, less £22,126 8s. 1d. transferred to successors, leaves £229,833 17s. 1d., or 53,449 florins at the current rate of £4 6s. to the florin. The higher receipts of the *camarlinghi generali* for this period are largely explained by the inclusion of unusually large amounts under the heading of "generalis et mixtus introitus"; £55,889 4s. 8d. *picc.* was received under this heading. Sums of 4,550 and 2,500 florins were received by the *camarlinghi generali* from *imposite* in this period and probably appear in their accounts as "generalis et mixtus introitus," see below, pp. 69–70 and note 33. There was also an increase in the tax on wine sold retail in Lucca, which produced an extra £1,542 16s. 4d. *picc.* in the year Dec. 1353–Nov. 1354.

were about 40,000 florins.[25] In 1356 49,254 florins were received[26] at a time when the payment to Pisa had been reduced to 33,000 florins, but in the next years receipts were lower: 40,812 florins in the eleven months January–November 1357, 37,831 florins in the year December 1357–November 1358, and 42,860 florins in December 1358–November 1359.[27]

If these receipts had represented its full revenues, Lucca would clearly have been in serious difficulties. It would have had deficits each year except December 1353–November 1354, 1356, and perhaps December 1349–November 1350, including a very large deficit in the year December 1357–November 1358, when its receipts of 37,831 florins would not have been sufficient even to cover the 40,000 florins payable to Pisa. In fact the records show that sizeable surpluses were transferred by each *camarlingo* to his successor at the end of his two-month period of office in the years 1351–1354; only in 1355 and 1356 did some *camarlinghi* have small deficits.[28] The explanation seems to be that there were sometimes revenues that did not pass through the hands of the *camarlingo generale* and were therefore not included in the *ragionieri*

25. Ragionieri 8, fols. 12r–14r (Dec. 1354–Jan. 1355), then unfoliated until Oct.–Dec. 1355, fols. 7r–10v. The revenues cannot be worked out for a twelve month period, but for the thirteen months Dec. 1354–Dec. 1355 they were £186,963 19s. 6d. *picc.*, or 43,480 florins at the rate of £4 6s. to the florin. The revenues must have been affected by the rising of May 1355; only £3,630 15s. 3d. were received in April, May, and June 1355, as against an average bi-monthly receipt of about £30,000. £31,147 16s. 10d. were received in July and August, £28,111 12s. 10d. in September, and £47,917 4s. 9d. in October, November, and December 1355.
26. Ragionieri 8, fols. 7r–9r, 19r–21v, 27r–29v, 43r–46v, 67r–70r. 4,803 florins were received and £186,697 10s. 7d. in *piccioli*, the equivalent of 44,451 florins at £4 4s. to the florin, a total receipt of 49,254 florins.
27. In the eleven months ending Nov. 1357 2,770 florins were received, plus £160,778 3s. 9d. in *piccioli*, the equivalent of 38,042 florins, a total of 40,812 florins: Ragionieri 8, fols. 73r–76r, 82r–84v, 15r–18r, 32r–35v and then unfoliated. For Dec. 1357–Nov. 1358 receipts were 7,831 florins, plus £125,366 11s. 6d. in *piccioli*, the equivalent of 30,000 florins, a total of 37,831 florins: Ragionieri 8, fols. 13r– 16r, 38r–41r, 10r–13r, 45r–48v; Ragionieri 9, fols. 77r–80v, 2r–6r. For Dec. 1358– Nov. 1359 receipts were 11,435 florins, plus £132,488 12s. 5d. in *piccioli*, the equivalent of 31,425 florins, a total of 42,860 florins: Ragionieri 9, fols. 29r–31r, 58r–61v, 88r–91r, 9r–12v, 36r–39v, 61r–63v.
28. There were deficits, none of them very large, in the accounts of April–June and July–August 1355 (Ragionieri 8, unfoliated); also Oct.–Dec. 1355 (Ragionieri 8, fols. 7r–29v); Jan.–Feb. 1356 (Ragionieri 8, fols.7r–18r); March–May 1356 (Ragionieri 8, fols. 19r–26r); and Oct.–Dec. 1356 (Ragionieri 8, fols. 67r–71v).

accounts for his treasurership.[29] If money was raised by a loan or *imposita*, it was usually repaid by assigning a particular *proventus* to the lenders, who would be allowed to appoint a special treasurer to receive it. As the *camarlingo generale* was not involved, it would not appear in his accounts, though the *ragionieri* would, of course, also audit the accounts of the special treasurer. There is much evidence of such loans in Lucchese records. A clear example of a large sum that did not pass through the hands of the *camarlingo generale* is the 5,500 florins 11s. 11d. received by Puccinello Galganetti between 7 December 1350 and 26 February 1351 as treasurer of an *imposita* on Lucca and the *contado* and paid by him directly to Pisa between 12 December 1350 and March 1351.[30] Merchants who had lent 8,000 florins, apparently in May 1345, had a special treasurer appointed to receive the revenues of the *dovana salis,* which were assigned for the repayment, and to distribute them to the lenders pro rata each month.[31]

In some cases the yield of a loan or *imposita* might be included in the receipts of the *camarlingo generale,* though they always seem to have been repaid without the money passing through his hands. The *camarlingo generale* received 3,400 florins from an *imposita* in November 1349–January 1350 and a further 333 florins in February and March 1350.[32] The *camarlingo generale* of April and May 1354 received over

29. The function of the *ragionieri* was to check the sums received and expended by each treasurer, in order to determine his personal responsibility and grant him quittance. They were not concerned to discover the total revenues of the commune.
30. Ragionieri 6, fols. 39r–40v. There are no details of the method by which this sum was repaid.
31. Anz. Av. Lib. 24, fols. 11r–11v, 31 Jan. 1346. Francesco di Bartolomeo Guinigi, the treasurer for this, had paid the 8,000 florins he received direct to Pisa in three payments between 4 June and 16 July 1345: Ragionieri 4, fols. 24r–25r. The composition of 14 October 1345, excluding the *proventus dovane salis* from the gabelles assigned to Pisa, refers to its assignment by Pisa to the Lucchese citizens who had lent 8,000 florins that year. The assignment was to begin on 1 May 1346: Capitoli 19, fol. 46r. There is a reference to another special treasurer appointed to receive revenues on behalf of merchants who had lent Lucca 2,500 florins: Anz. Av. Lib. 24, fol. 8r, 26 Jan. 1346. There had been a similar loan of 2,500 florins to pay the Duke of Athens, 8 July 1343. Special treasurers were appointed to receive this sum, plus 250 florins interest on behalf of the lenders. Their audited accounts are to be found in Ragionieri 4, fols. 32r–34v. 300 florins was apparently still outstanding in October 1345: Capitoli 19, fols. 46r–46v. There was also a loan in 1352 to raise the 2,333 1/3 florins due to Florence. A hundred citizens were to lend the money, which was to be repaid from the *dovana salis:* Anz. Av. Lib. 34, fols. 35r, 18 June, 37r–39v, 19 June, 39v–40v, 21 June 1352.
32. Ragionieri 5, fols. 54r, 68v. The audited account of Jacobo Sbarra, the treasurer for this *imposita* of November 1349 shows his receipts 5 Dec. 1349–29 April 1350 and his

4,550 florins from a sum of 5,000 florins imposed in Lucca and the *contado* in April of that year,[33] and there are details of various other sums, some of them substantial, received by *camarlinghi generali* later in 1354 and in 1355-1356.[34]

Recourse to *imposite* intensified in 1357-1358, which seem to have been particularly difficult years. In June and July 1357 a total of 2,035 florins and £565 11s. 6d. was raised by an *imposita* on the five *porte* of the city and on *cives silvestres* and was paid to the *camarlingo generale*,[35] and in September 1357 a group of eighty citizens lent 4,000 florins needed to buy off an armed company.[36] The same citizens had to lend Lucca

---

payments to the *camarlingo generale:* Ragionieri 5, fols. 73r-74v. There are no details of of the repayment of this *imposita*. It seems to be identical with the one recorded as collected in December 1349 and January 1350 in the series Imposte Diverse e Straordinarie nos. 5 and 6, except that the treasurer is there given as Puccinello Galganetti.

33. The audited accounts of the treasurer for this *imposita* show he received 4,5503/4 florins and £302 5s. *picc.:* Ragionieri 7, fols. 70r-71r. The *camarlingo generale*'s account for April and May includes the unusually large sum of £20,865 19s. 6d. under the heading "generalis et mixtus introitus." This is said to include 4,500 florins paid in florins: Ragionieri 7, fols. 7r-7v. Details of this *imposita:* Anz. Av. Lib. 37, fols. 28v-30r, 9 April 1354. Imposte Diverse e Straordinarie 7 appears to be the records of its collection in the Six Miles and vicariates.

34. There are audited accounts of further *imposite* in 1354-55, where the money received was paid to the *camarlingo generale:* 2,500 florins, imposed 1,500 on the city and 1,000 on the *contado* in November 1354; an unspecified sum that produced 598 florins and £1,975 6s. 7d. in March 1355; 3,3391/4 florins and £267 2s 10d. from an *imposita* of 3,500 florins on citizens and 1,500 florins on the Six Miles and vicariates in July 1355: Ragionieri 8, unfoliated. A further sum of 869 florins and £210 13s. 11d. was received from the latter 3 Oct. 1355-8 Aug. 1356: Ragionieri 8, fols. 5r-6r. There were also sums that did not pass through the *camarlingo generale*'s accounts: Francesco di Parente Onesti received 2,975 florins and £3 8s. 4d. from an *imposita* on the city and *contado* in April and May 1355. Although he also held the office of *camarlingo generale*, his *exitus* shows that he paid 3,000 florins representing this sum directly to Pisa in seven payments 25 April-5 May 1355. He thus remained Lucca's creditor for 24 florins 19s. and 4d.: Ragionieri 8, unfoliated. In June 1356 various small sums totalling 85 florins £2 13s. 2d. received from an *imposita* were used for the expenses of embassies without passing through the hands of the *camarlingo generale:* Ragionieri 8, fols. 5r-6v. Details of the assessments and payments for this are contained in Imposte Diverse e Straordinarie 8.

35. Ragionieri 8, fols. 60r-61r.

36. Anz. Av. Lib. 39, fols. 48v-49r, 11 May 1358. Lucca and Pisa were to pay the company jointly 11,000 florins and 4,000 florins in gifts: A.S.P. Comune A 62, fols. 24r-24v, 4 Sept. 1357. Pisa needed a total of 25,000 florins and Lucca's share of this was 4,000 florins with a further 4,000 florins to come from the Pisan and Lucchese clergy: ibid., fols. 26r-26v, 5 Sept. 1357. Lucca's petition for a reduction and for *proventus* to be assigned: ibid., fol. 26r, 10 Sept. 1357. The *dovana salis* was assigned and the repayments with lists of citizens and sums received are included in the

another 4,000 florins in February 1358, when Pisa asked that everything due under the composition ending 1 April be paid as soon as possible. At the same time there was to be an *imposita* of 6,500 florins in the city and the *contado*.[37] In May 1358 Pisa demanded the immediate payment of all sums outstanding and also an advance of 4,000 florins to pay its forces. This was to be repaid with 10% interest from sums due later under the composition. Again Lucca had to resort to loans to raise the money. The same citizens who had lent 4,000 florins earlier in the year were to advance this sum, and the *dovana salis* and the *gabella maggiore* were assigned for the repayment of this and of the *imposita*.[38] The repayment of these sums from money not passing through the hands of the *camarlingo generale*—no receipts from the *dovana salis* are recorded for 1358 and nothing from the *gabella maggiore* for June and July—would explain his exceptionally low receipts in 1358.[39]

It is easy enough to find records of money that by-passed the *camarlingo generale* completely or was received by him from an extraordinary loan or *imposita* to be repaid later from money not passing through his hands. Unfortunately it is difficult to be sure how complete these records are. Consequently Lucca's total resources cannot be ascertained with any degree of reliability, nor can one estimate how heavily burdened the city was by the sums owed to Pisa and the other charges that were paid

---

accounts of the treasurer of the *dovana salis* for 14 Sept. 1357–26 March 1358: Ragionieri 9, fols. 32r–44v. A dispute about the authorisation of interest payments to these citizens was settled in the Council of Fifty on 11 May 1358: Anz. Av. Lib. 39, fols. 48v–49r; Ragionieri 9, fols. 43r–44v, also fols. 101r–108v.

37. Anz. Av. Lib. 39, fols. 8v–9r, 30 Jan., 10r–11r, 1 Feb. 1358; complaints about this *imposita:* fol. 41v, 25 April 1358. Francesco Dati, the *camarlingo generale* for Feb. and March 1358, was also treasurer for this *imposita* of 4,000 florins: Ragionieri 9, fol. 60r. His receipts of exactly 4,000 florins were entered in his accounts as *camarlingo generale:* fol. 48r. Michele del Caro was the treasurer for the *imposita* of 6,500 florins. He is recorded as having received 2,9421/2 florins from this (Ragionieri 9, fol. 12r), but it is not clear what period this covered. He paid 3,809 florins to the *camarlingo generale* as treasurer for this *imposita* in Feb. and March 1359 (fol. 61r), and a further 730 florins and £2 2s. *picc.* in April and May (fol. 90v). He also lent, apparently personally, 650 florins in Feb. and March 1359 (fol. 60v).

38. Anz. Av. Lib. 39, fols. 52r–52v, 16 May, 57v–58r, 25 May, 58v–59r, 27 May 1358. Michele del Caro received this as treasurer for these loans. His audited accounts show the names of Lucchese citizens and the sums repaid to them 1 June–5 Aug. 1358: Ragionieri 9, fols. 28r–37v. There was a further loan of 3,200 florins from 120 Lucchese citizens decreed on 17 July 1359. 3,0691/4 florins were received 5 Aug.–11 Sept. 1359 and mostly paid directly to Pisa: Ragionieri 9, fols. 57r–59v.

39. Only 37,831 florins December 1357–November 1358, despite the inclusion of 4,000 florins received from a loan from eighty Lucchese citizens in the receipts for February and March 1358: Ragionieri 9, fols. 45r–48v.

directly. It is probable, however, that Lucchese revenues were lower during much of the period of Pisan rule than they had been earlier or were to be later. Certainly they cannot have approached the figure of 110,000 florins that Bongi calculated for 1337, and for much of the period they seem to have been appreciably lower than the 70,000-79,000 florins envisaged in 1342.[40] The revenues were probably also less than they would be in the 1370s, when they averaged 60,000-65,000 florins a year in 1373-1375 and 65,000-70,000 in 1375-1379.[41] Lucca would therefore have found it difficult to provide for necessary expenditure even if left to its own devices, and the financial relations of Pisa and Lucca must be viewed in the context of these reduced revenues. The *ragionieri* accounts together with references to financial matters in the council records suggest that Lucca's financial situation was always precarious, even though there was rarely a deficit for more than a short period. Revenues barely covered expenditure, and it was often necessary for Lucca to anticipate its income by borrowing from a small number of wealthy citizens or levying a more general *imposita*. Only in December 1353-November 1354 can there have been much of a surplus, taking a whole year together. Of course, a surplus was not really to be expected. Had Lucca's revenues regularly been in excess of its expenditure, the opportunity would have been taken to reduce the gabelles. In fact it was necessary to increase some of these, perhaps only temporarily, in the early 1350s.[42] By 1357-1358 there are signs of a deterioration in Lucca's financial position, even before the outbreak of hostilities with Florence involved it in the kind of financial crisis that wars always brought.

40. *Inventario*, 2:28. He calculated the revenues at £353,359 17s. 10d. *picc.*, the equivalent of 110,000 florins. He reached a figure of £325,910 12s. *picc.* for the previous year, though this was on the basis of surviving figures for only four and a half months, 15 Nov. 1335-1 April 1336. Also S. Bongi, *Bande lucchesi del secolo decimoquarto* (Bologna, 1863), p. 319. Nor, of course, were they approaching the 79,000 florins envisaged in the agreement between Pisa and Lucca, 14 August 1342: Capitoli 19, fols. 11r-13v, and *Memorie e documenti*, 1:335-336, doc. I. Many individual *proventus* show a marked decline between the late 1330s and mid-1340s, and there are a number of references in Lucchese sources to a fall in the revenues: a letter of 30 Oct. 1349 speaks of "diminutione nostrorum introytuum et gabellarum qui pro dimidia solito non respondent" (original in Anz. Av. Lib. 47, corresponds to no. 447 in *Regesto*) and another of 19 Oct. 1348 of "nostrorum facultatuum que iam causis vobis notis ad infima devenerunt" (Anz. Av. Lib. 47; *Regesto* no. 406, also no. 460, 19 June 1350).

41. For the revenues for these years series Camarlingo Generale, nos. 79-83 and Ragionieri, nos. 11-14.

42. Anz. Av. Lib. 37, fols. 79r-79v, 11 Dec. 1354. This refers to provisions increasing the *introitus* and gabelles from 13 Jan. 1351 until 1352, with an extension for three

It is clear that Lucca had to pay over the vast majority of its revenues to Pisa. But these sums were to cover the costs of the custody and defence of Lucca and its *contado,* and the salaries of many officials, including all those appointed in Lucca by the Pisans, the same costs that had absorbed a great proportion of the revenues before 1342. The main expense was certainly the payment of hired soldiers and guards. As they were paid by Pisan officials, Lucchese records contain no details of their number and cost, and Pisan sources, where such information might be found, are not very full. There is a list of payments to foot-soldiers garrisoning the walls and towers of Lucca and certain fortresses in the *contado* for the period April to July 1355,[43] but even if one could be sure that it is complete, the list is only of limited value. These were the months when Emperor Charles IV was in Italy and his presence encouraged the Lucchese to rebel against Pisa; the garrison at that period may not be typical of more ordinary years.[44] In any case the list covers only foot-soldiers, and cavalrymen were probably a greater expense. One is

more years, 21 Dec. 1351. See also *Regesto* no. 505. As these increases were therefore due to expire on 1 Jan. 1355, the council extended them for another year. These earlier decrees do not survive, so it is unclear what gabelles were affected and how large the increase was. The series Proventi Contratti, which includes details of the rates at which the various *proventus* were exacted, does not show any signs of increases, so they may not have been very significant. There was an increase in the retail wine tax in 1354, administered separately as "augmentum vini venalis," but its yield was not very great (see above, note 24). There is little sign in Lucca of the general upward trend in the rates of the gabelles discernable in Florence for these years, even though this was not continuous: C. de la Roncière, "Indirect Taxes or 'Gabelles' in the Fourteenth Century: The Evolution of Tariffs and the Problems of Collection," in *Florentine Studies,* ed. N. Rubinstein (London, 1968), pp. 149–162. In Lucca some old levies were even dropped, notably the tax on the Six Miles and *contado* in lieu of military service, known as the *taglia delle cinquantasettemila lire e la paga dei pedoni: Inventario,* 2:81–89; Capitoli 19, fols. 11v, 45v. The only *proventus* permanently instituted under Pisan rule seems to have been the *proventus meretricium,* which was not very significant financially: *Inventario,* 2:27–28. I hope to discuss the development of Lucchese revenues in the fourteenth century more fully in a future study.

43. A.S.P. Comune A 122. It is difficult to be sure how complete this is. The list of forces Lucca was to pay, which had been included in the agreement of 4 July (Capitoli 19, fols. 3v–4r), had long since been superseded. It had in any case left many salaries and numbers of garrisons to be decided later. Also Pisa controlled more fortresses in the Lucchese *contado* in 1355 than it had in 1342, though some were in the vicariates it was ruling directly and which were presumably not maintained from Lucchese resources. There are some mandates for payments for forces in Lucca and for fortresses in the Lucchese *contado* in other volumes of the *Provvisioni* of Pisa, but they are far less complete even than Comune A 122.

44. In fact the *cerne* of the Pisan *contado* had been sent to reinforce the garrison of Lucca and were only withdrawn at the end of April 1355: A.S.P. Comune A 60, fol. 1r, 30

therefore obliged to use more general evidence to determine the costs of defence and their relation to the total revenue. In a period of four and a half months from mid-November 1335 to 1 April 1336 £71,566 2s. 4d. *picc.* out of a total expenditure of £113,532 17s., or almost two-thirds, was spent on mercenary soldiers.[45] In the period after 1369, although Lucca pursued an unadventurous foreign policy and tried to keep its military expenditure to a minimum, nearly a third of its total expenditure was on mercenaries. In the period January–June 1376 10,206 florins out of a total of 34,107 florins and in the year 1377 21,311 florins out of a total of 65,571 florins were spent on hired soldiers.[46] This is for mercenary soldiers alone, and does not include the cost of garrisoning fortresses and providing arms, or other defence expenditure. Though these comparisons are of rather limited value in view of the fact that the number of forces, castellans, sergeants, and guards maintained while Lucca was under Pisan rule is unknown, the very fact that Lucca was held by Pisa was likely to increase rather than reduce the number of guards needed. Since Pisa was responsible for the payment of many salaries and general administrative costs in addition to defence expenditure, it seems probable that the sums Lucca was paying to Pisa were not disproportionate to the expenditure they were intended to cover.

The sums paid by Lucca amounted to about a quarter of Pisa's total revenues. In 1355 the Pisans informed Emperor Charles IV that their annual revenues were about 141,000 florins, including 36,000 florins a year from Lucca.[47] This is a surprisingly low proportion and must easily

---

April 1355, printed as doc. II in G. Mancinelli, "Carlo IV di Lussemburgo e la Repubblica di Pisa", *Studi storici* di A. Crivellucci 15 (1906), pp. 358–360. The costs included in A.S.P. Comune A 122 amounted to £2,218 10s. *pis.*, plus £3,020 *lucch.* in April 1355. For a year at the same rates the cost would be £26,622 *pis.* and £36,246 *lucch.*, but the rates for April 1355 cannot be regarded as typical.

45. *Inventario*, 2:28–29.

46. Ragionieri 13, fols. 6r–93r (first semester), 33r–143r (second semester), (various foliations). Series Camarlingo Generale no. 103, Mandatorie, shows a total expenditure of 35,862 florins and £3 18s. 9d. *picc.* authorised by the Anziani for defence. For the first semester of 1376: Ragionieri 12, fols. 9r–76r. For the high cost of mercenaries and warfare in other cities, see W.M. Bowsky, *The Finance of the Commune of Siena, 1287–1355* (Oxford, 1970), pp. 43–46, and for the late fourteenth and early fifteenth centuries, Becker, *Florence in transition*, 2:160–165, 190; A. Molho, *Florentine Public Finances in the Early Renaissance, 1400–1430* (Cambridge, Mass., 1971), pp. 3–4, 9–11, 15; P. Silva, "Il governo di Pietro Gambacorta in Pisa," *Annali della R. Scuola Normale Superiore di Pisa* 23 (1912), p. 108. But much depended on how active a foreign policy was pursued and whether it were a time of peace or war.

47. A.S.P. Comune A 60, fols. 2r, 10 May 1355, printed as doc. V in Mancinelli, "Carlo IV," p. 363.

have been absorbed by Lucchese expenses. Indeed in some years at least much of the money paid by Lucca never seems to have reached Pisa, but was spent in Lucca itself by the Pisan treasurer there in paying the Pisan forces in Lucca and other local expenses. The only register of Pisan letters for this period, which covers the year 1361, includes a number of letters urging the Pisan rectors to ensure that their forces were paid from the revenues due to Pisa and forbidding the use of Lucchese funds for any other purposes in terms that suggest that it was the normal practice to use Lucchese revenues locally for the payment of Pisan forces.[48] It therefore seems quite possible that possession of Lucca brought no direct financial benefit to Pisa and that it may at times have been a burden. In October 1349 Pisan citizens and *contadini* are found complaining of the burden of guard duty on the walls and towers of Lucca and the Augusta,[49] and after the unsuccessful rising of May 1355 Pisa seems to have been obliged to contribute to the costs of the defence and administration of Lucca out of its own pocket.[50]

It might be thought that Lucca, as a subject city, would be in a weak negotiating position in financial matters; that it might petition for relief, but was hardly in a position to bargain; that in the last resort it would have no option but to accept whatever terms the Pisans chose to offer. But there is evidence in some cases at least that the compositions were the result of long drawn out negotiations and hard bargaining, and that Lucca was often successful in obtaining the terms it wanted. In 1345, although the negotiations for a new composition had begun by 11 August, no agreement was reached until 11 October, despite a number of embassies from Lucca to Pisa, several council meetings in which the

---

48. A.S.P. Comune A 206, fols. 12r, 24 Jan., 40r, 5 March, 47v, 16 March, 69r, 16 April, 184v, 20 Oct. 1361. Also *Regesto* nos. 589 (17 Sept. 1353), 592 (7 Oct. 1353), 601 (13 Nov. 1353). But there are also mandates for payments to men serving in Lucca among the mandates to the ordinary Pisan treasurers, for example in A.S.P. Comune A 119 (1353).
49. A.S.P. Comune A 56, fols. 67r–67v, 12 Oct. 1349.
50. A.S.P. Comune A 60, fol. 32v, 7 June 1355: "licet pisani propter defectum multorum civium lucanorum graventur multis et variis expensis magis quam soleant pro custodia civitatis lucane pro quibus expensis opportet pisanos ponere manus ad borsas suas nicchilominus propter affectionem quam habent ad comune lucanum placet eis et contenti sunt quod compositio fiat pro anno presenti de florenis trigintasex milibus auri more solito. Et non augeatur non obstantibus hiis que supra dicta sunt''; and similar expressions: fol. 37v, 11 June 1355. There were, of course, offices and other benefits for individual Pisan citizens, including members of the most important families. The lack of financial benefit to Pisa from its possession of Lucca may be contrasted with Venice, which drew very substantial sums from its subject cities: F. C. Lane, *Venice: A Maritime Republic* (Baltimore, 1973), pp. 237–238.

matter was discussed, and perhaps even a visit of messer Dino della Rocca to Lucca.[51] The agreement when finally reached embodied a major concession to the Lucchese, permitting the retention of the system under which Pisa administered Lucchese revenues, rather than forcing Lucca to collect its own revenues and pay Pisa a fixed sum each year, as the Pisans had desired.[52] Though Pisa got its way on this point in the composition agreed 28 October 1348, the negotiations were again long drawn out, involving at least five embassies to Pisa in August and September and the calling in of messer Francesco Castracani by the Lucchese to intercede for them.[53] Less is heard of the negotiations for subsequent compositions, perhaps because once the pattern was set many clauses were simply carried over from one agreement to the next, and only relatively minor variations and disputed points remained to be settled. But Lucca's ability to obtain concessions, or Pisa's willingness to grant them, can be seen again in 1355. Pisa recognised that, despite the increased expenses of this crisis year and its own financial difficulties, it would need to make concessions. There was no question of increasing the Lucchese contribution, but Pisa hoped that Lucca could be induced to agree that the annual payment should remain at 36,000 florins, as in previous years. Failing this, Pisa's negotiators were authorised to agree to a smaller sum: "discendatur paulatim ad componendum cum eis de trigintaquinque milibus seu trigintaquattuor usque in trigintatribus florenis auri prout melius fieri poterit."[54] Nothing is known of the negotiations, but the resulting agreement called for the smallest of the sums authorised.[55]

51. A.S.P. Comune A 54, fol. 27v, 11 Aug. 1345; Capitoli 19, fols. 45r–48v, 11 Oct. 1345. For the negotiations: A.S.P. Comune A 54 fols. 34v–35r, 23 Aug. 1345; Comune A 55, fols. 17v, 23 Aug., 18r–18v, 7 Sept. 1345.

52. A.S.P. Comune A 54, fol. 27v, 11 Aug. 1345. Lucchese refusal of the Pisan proposals: Comune A 54, fols. 34v–35r, 23 Aug.; Comune A 55, fols. 17v, 23 Aug., 18r–18v, 7 Sept. 1345.

53. Anz. Av. Lib. 28, p. 259 (modern pagination; no foliation), 5 Sept., p. 262, 11 Sept., p. 267, 19 Sept., p. 268, 22 Sept. 1348: authorisation for the payment of ambassadors without giving the precise date of the embassies. Also *Regesto* nos. 387, 393, 395, 397, 399, 401, 403–406, 408–409, 1004. For an ambassador to messer Francesco Castracani and a dinner held in his honour 25 Sept.: Anz. Av. Lib. 28, p. 271, 26 Sept. 1348. Lucca apparently finally left the terms to the discretion of Pisa (Capitoli 19, fols. 49r–49v), but wrote on 19 October asking them to have regard to Lucchese resources "que iam casis vobis notis ad infima devenerunt" (Anz. Av. Lib. 47; no. 406 in *Regesto*).

54. A.S.P. Comune A 60, fol. 32v, 7 June 1355.

55. A.S.P. Comune A 60, fol. 37v, 11 June 1355; Capitoli 19, fols. 67v–68r, 16 June 1355.

Each composition from 14 October 1345 to 1 June 1361 had stipulated that Lucca was not to be liable for any payments beyond the annual sum laid down, 2,333 1/3 florins as its share of the annual payment to Florence, the salaries and other charges for which it was directly responsible, and a sum of 800–1,000 florins to be spent on the repair of fortresses. Lucca was specifically exempt from any *prestantia, mutuum,* or *imposita.* This guarantee against arbitrary extra levies had not invariably been observed. It was violated in April 1348, when Pisa demanded a loan of 6,000 florins. The demand was particularly untimely, coinciding as it did with the outbreak of plague in Lucca. The Lucchese replied with an eloquent plea to be excused because of their poverty; the effects of the plague, which was raging so fiercely that the cemeteries could take no more bodies; and their lack of revenues, since all their *proventus* and gabelles were in the hands of Pisa. They also urged that such a demand was in any case contrary to the composition.[56] The Pisans, however, insisted, stressing their need and writing, "necessitas caret lege. Nos enim modo sumus in necessitate extrema. Unde si vos gravamus, quamquam gravamen sit modicum, exinde reddimur merito excusari."[57] The Lucchese were obliged to make the loan.[58]

In this case Pisa ignored the terms of the composition and made a heavy demand in the face of strong protests from the Lucchese. There

56. Anz. Av. Lib. 55, fol. 113r, 5 April 1348; no. 367 in *Regesto.* Also *Regesto* no. 371 (10 April 1348). An embassy was sent on 3 April; payment to the ambassadors for two days: Anz. Av. Lib. 28, p. 215, 12 April 1348.

57. Original letter in Anz. Av. Lib. 47; no. 372 in *Regesto,* 10 April 1348. The Pisans also pointed out that they had imposed even heavier burdens on their own citizens. Also *Regesto* no. 368 (7 April 1348).

58. Anz. Av. Lib. 28, p. 217, 17 April, p. 219, 25 April, p. 225, 13 May 1348: details of collection. Sixty citizens lent the money and the *dovana salis* was assigned for its repayment: A.S.P. Comune A 56, fols. 27v–28r, 4 July 1353, referring to repayment of loan of April 1349 (Pisan style, i.e. 1348). There had also been an extraordinary levy in June 1344 before the first composition. Lucca was obliged to raise 6,000 florins from its citizens in a loan "pro sobventione comune pisano facienda." In fact receipts were 6,541 florins, of which 6,460 florins were paid to Pisa in five different payments 15 June–11 Aug. 1344: Ragionieri 4, fols. 10r–13v. The *proventus farine* was assigned for the repayment of this on 12 June 1344, and a total of £25,634 2s. 6d. was received from it Nov. 1344–20 Nov. 1345: Ragionieri 4, fols. 101r–107v, 109r–111r, 112r–114r. In the composition of October 1345 1,400 florins were said to be still outstanding and the *proventus farine* was not to be included among the *proventus* assigned to Pisa until it had been paid off: Capitoli 19, fol. 46r. The contract for the sale of the *proventus farine* for the year beginning 1 November 1345 provided for £1,647 18s. 7d. *picc.* to go to the citizens who had lent 6,500 florins in June "pro subventione facta pisano comuni." In addition 3,105 florins were to be paid to three Pisan citizens who had lent Lucca 3,354 florins at a date unspecified: Proventi Contratti 23, fols. 135r–138v.

were, however, very few demands of this kind in peacetime. Whether because of the strength of Lucchese protests, or a more general desire not to arouse discontent, or a feeling that agreements ought to be kept and subjects treated well, the Pisans refrained from making extraordinary levies on Lucca for about ten years, despite serious financial difficulties and the need for extraordinary levies in Pisa itself. In 1345 there had been a large *prestanza* of 30,000 florins in Pisa, but none in Lucca.[59] In 1350 Pisan expenditure was said to exceed the revenues by 12,000 florins a year. Various emergency measures were proposed to remedy this, none of them affecting Lucca.[60] It is not perhaps surprising that the Pisans should have demanded no extraordinary financial contributions from Lucca in 1355, in view of the recent rebellion there.[61] But in July 1357, when there was a *prestanza* in Pisa and the Pisan *contado*, Lucca was unaffected although by that time calm had been restored.[62] Lucca did have to contribute 4,000 florins toward the sum required to buy off an armed company in September 1357.[63] It was also asked in May 1358 to pay in advance 4,000 florins due later under the composition, [64] but apparently did not have to contribute when an *imposita* of 12,000 florins was levied on the Pisan *contado*.[65]

But this was in peacetime. In 1362 the war with Florence was renewed. Pisa therefore found itself in need of large sums of money to meet war expenditure and naturally looked to Lucca, which was also involved in the war, to bear a share of the cost. The composition of 1 June 1361 still contained the clause exempting Lucca from any *prestanza* or *imposita*, but that of 1 June 1362 stipulated that for the next two years extraordinary expenses were to be borne three-quarters by Pisa and one-quarter by Lucca, and that Pisa could, if necessary, assign Lucchese *pro-*

59. A.S.P. Comune A 55, fol. 15r, 13 Aug. 1345. This applies only to extraordinary levies imposed by Pisa. Lucca itself was, of course, obliged to impose *imposite* and loans in order to raise the money for necessary expenditure, as has been seen.

60. A.S.P. Comune A 57, fols. 8v, 9v–10r, 12r–14r, 15r–16r, 16r–18r.

61. No attempt was made to obtain from Lucca any of the 20,000 florins that had to be paid to Charles IV on his departure (A.S.P. Comune A 60, fols. 24r–24v, 4 June 1355), and other means were found to raise the money for the pay of the cavalry and footsoldiers in Lucca (fol. 39v, 12 June 1355).

62. A.S.P. Comune A 62, fol. 7v, 7 July 1357.

63. A.S.P. Comune A 62, fols. 24r–24v, 4 Sept., 26r, 5 Sept. 1357. The Lucchese clergy also had to make a contribution. In fact these were not contributions towards the expenses of Pisa generally; rather, Pisa had made terms on Lucca's behalf as well as its own.

64. Anz. Av. Lib. 39, fols. 52r–52v, 16 May, 57v–58r, 25 May 1358. Interest of 10% was to be paid, and the *dovana salis* and the *gabella maggiore* were assigned as security for its repayment: Anz. Av. Lib. 39, fols. 58v–59r, 26 May 1358.

65. This is mentioned in A.S.P. Comune A 64, fol. 15v, 23 Aug. 1359. Its precise date is not clear.

ventus to Pisan citizens for the repayment of loans.[66] These conditions were strictly observed. Lucca was never asked to contribute more than a quarter of any levy, but the sums required under these terms in the next two years were large: in July 1362 5,333 florins as Lucca's quarter share of 21,332 florins required for the war,[67] and in August 1362 £233 per day for six months as its share of a "seca" of £933 per day.[68] There were already signs of financial strain in 1361 and 1362. Lucca was having difficulty raising the money for payments due to Pisa under the composition and was obliged to levy *imposite* and seek loans from its own citizens. There had been one *imposita* of 8,000 florins in April 1361 to cover a deficit of 6,450 florins in the payments to Pisa and certain other debts,[69] and another of 5,200 florins in October of the same year.[70] There were complaints of over-taxation and unfairness in the assessments, and arrangements had to be made to relieve individuals.[71] Other complaints alleged that some citizens were leaving Lucca or were making fraudulent alienations of their property, with secret agreements safeguarding their rights over it, in order to escape taxes and *imposite*.[72] In April 1362 Lucca tried to levy an *imposita* of 8,000 florins to raise 5,000 florins towards buying off an armed company led by Anichino and 4,000 florins owed to Pisa.[73] The attempted levy gave rise to so many com-

66. Capitoli 19, fols. 107r, 116r. On 3 July 1362 it was decreed by the Pisan Anziani that there was not to be any *imposita, mutuum, datium* or *collecta* in Lucca or the Lucchese *contado* without a decree of the Pisan Anziani: fol. 121r.

67. Anz. Av. Lib. 42, fols. 57v–58r, 12 July 1362. It was to bear 10% interest and be included in the Pisan public debt. Arrangements for raising this sum: Anz. Av. Lib. 42, fols. 59r, 13 July, 59v, 16 July, 61r, 21 July 1362. Accounts of this loan: Ragionieri 10, fols. 73r–74r; also fol. 111v. Payment to the scribe for writing it in the Pisan public debt: fol. 68r.

68. Anz. Av. Lib. 42, fol. 61v, 16 Aug. 1362. This apparently amounted to 12,000 florins over six months. Arrangements for raising it: Anz. Av. Lib. 42, fols. 62r, 16 Aug., 62v, 17 Aug., 63r, 20 Aug. 1362. There were a number of embassies to Pisa about this "seca": Ragionieri 10, fols. 69r, 70v, 71v.

69. Anz. Av. Lib. 41, fols. 32r, 14 April, 33v, 16 April, 34r–35r, 17 April, 37v–38r, 19 April, 41v–42r, 26 April, 46r, 4 May 1361. Series Imposte Diverse a Straordinarie 12 is a fragment of the assessments and payments for the 6,000 florins of this *imposita* that were allotted to the city.

70. Anz. Av. Lib. 41, fols. 102v–103r, 8 Oct. 1361. Details: fols. 104r–114r, 9, 13, 15, and 19 Oct., 112v, 18 Oct., 113r–114r, 20–23 Oct. 1361. Accounts of the treasurer for this: Ragionieri 10, fols. 29r–32r.

71. Anz. Av. Lib. 41, fols. 46v–47r, 10 May, 47r–47v, 11 May, 117v–118r, 20 Oct., 124v, 5 Nov., 125r, 6 Nov., 8 Nov., 126r–126v, 19 Nov. 1361.

72. Anz. Av. Lib. 41, fol. 76r, 24 July 1361. Penalties for failure to pay: fols. 85r–85v, 3 Aug. 1361. The Pisan rectors were ordered to act against men declaring themselves *forenses* to avoid taxation: A.S.P. Comune A 206, fol. 195r, 11 Nov. 1361.

73. Anz. Av. Lib. 42, fols. 22v–23r, 3 April 1362. Pisa had at first asked for 6,000 florins, but later agreed to a reduction. Three Lucchese citizens, who had been sent to Pisa as

plaints—both that some assessments were so heavy that men would be obliged to abandon Lucca and become vagabonds, and also that the levy had been distributed unfairly, sparing the rich and taxing the poor excessively—that it had to be cancelled and the money raised from a small group of wealthy citizens.[74] 1362 was also a plague year, which must have aggravated these financial problems.[75]

The situation deteriorated in 1363. In April Pisa tried to raise a loan of 50,000 florins and pressed Lucca for 12,500 florins as its quarter share of this.[76] In June there was another *imposita* of 50,000 florins, of which Lucca's share was again 12,500,[77] and in August Pisa was trying to raise

ambassadors for this, were paid their salary for 4–7 April 1362 and the cost of letters from the Pisan chancery reducing the sum to 5,000 florins: Ragionieri 10, fols. 48v–49r, and 40v (a different set of foliation). For the *imposita:* Anz. Av. Lib. 42, fols. 24r, 8 April, 24v, 9 April 1362; and details: fols. 25r, 22 and 23 April, 25r–25v, 24 April 1362. There was also a small *imposita* of 1,000 florins for the defence of Pietrabuona: Anz. Av. Lib. 42, fols. 2r, 8 Jan., 8r, 17 Feb., 9r, 18 Feb. 1362. Imposte Diverse e Straordinarie 13 records the assessments and payments for this.

74. Anz. Av. Lib. 42, fol. 40r, 21 May 1362. Other levies this year were raised from relatively limited groups of citizens: Anz. Av. Lib. 42, fols. 48r–48v, 10 and 11 June, 59r, 13 July, 59v–60r, 12 July 1362 (a loan of 2,000 florins owed to Pisa). Imposte Diverse e Straordinarie 14 apparently refers to the loan decreed 12 July 1362. There is an account of an "imposita sive mutuum" of 1,600 florins in August 1362 in Ragionieri 10, fols. 47r–49v.

75. Anz. Av. Lib. 42, fol. 75r, 7 Nov. 1362.

76. Anz. Av. Lib. 42, fol. 117r, 5 April 1363. Interest of 10% was to be paid. Despite a number of council meetings on the subject, there was difficulty reaching agreement on the methods of raising the money: Anz. Av. Lib. 42, fols. 118r–118v, 5–7 April, 119r–119v, 7 April, 119v, 19 April, 120r, 20 May 1363. References to the repayment of this loan by Pisa: Anz. Av. Lib. 42, fol. 135v, 27 June 1363; Anz. Av. Lib. 43, fol. 37r, 4 and 6 July 1363; *Regesto* no. 935. There were a number of embassies and letters to Pisa about this levy: Ragionieri 10, fols. 102r, 106v, 107r, 107v–108r.

77. Anz. Av. Lib. 42, fol. 132v, 19 June 1363. This *imposita* was decreed by Pisa on 10 May and was additional to the 50,000 florins *imposita* of April 1363. Pisa was to pay 29,000 florins, its *contado* 8,500 and Lucca 12,500. Interest was now only 5%. Lucca seems to have had difficulty raising the money, for on 27 June payment was authorised for two days to Turellino Bonucci who "ivit Pisam si poterat invenire aliquem civem pisanum vel aliquos qui lucano comuni mutuare vellent florenos XII^m V^c petitos per comune pisanum comuni lucano": Ragionieri 10, fol. 101v. There were a number of embassies to Pisa to try to obtain a reduction: fols. 102r, 120r, 122r. The full sum was apparently levied: fols. 112v, 119v–120r, 126r; but later two ambassadors were sent to Pisa to ask "quod placeret eis esse contentos de exoneratione facta de imposita facta florenorum XII^m V^c auri et quod summa exonerata non reponeretur": fol. 127r. Lucca does seem to have obtained some reduction, for it thanked Pisa for this: Anz. Av. Lib. 43, fol. 37v, 16 July 1363. Arrangements for raising the money: Anz. Av. Lib. 42, fols. 134r–135r, 19–20, and 22–24 June, 135r, 26 and 30 June 1363.

60,000 florins, 15,000 of it from Lucca.[78] Pisa was by this time hard pressed itself; money was needed to pay its forces and to raise sums due to an armed company at a time when most of its *proventus* were pledged for the repayment of earlier loans. For Lucca the latest demand was a further heavy burden, and it sent an embassy "ad exponendum gravamina et impossibilitates comunis et civium lucanorum et ab eis gratiam et misericordiam implorandum."[79] Despite its own serious financial position Pisa responded to this appeal, agreeing that the 15,000 florins originally demanded should be reduced to 12,000.[80]

Early in 1364 there was apparently an increase in the gabelles in Lucca. Neither Lucchese nor Pisan records give any details of the circumstances of the increase, in particular whether or not it was intended as a temporary war measure, but it seems to have represented a significant burden, for Lucca sent no fewer than three embassies to Pisa on this matter in February 1364.[81] The instructions for one of these embassies give some details of the nature of the increases and prognostications about their probable effect. They ask the Pisan Anziani "quod placeat eis moderari gabellas cum sint nimis et intolleribiliter augmentate propter quod pauperes et artifices habitantes in civitate lucana et eius burgis non possent substinere et habent materiam absentandi se cum familia tam cives quam forenses. Et dicta occasione introitus non crescunt sed potius decrescunt et satis minus valent nunc quam valerent ante dictam augmentationem ut videri et percepi potest per libros introytus dictarum gabellarum." The instructions specifically mention the gabelle on wine,

78. Anz. Av. Lib. 42, fols. 143v–144v, 29 Aug. 1363. Pisa had originally asked for this on 8 August and wrote on 28 August, expressing surprise that no *imposita* had yet been levied.
79. Anz. Av. Lib. 42, fols. 143v–145r, 29 Aug., 145r, 30 Aug. 1363. Payment of ambassadors to Pisa for five days: Ragionieri 10, fol. 129v.
80. Anz. Av. Lib. 42, fols. 143v–145r, 29 Aug., 145r, 30 Aug., 145v, 4 Sept. 1363. Raising the money: fols. 145v–147r, 4–6 Sept. 1363. Ragionieri 10, fol. 121v, records a provision of 20 Sept. in connection with fifteen citizens "deputatorum super exonerum de florenis M VIII^c auri de imposita facta de dicto mense."
81. Ragionieri 10, fol. 130v: payment to two separate embassies to the Pisan Anziani in February 1364 "occasione aumentationis ghabellarum." One ambassador was paid for two periods of nine and seven days. There was a different embassy for six days beginning on 7 February, "occasione augmenti ghabellarum lucane civitatis": fol. 141v. The increase seems to have been connected with a new composition between Pisa and Lucca, since the Lucchese asked that the provision concerning increased gabelles should not be applied to anything due before that date: *Regesto* no. 1014 (original in Anz. Av. Lib. 51, undated, but Feb. 1364). Three Pisan citizens had been authorised to negotiate agreements between Pisa and Lucca about the expenses of the war despite the composition: Anz. Av. Lib. 42, p. 301 (modern pagination; no foliation), 20 Sept. 1363.

stating that gabelle and transport costs so exceeded the value of the wine itself that it was no longer brought to Lucca and *contadini* were discouraged from producing it. They also ask for the abolition of gabelle on goods not traditionally subject to it, especially cereals, which hads not previously paid gabelle on entry to Lucca. The rest of the clauses are concerned with the coinage in which the gabelles were to be exacted and the methods of calculating the amount due in different Lucchese and Pisan coins. In some cases they seem to refer to errors and confusion that resulted in increases in the gabelles beyond what had been intended. The case of the *proventus farine* is cited, where 3s. of Lucchese *piccioli* a *staio* instead of 2s. 6d. were being exacted, and the same is said to have happened in other gabelles.[82] The ambassadors were to ask for a clear declaration of the rates of the gabelles and the money in which they were to be paid "ut cesset obscuritas monetarum," and they were to press particularly that the exaction should be in Lucchese money. Unfortunately nothing is known of the outcome of these embassies, though it seems probable that the increases in the gabelles were only intended as temporary war measures.[83]

There are references to other financial matters, of which little is known in detail because of the lack of council records for these months. In or before May 1364 there was an *imposita* of £9,000 in Lucca, apparently for the war or for local defence, since it is described as "pro solvendo balistrariis et magistris lapidum et lignaminis." This was a relatively modest sum. Although it gave rise to an embassy to Pisa, the issue was the claims of certain Lucchese citizens that they were exempt from such payments, not protests from Lucca or pleas that the sum be reduced.[84] At the end of 1363 or early in 1364 Lucca had made rep-

---

82. "Item quia error et deceptio est in exactione gabellarum in eo et de eo quod ultra augmentationem exigitur tertia pars plus videlicet quia pro duobus soldis lucanorum parvorum exiguntur tres sicut apparet in proventu farine ubi solvebantur soldi duos parvorum lucanorum pro quolibet stario qui valent soldos i et denarios viii pisanos in quo proventu exiguntur soldi tres parvorum pro quolibet stario predicto de quo ad rationem denariorum quatuor pisanorum pro quolibet cinquino et soldorum quatuor pro quolibet grosso solvi deberent tantum cinquini quinque qui valent ad parvam lucanam monetam soldos duos et denarios sex. Ita quod error et deceptio est de denariis sex parvorum lucanorum in et pro quolibet stario predicto.

"Et similis error et deceptio est in aliis exactionibus gabellarum": Anz. Av. Lib. 51, Feb. 1364; no. 1014 in *Regesto.*

83. See below, pp. 108–109.

84. Two ambassadors were paid for four days in Pisa May 1364 "occasione imposite facte in civitate lucana librarum VIIII^m pro solvendo balistrariis et magistris lapidum et lignaminis quam quidam cives lucani compositati solvere recusabant": Ragionieri 10, fols. 145v, 148r.

resentations about the exaction of the *dovana salis* in the *contado*; apparently a remission granted by the Pisan Anziani of part of the sum due previously was not being observed.[85] But both these cases were relatively minor. Apart from the increase in the gabelles, the significance of which is difficult to gauge, it seems that Lucca was not being called upon to furnish the kind of sums in 1364 that it had had to supply the previous year.

Although Lucca might feel that the war with Florence in no way served its interests and that it had nothing to gain from such a war, Lucca was involved in it and was quick to claim a share in any victories.[86] It was therefore not unreasonable that Lucca should contribute towards its costs. Nor can a quarter share be regarded as excessive. It was in line with the sums that Lucca had been paying to Pisa under the compositions: according to the Pisan declaration to Charles IV in 1355 Lucca's contribution of 36,000 florins represented about a quarter of Pisa's annual revenues of 141,000 florins.[87] Indeed Lucca had later paid more than 36,000 florins, and was probably being treated generously in being required to pay only a quarter of the extraordinary levies for the war. Pisa was certainly a larger and richer city than Lucca, but hardly three times as large.[88] Also, although Lucca was called upon to contribute conspicuous sums in 1362 and 1363, it was left free to distribute the burden among its citizens and subjects as it thought best. It any case the levies took the form of interest-bearing loans, included in the Pisan public debt or with *proventus* assigned for their repayment, and there is evidence that repayment of these loans was begun even before hostilities were over.[89] It is important to note that the Lucchese were treated no worse than the Pisans in this respect. Certainly the Lucchese were not

---

85. Payment of two ambassadors for four days in Pisa "pro factis lucani comunis et comitativorum lucani comunis qui gravabantur ad solvendum quintam partem imposite salis eis in preterito remissam per dominos Anthianos pisani populi," and also "pro habendo provisione dicti salis": Ragionieri 10, fol. 129v. The payment was authorised on 23 Jan. 1364, but the date of the embassy is not clear. Also fol. 141v.

86. Lucca asked to be allowed to run a *palio:* Anz. Av. Lib. 43, fol. 38r, 23 July 1363 (*Regesto* no. 938 gives an incorrect version of this), fol. 38v, 2 Aug. 1363, (*Regesto* no. 941). Payments for celebrations, rewards to messengers who brought good news, and similar expenditures: Ragionieri 10, fols. 139v–140r, 157r–157v, 160v .

87. A.S.P. Comune A 60, fol. 2r, 10 May 1355.

88. D. Herlihy, *Pisa in the Early Renaissance* (New Haven, 1958), pp. 35–43 on the relative size of Pisa and Lucca.

89. Anz. Av. Lib. 42, fols. 135v–136r, 27 June 1363; Anz. Av. Lib. 43, fol. 37r, 4 July, 6 July 1363. Payment to the Pisan notary who wrote the 12,500 florins lent by Lucca July 1363 "in credito pisani comunis seu in massa mutuum": Ragionieri 10, fol. 161v.

asked to pay anything that the Pisans were not also paying, or to make any sacrifices that the Pisans were not also making. Nevertheless the sums Lucca was required to pay were very large. In 1363 the Lucchese had to raise two loans of 12,500 florins and one of 12,000, a total of 37,000 florins. Since Lucchese revenues were in Pisan hands, this could only be done by levying forced loans and *imposite*. The signs of strain are clear in the records of 1362 and 1363. But warfare always placed a severe strain on the finances of medieval Italian communes—there were similar financial problems in Florence at this time for the same reasons[90]—and these war years were quite exceptional.

Unfortunately it is impossible to say how quickly Lucca recovered once peace was restored. Lucchese revenues were administered directly by Pisa for the rest of the period of Pisan rule, so that only the few hundred florins required for the *familia* of the Anziani and other very local expenses are recorded as passing through the hands of the *camarlingo generale*. Again Lucca apparently preferred this system, which denied it control of its own revenues. In the negotiations for the composition of 1 June 1361 the Lucchese offered to assign the revenues to Pisa. When this was refused, they seized the opportunity of making a contract with an individual Pisan citizen, Frammuccio di messer Frammuccio, to collect all Lucchese revenues and pay all the expenses for the duration of the composition, even though this meant offering him "aliquam congruam additionem pecunie."[91] In 1362 Pisa agreed to take over the direct control of Lucchese revenues for two years, and this continued for the rest of Pisan rule. When Lucca regained control of its revenues on 25 March 1369, Sercambi at least regarded it as a gain, though perhaps from a political rather than a financial viewpoint. He wrote, "Le quali gabelle funno buono fondamento alla libertà di Lucha, però che molti Pisani et officiali, socto tale colore dimoravano in Lucha."[92]

The financial relations of Lucca and Pisa in the last few years of Pisan rule will be discussed below in connection with the rule of Gio-

90. M.B. Becker, "Economic Change and the Emerging Florentine Territorial State," *Studies in the Renaisance* 13 (1966), esp. pp. 24–25, 27, 30–31, 33; *Florence in Transition*, 2:160, 176–178.

91. Anz. Av. Lib. 41, fol. 52v–53r, 9 June 1361. There are many subsequent references to this contract: especially Anz. Av. Lib. 41, fols. 102v–103r, 8 Oct. 1361; Anz. Av. Lib. 42, fols. 7v, 14 Feb., 37v, 13 May 1362. He was authorised to continue to exact the revenues after the expiry of the contract until a new composition was made: Anz. Av. Lib. 42, fols. 46r, 7 June, 46v, 10 June 1362; the closing of his account: fols. 65r–65v, 20 Sept. 1362. His accounts are in Ragionieri 10, fols. 2r–9v, 11r–23v (different sets of foliation), also fols. 27r–29r.

92. Sercambi, 1:161.

vanni dell'Agnello. The picture is far from clear, but it seems possible that there were still increases in the gabelles and extraordinary levies even after the Florentine war had come to an end. It is difficult to assess how serious these impositions were, but it is worth remembering that whatever the financial burdens Lucca had to bear during Pisan rule, the Lucchese were still in a position to purchase their freedom from Charles IV. This certainly involved heavy payments even if the figure of 300,000 florins given by Sercambi is an exaggeration.

V

External Relations

THE MAIN REASON for the increased financial demands that Pisa made on Lucca after 1362 was the war with Florence. One of the consequences of Pisan rule was that it involved Lucca very closely in Pisan internal and external relations. The "liga, societas et fraternitas" of 4 July 1342 had provided for mutual aid and assistance in war and peace against their common enemies, and even the loosest and most informal association between a dominating and a subject city involved the control of the external relations of the subject city.[1] Lucca therefore had to follow closely any developments in Pisa's external relations, and each fluctuation in the internal government of Pisa was also reflected in Lucca.

In 1342 Pisa was under the nominal authority of Ranieri della Gherardesca, count of Donoratico; he was therefore elected to a similar position in Lucca. On his death in 1347 Pisa was ruled in the name of the Anziani, and Lucca was obliged to elect the Anziani of Pisa captains, governors, and defenders of Lucca, with the right to appoint vicars. Factional divisions in Pisa were accentuated on the death of Count Ranieri, and the choice of rectors and vicars for Lucca tended to reflect the balance of the two Pisan factions. Thus from 1347 until 1355 many of the rectors and vicars sent to Lucca were adherents of the predominant Bergolini faction. In 1355 there were disturbances in Pisa during the visit of Emperor Charles IV; the Bergolini fell from power and some were driven into exile. Not only were the rectors and vicars sent to Lucca after 1355 predominantly supporters of the Raspanti party, but the three Pisans in office at the time of the disturbances, who were all Bergolini, were replaced on 1 June 1355 by three Raspanti, though their term of office still had two months to run.[2] In 1364, when in the after-

---

1. Capitoli 19, fol. 7r. For other cities see for example G. Romano, "Delle relazioni tra Pavia e Milano nella formazione della signoria viscontea," *Archivio storico lombardo* 19 (1892), esp. pp. 577–578; S. Favale, "Siena nel quadro della politica viscontea nell'Italia centrale," *Bollettino senese di storia patria* 43, n.s.7 (1936), pp. 316–319.
2. *Inventario*, 1:107–118. After 1 June 1355 the semesters were 1 Dec.–31 May and 1 June–30 Nov., instead of 1 Feb.–31 July and 1 Aug.–31 Jan. A list of Raspanti and Bergolini 1355 is printed in Mancinelli, "Carlo IV," pp. 355–357. Also P. Silva, "Il governo di Pietro Gambacorta in Pisa e le sue relazioni col resto della Toscana e coi Visconti," *Annali della Reale Scuola Normale Superiore di Pisa*, sez. Filosofia e Filologia 23 (1912), pp. 10–32.

math of the unsuccessful war with Florence Pisa elected Giovanni dell'Agnello as doge, this change in the internal government of Pisa was again reflected in Lucca—the Lucchese had to elect him to a similar position in their city.

These changes in the internal balance of the various groups in Pisa,though reflected in Lucca, probably did not make much difference to Pisan rule there. It can after all have mattered little to Lucca whether the Pisan rectors were Raspanti or Bergolini; both were equally committed to maintaining the Pisan hold on Lucca.[3] The consequences of Lucca's involvement in Pisan foreign relations were felt much more sharply. The capture of Lucca in 1342 might have decided the fate of the city itself, but it left many matters unsettled. Pisa and Florence were still at war, and many places in Lucchese territory were in the hands of the Florentines, the Antelminelli, or other enemies. Now that it had a league with Pisa, Lucca was naturally expected to follow the Pisan line in foreign policy and to contribute men and money to the Pisan war effort. In particular the Lucchese were expected to join with Pisa in attempts to recover parts of Lucchese territory that were in revolt or were being held by the enemy.

Peace was made with Florence on 9 October 1342 on terms disadvantageous to the Florentines. Pisa was confirmed in the custody of Lucca, and Florence was to retain no rights there, except that the duke of Athens was to name the *podestà* of Lucca each semester for the remaining fourteen and a half years of Pisan custody. Several important points were left for settlement at a later date. The destiny of certain Lucchese lands that were held by Florence—Barga, Coreglia, Pietrasanta, and other places in the Garfagnana and Versilia—was left to the decision of the duke of Athens on the one side and messer Tinuccio della Rocca on the other. So was the indemnity Pisa and Lucca were to pay to Florence, though it was stipulated that this should not be less than 60,000 florins or more than 150,000 and that it was to be paid within fifteen years. It is apparent that the indemnity was meant to compensate Florence for the money it had spent in attempting to purchase Lucca. It was laid down that Pisa was only bound to this payment while it retained custody of Lucca; otherwise the Lucchese were to pay it. Lucca was a full party to this treaty; it sent syndics to the negotiations as if it were a free commune, and the agreement was between Pisa, Lucca, and Florence on an

---

3. The Pisan chronicler records that when in 1355 it was believed that Charles IV was about to free Lucca "lo popolo di Pisa, e Raspanti, e Bergulini per la città, ciascuno si baciava in bocca, dicendo: Siamo fratelli, e cacciamo questo lupo, che ci vuol toller Lucca," *Cronica di Pisa* [hereafter *Cron. Pis.*], R.I.S. 15, col. 1030.

apparently equal basis. There was no question of Lucca's being named as an adherent or appearing only as a subject city. But clearly Lucca can have had little say in the actual terms.[4]

Lucca also participated along with Pisa in negotiations with marchese Spinetta Malaspina, which produced an agreement on 14 April 1343,[5] and in negotiations for a league with Florence in February 1343. A meeting of the Lucchese General Council with many *invitati* authorised the city's two syndics to conclude this league for two years, renewable for five years, with a *taglia* of 2,000 cavalry for use against common enemies.[6] Lucca also participated fully in negotiations leading to a further agreement with Florence on 15 November 1343, after the expulsion of the duke of Athens. The terms included an undertaking by Pisa and Lucca not to intervene in the parts of the Valdinievole, Garfagnana, Valdriana, and Lower Valdarno that had once been part of the Lucchese *contado* but were now held by Florence, and an undertaking by Florence not to interfere in Lucca and Lucchese territory, including the parts of Versilia, Lunigiana, the Garfagnana, Valdinievole, and Valdriana that Lucca still held, or to impede Pisa and Lucca in the recovery of Lucchese possessions in Versilia and Lunigiana. Pisa and Lucca were to compensate Florence for the price it had paid to Mastino and Alberto della Scala for Lucca by payment of an indemnity of 100,000 florins over fourteen years at the rate of 7,000 florins each year on the feast of St. John.[7]

Meanwhile, within a few days of its acquisition of Lucca Pisa set about reducing Lucchese fortresses in the Garfagnana that were held by the Antelminelli and others, demanding Lucchese assistance in this.[8]

---

4. The peace terms are in Capitoli 19, fols. 15r–19v, printed in *Memorie e documenti*, 1:338–348. It is recorded with some variations in G. Villani, *Cronica*, ed. F. G. Dragomanni (Florence, 1844–1845), Lib. XII, cap. viii, and in *Cron. Pis.*, cols. 1012–1013. G. Tommasi, "Sommario della storia di Lucca," *Archivio storico italiano* 10 (1847; repr. 1969), p. 210. Pardon of Lucchese *banniti* on these terms: Anz. Av. Lib. 18, fols. 50r–50v, 12 Nov. 1342.

5. *Cron. Pis.*, col. 1014; Tommasi, "Storia di Lucca," p. 216; G. Rossi–Sabatini, *Pisa al tempo dei Donoratico, 1316–1347* (Florence, 1938), p. 125.

6. Anz. Av. Lib. 21, fols. 2r–3v, 20 Feb. 1343. The *sindicatus* was authorised in the General Council by a vote of 213 in favour to 21 against.

7. There were also various clauses about the re-admission of exiles and the treatment of debtors: Capitoli 19, fols. 22r–37r; Capitoli 24, pp. 107–134 (not foliated); G. Villani, XII, xxv; and a confused account of these events in Sercambi, 1:90. Tommasi, "Storia di Lucca," p. 216. There were also agreements with Pistoia (9 Dec. 1343, Capitoli 19, fols. 38r–40r) and San Gimignano (5 Feb. 1344, Capitoli 19, fols. 43r–44r), in which Lucca again participated, sending its syndics.

8. Anz. Av. Lib. 17, fol. 39r, 12 July 1342: Pisa announced that it was sending messer Rosso Zacci "cras de mane tempestive" to recover places outside Lucchese obedience

When the Pisan captain took Gallicano, he offered it certain pacts that were confirmed by the Lucchese Anziani on 2 August 1342.[9] There are a number of references in Lucchese documents to these and later operations for the defence or recovery of Lucchese territory. Payments were made for the army in the Garfagnana, especially for the defence of Casoli and for operations at Corsena in 1343,[10] and later for an army sent against Pietrasanta and Monteggiori and for the repair of the defences at Vegghiatore.[11] In 1344 there was rather more serious fighting, for the sons of Castruccio Castracani and other Antelminelli exiles had obtained the assistance of Luchino Visconti and also of the bishop of Luni, who was a member of the Malaspina family and who was in possession of Pietrasanta and other Lucchese territories. The Lucchese had assisted Pisa in the preparation of defences at Rotaio and helped to man these, but the invaders breached them on 5 April 1344 and passed on first into Lucchese territory and then into that of Pisa, plundering and burning as they went. They achieved little, however, and suffered much from heat and disease, so that they had to retreat through the Garfagnana. There they laid siege to Castiglione, but were beaten off by the forces of Pisa and Lucca.[12] There was a further attack early in 1345, but peace was

---

and asked Lucca to second its efforts. This was agreed in council by a vote of 58-0: Anz. Av. Lib. 17, fols. 39v-40r. There are references to Lucchese *balistarii* selected to go to the Garfagnana: Anz. Av. Lib. 18, fol. 2v, 5 Aug. 1342.

9. Anz. Av. Lib. 19, fols. 2r-3r, 2 Aug. 1342: they were confirmed by the Lucchese Anziani "si et in quantum predicta placeant dominis Anthianis pisani populi. Et non aliter vel alio modo." The terms had been offered by the Pisan captain 15 July 1342. Also *Cron. Pis.*, col. 1014.

10. Ragionieri 3, fols. 36r-37v: account of ser Bonaiuncte vocato ser Meliano de Fabrica for sums spent on behalf of Lucca "in exercitibus factis in Garfagnana," mostly in March 1343. Also Anz. Av. Lib. 54, fol. 51v, March 1343; no. 156 in *Regesto*.

11. Ragionieri 3, fols. 86r-87r, 27 April-26 May 1343. Fols. 89r-90v: Coluccino Savini accounted for £11,360 4s. 4d. *picc.* as fines imposed on Lucchese citizens and communes of the *contado* on the occasion of the sending of an army to the Garfagnana and vicariate of Valdilima and Corsena, and a further £11,849 3s. *picc.* for the army sent against Monteggiori Feb.-May 1343. Ragionieri 3, fols. 30r-32r has an account for work done at Vegghiatore and Monteggiori May-June 1343. An army was sent against Pietrasanta in September 1343: Anz. Av. Lib. 21, fols. 46r-46v, 25 Sept. 1343. Fines and compositions for citizens who did not go with this army: Ragionieri 4, fols. 18r-20v, Sept.-Oct. 1343.

12. G. Villani, XII, xxiv, xxvi, xxix, xxxviii; Sercambi, 1:89-90; Ranieri Sardo, *Cronaca di Pisa*, [hereafter Sardo], ed. O. Banti (Rome, 1963), pp. 94-95; *Cronica Senese* [hereafter *Cron. Sen.*], R.I.S. n.s. 15 (Bologna, 1935), pp. 544-545; Tommasi, "Storia di Lucca," pp. 216-217; Rossi-Sabatini, *Pisa al tempo dei Donoratico*, pp. 226-230. Levies on Lucca for the expenses of work at Rotaio and other defences in the area in March

concluded in May through the efforts of Filippo Gonzaga of Mantua. The terms called for Luchino Visconti to surrender Carrara, Massa, Pietrasanta, and various places he held in the Garfagnana against a payment of 80,000 florins, the cancellation of sentences against certain Lucchese exiles, and provision for the sons of Castruccio Castracani.[13]

Lucca had cooperated with Pisa in all this. It had contributed men and money and seconded Pisan efforts at the defence or recovery of its territory. The terms of the surrender to Pisa in 1342 had stipulated that any Lucchese possessions that were recovered by the efforts of Lucca or Pisa should be restored to Lucca. The Lucchese reminded the Pisans of this in an embassy early in June 1345, asking that the vicariates recently recovered should be staffed with Lucchese officials and their revenues paid to the Lucchese *camera*, and stressing the satisfaction that this would give to Lucca.[14] But the Pisans retained the vicariates of Pietrasanta and

---

1344: Ragionieri 4, fols. 55r–59v; account of money for paying hired foot-soldiers "ad reparationem inimicorum" in Versilia in March 1344: Ragionieri 4, fols. 60r–63r; *secas* and fines, and expenditure mainly on defence: fols. 67r–76v. Lucchese were serving as *balistarii* in the Pisan army in numbers like 160 and 300 and served on Pisan territory as well as their own: Anz. Av. Lib. 22, fols. 31r–31v, 26 May 1344. Accounts of the treasurer for fines for failure to serve, etc., which give details of the defence works and how they were forced: Ragionieri 4, fols. 54r–59v (various foliations). Other references to the Lombard invasion: Anz. Av. Lib. 22, fols. 20v, 14 April, 21r, 15 April 1344; Anz. Av. Lib. 23, fols. 3v, 4r, 10 Jan., 31v, 25 June, 35r, 11 July, 43v, 27 Aug., 47v, 15 Sept. 1345; Anz. Av. Lib. 24, fols. 65v–66r, 18 Aug. 1346. Also Anz. Av. Lib. 55, fols. 5v, no. 262 in *Regesto;* 32r–32v, no. 309 in *Regesto.*

13. G. Villani, XII, xxxviii; *Cron. Pis.,* col. 1017; *Cron. Sen.,* p. 545; Sercambi, 1:91, where he gives the date as September 1346. Tommasi, "Storia di Lucca," p. 217. Arrangements for carrying out the provisions concerning the sentences: Anz. Av. Lib . 23, fols. 42r, 16 Aug., 43r, 25 Aug., 76r, 19 May 1345; also Anz. Av. Lib. 54, fols. 97r–99v, 17–19 May 1345, nos. 209–217 in *Regesto.*

14. Capitoli 19 fols. 5r–5v, cap. ix. The Lucchese petitioned the Pisan Anziani "quod velint et eis placeat reformare vicarias presentialiter recuperatas officialibus lucanis more consueto. Et quod introitus dictarum vicariarum veniant ad lucanam cameram more aliorum introituum pisano comuni assignatorum reservata eis custodia fortilitiarum terrarum dictarum vicarie prout eis videbitur convenire. Et hostendit dictis dominis de Pisis quod in isto principio hec reformatio erit lucanis multum acceptabilis et erit principium bone spei et dilectionis hostentio. Ex quo principio cives lucani tam presentes quam absentes ex inde suscipient magnum contentamentum unde introitus comunis lucani et aliter de die in diem melius convalescent. Et per pacta pacis comune pisanum tenetur terras lucani comunis recuperare absque aliqua redentione solutione vel gravamine. Que pacta et alia comune lucanum infallibiliter credit quod a comune pisano semper serventur et augmententur de bono in melius ad gloriam et bonum et pacificum statum utriusque comunis": Anz. Av. Lib. 54, fols. 99v–100r, 9 June 1345; no. 218 in *Regesto.*

Massa directly under their own rule. They also administered Cerruglio directly and allowed the vicariate of Coreglia to remain in the possession of messer Francesco Castracani. Lucca drew no revenues from these lands for the rest of the period of Pisan rule and had to make representations about the treatment of Lucchese citizens and *contadini* in the vicariate of Pietrasanta and other lands that had once been Lucchese, but were now under Pisa.[15] However, Lucca may well have been glad that these territories had at least been recovered from the Malaspina or Luchino Visconti, in whose hands their loss would have been more permanent. The terms of some other agreements made in these first years, especially with Florence, were perhaps less acceptable, since they meant the recognition of territorial losses to a completely extraneous power. But some of these lands had in fact been lost some years previously, and in any case Lucca had no effective way of protesting. There was no outside power to which Lucca might look for assistance, and Pisa had no difficulty in controlling Lucca's relations with other states.

This situation was to change in 1354–1355 with the Italian expedition of Emperor Charles IV. This imperial expedition brought about a crisis for the Pisan rulers of Lucca, as it did for those in power in many other cities. Imperial expeditions always aroused the fears of those who had something to lose and the hopes of those who had something to gain. The Pisan Bergolini had to fear for their position in their own city and for the authority of Pisa over Lucca. The Lucchese hoped to induce the emperor to free them from Pisan rule, especially since the original fifteen-year agreement for Pisan custody of Lucca was due to expire in 1357. These were by no means wild dreams; Lucca was to obtain its freedom by a grant of the same emperor in 1369 and came near to doing so in 1355. Even the Antelminelli, the sons of Castruccio Castracani and

---

15. The Pisan Anziani had instructed the Lucchese to name a vicar for Massa "ad beneplacitum": Anz. Av. Lib. 54, fol. 58r, 6 May 1343; nos. 172–173, 175 in *Regesto*. But this does not seem to have been observed later; it was under Pisa: A.S.P. Comune A 64, fol. 14v. There are a number of other references to Pisa ruling Lucchese vicariates directly, especially Pietrasanta: A.S.P. Comune A 56, fols. 4r, 45r; Comune A 64, fol. 15v. For Coreglia under Francesco Castracani and later his widow: Anz. Av. Lib. 55, fols. 5v–6v, 16 Jan. 1346; A.S.P. Comune A 60, fols. 37r, 40v; Comune A 62, fols. 21v, 51r. Pisan authority in Cerruglio: Anz. Av. Lib. 55, fols. 64r–64v, 30 Sept. 1347. Lucca claimed that it had no jurisdiction there in reply to a complaint (nos. 342–343 in *Regesto*), but the men of Cerruglio could be summoned in Lucchese courts: Capitoli 19, fols. 93v, 109v, 117r. Clauses concerning the treatment of Lucchese citizens and *contadini* in Pietrasanta and other Lucchese lands now under Pisa are included in compositions: Capitoli 19, fols. 90r, 102r, 111v, 119r; also in Coreglia: fols. 104r, 111r, 118v. Giovanni dell'Agnello later incorporated some of these lands into the Pisan *contado*.

their uncle messer Francesco, hoped to have their claims to Lucca satisfied with imperial support. The Pisans, of course, hoped to prevent any threat to their authority and if possible to have it confirmed by the grant of an imperial vicariate over Lucca. They therefore sent ambassadors to the emperor, who gave reassurances about the continuation of Bergolini rule in Pisa and granted an imperial vicariate over Lucca on 27 December 1354.[16]

The situation was made more serious for those in power in Pisa by the fact that Charles IV and his entourage made extended visits to both Lucca and Pisa before and after his imperial coronation in Rome.[17] This made it easier for the Lucchese to plead their cause with the emperor, offering him gifts and doing everything possible to win his favour.[18] They were also in a good position to profit should the Pisans do anything to offend him. The emperor had promised Pisa that Lucca should remain under Pisan rule. He claimed that he had made this clear to the Lucchese and was not going to change his mind even if he was offered Lucca full of florins. On 9 May 1355 he confirmed the imperial vicariate he had granted the Pisans over Lucca,[19] but he seems also to have encouraged the Lucchese to hope that he would grant them their freedom. There were rumours in Lucca, Pisa, and elsewhere that he was about to free Lucca or had already done so. Matteo Villani records rumours that Charles IV had reached an agreement with Lucchese exiles to free the city when the fifteen years of Pisan custody expired, in return for a payment of 120,000 florins to be made in France.[20]

16. Boehmer, *Regesta Imperii,* 8:157, rough copy in Capitoli 31, pp. 273–275 (no foliation); Sercambi, 1:98–101; M. Villani, IV, xxxv; *Cron. Pis.,* cols. 1026–1027; *Cron. Sen.* pp. 575–576, 582; Mancinelli, "Carlo IV," pp. 321–324; Tommasi, "Storia di Lucca," pp. 216–217.

17. He entered Pisa on 18 January and remained there till 22 March, returning after his coronation, 6 May 1355: Sardo, pp. 101, 114–115, 122; *Cron. Pis.,* col. 1027; *Cron. Sen.,* pp. 576–577. He made two visits to Lucca before his coronation (Sercambi, 1:102–104, 108–109) and planned that he and the empress should spend the summer there: A.S.P. Comune A 60, fol. 2v, 10 May 1355; Mancinelli, "Carlo IV," doc. V, p. 363.

18. Sardo, p. 110; M. Villani, IV, lix, V, xxxi; Sercambi, 1:102, 105.

19. "Et quod ipse dominus imperator dixit ipsis Anthianis quod ipse dixit lucensibus quod ipse intendebat quod ipsi essent omnino sub gubernatione et regimine pisani comunis. Et quod si darent sibi castrum Luce plenum florenorum non faceret aliud": A.S.P. Comune A 60, fols. 2r–2v, 10 May 1355; Mancinelli, "Carlo IV," doc. V, p. 363. The confirmation of 9 May: A.S.P. Comune A 29, Protocolli di Capitoli, fol. 117r; J. C. Lünig, *Codex Italiae Diplomaticus* (Frankfurt, 1725-35), 1:1085, where wrongly dated 9 March; Mancinelli, "Carlo IV," pp. 341–345.

20. M. Villani, V, xix, xxviii; *Cron. Sen.,* p. 580, also mentions a promise made by the emperor's seneschal, with Charles IV's knowledge, to free Lucca. Also *Cron. Pis.,* col. 1031.

These rumours were also rife in Pisa. On the very day that rebellion broke out in Lucca they were described as defamatory rumours put about by the Gambacorta to the effect that the emperor had sold Lucca to the Lucchese for 150,000 florins. Again the emperor denied that he had any intention that Lucca should be under any rule but that of Pisa.[21] The Lucchese chronicler Sercambi also records that the emperor had promised to free Lucca and that in mid-May he was negotiating the terms of the implementation of this with the Lucchese.[22] The Pisan position in Lucca was weakened by the fact that they had granted Charles IV the lordship of Pisa and Lucca; the Pisan garrison of the Augusta and of the walls and towers of Lucca had been replaced by imperial forces.[23] This had again encouraged the Lucchese, who hoped that it would be easy to get the imperial garrison replaced by their own men, especially after the rising in Pisa on 20 May 1355. According to Sercambi agreement was actually reached between the Lucchese and the emperor's officials on 21 May, but Pisa was warned of the impending danger when ser Bonagiunta Guarzoni and ser Bardino da Pescia, ghibellines from places that had once been part of the Lucchese state, together with Giovanni Marsiglio, a captain who had remained in the Augusta despite the fact that he had been in Pisan service, were able to raise a white banner on the "torre ghibellina," which was the agreed signal to summon aid from Pisa.[24]

The first open act of rebellion came when Giovanni Damiani and Francesco Grifo, the new Pisan rectors appointed after the fall of the Bergolini, were refused entry by the German garrison of the Augusta

---

21. "Quod Gambacurte et eorum seguaces diffamaverant eum populo pisano quod ipse debuerit vendidisse civitatem lucane [*sic*] civibus lucensibus pro centumquinquaginta milibus florenorum auri. Et sub isto falso colore convocaverant contra maiestatem suam populum pisanum. Et quod nunquam cogitavit nec consentiret aliquo modo quod civitas lucana pro honore suo et sacri imperii commodis esset sub alio regimine seu gubernatione quam sub regimine seu gubernatione pisani comunis": A.S.P. Comune A 60, fol. 5r, 21 May 1355; Mancinelli, "Carlo IV," doc. VII, pp. 477–478. Also M. Villani, V, xxxi; *Cron. Pis.,* col. 1030.

22. Sercambi, 1:105–106.

23. "Di che, lo dì, si disse che llo inperadore ci aveva levato Luccha," according to the Pisan chronicler Sardo, p. 127, also pp. 121–123; *Cron. Sen.,* p. 580. Pisa had also removed the *cerne* of the Pisan *contado* sent earlier to reinforce the garrison of Lucca: A.S.P. Comune A 60, fol. 1r, 30 April 1355; Mancinelli, "Carlo IV," pp. 337–338 and doc. II, pp. 358–360.

24. Sercambi, 1:105–107; *Cron. Pis.,* col. 1031; Mancinelli, "Carlo IV," pp. 446–447. For the Pisan signal system: A.S.P. Comune A 56, fols. 41v, 53r; G. Civitali, *Storia di Lucca . . . sino al 1572,* manuscript history in Archivio di Stato in Lucca, series Biblioteca Manoscritti 38, fol. 283r.

when they arrived to take up their office.[25] The Pisan Anziani lost no time in taking counter-measures. They ordered the men of the quarter of Kinzica in Pisa and the *cerne* of the *capitanerie* of Piedimonte, Calci, and both valleys of the Serchio, together with certain Pisan officials, to proceed to Lucca without delay, and they were outside Porta S. Pietro early the next morning. But the Lucchese had also been receiving reinforcements from the *contado* and had taken the squares and all the gates except Porta S. Donato.[26]

There was fierce fighting during the night of Thursday 21 May and throughout Friday 22 May with the cry of "moriantur gebellini et vivant guelfi."[27] Pisan rule in Lucca hung in the balance. Sercambi (b. 1348), not old enough to have been an eyewitness but likely to have been well informed, attributes the eventual failure of the Lucchese to divisions among themselves rather than to the superior strength of the Pisans. He asserts that the Lucchese would have been victorious, despite the reinforcements that arrived from Pisa, if certain Lucchese had not joined the Pisans in the Augusta. These divisions gave the Pisans new heart and discouraged the Lucchese.[28] In addition, whatever his earlier attitude may have been, the imperial captain in Lucca seems to have come out on the Pisan side at a crucial point.[29] By the morning of Saturday 23 May some Lucchese had fled from the city, seeing that their cause was lost, and the rest were reduced to begging the Pisans for mercy.[30]

Pisa treated the Lucchese leniently. There were no reprisals. A general amnesty was declared, and very shortly after the revolt was suppressed the Pisans can be seen as anxious above all to reassure the Lucchese and prevent any emigration from the city for fear of reprisals. Luc-

25. "Di che fu la novella in Pisa che lLucha era venduta": Sardo, p. 129, 21 May 1355.
26. A.S.P. Comune A 60, fol. 6r, 21 May 1355. The quarter of Ponte joined that of Kinzica against Lucca: fol. 6v, 22 May 1355; Mancinelli, "Carlo IV," pp. 447–449 and docs. VIII and IX, pp. 478–480; Sardo, pp. 129–130; Sercambi, 1:107–108; *Cron. Pis.,* col. 1031; *Cron. Sen.,* p. 580.
27. A.S.P. Comune A 60, fol. 6r, 21 May 1355; Mancinelli, "Carlo IV," doc. VIII, pp. 478–479; M. Villani, V, xxxiv; Sercambi, 1:107–108; *Cron Pis.,* cols. 1031–1032.
28. Sercambi, 1:108–109. *Cron. Pis.,* cols. 1031–1032, says nothing of this, but attributes the Pisans' eventual success to their own efforts and the courage of Giovanni Marsiglio. Also *Cron. Sen.,* p. 580. Sercambi, though in a position to be well informed, was also likely to preserve legends about the period of Pisan rule, but the account of divisions among the Lucchese is confirmed by Matteo Villani, who relates that the Antelminelli and certain *popolari,* who had suffered less than the rest under Pisan rule, were able to persuade the populace that they would get favourable terms if they surrendered: M. Villani, V, xxxiv.
29. *Cron. Sen.,* pp. 580–581; Mancinelli, "Carlo IV," p. 449.
30. Sercambi, 1:108; Sardo, p. 130.

chese ambassadors asked at the end of May "quod de pactis et conventionibus factis et promissis lucensibus pridie tempore rumcris Luce suscitati per lucenses contra comune pisanum per Anthianos pisani populi fiat scriptura de gratia comunis lucani quam obstendere possint lucensibus civibus ad hoc ut tutius morentur in civitate lucana et ut illi qui pro timore recesserunt confidenter redeant ad civitatem lucanam,"[31] and a concession early in June was made "ad hoc ut mercatores et alii non recederent de civitate lucana."[32] Though the crisis caused by Charles IV's expedition and the rebellion in Lucca had increased Pisan expenditure, and at least part of this could be regarded as the fault of the Lucchese, Pisa lowered its financial demands for the next two years.[33] This leniency was the more remarkable as there continued to be threats to Pisan possession of various parts of the Lucchese *contado* from the Antelminelli and other exiles, and as there were people in Lucca itself who sided with the exiles or whose attitude gave rise to suspicion. At the end of May Altino degli Antelminelli, an illegitimate son of Castruccio Castracani, raised Monteggiori in rebellion, and when he was captured on 10 June letters found on him showed widespread plots against Pisa.[34] Later in the summer Arrigo and Valerano, the sons of Castruccio, and their ghibelline followers came to terms with guelf exiles of Lucca, led by members of the Obizi and Salamoncelli families, for a joint attack on Lucchese territory. They took Verrucola Gherardinga, Verrucchio, and Capraia and laid siege to Castiglione Garfagnana, but were driven off on 12 August 1355 and withdrew to Frignano.[35]

31. A.S.P. Comune A 60, fols. 9v, 25 May, 14v, 29 May 1355. A group of Lucchese had concentrated at Segromigno and although Pisa mounted an expedition against them, agreement was reached without fighting and they were allowed to return to Lucca: Sercambi, 1:110–111. Series Imposte Diverse e Straordinarie no. 11 is connected with this expedition. M. Villani, V, xxxix, claims that the Lucchese were treated harshly.

32. A.S.P. Comune A 60, fol. 37v, 11 June 1355. The general amnesty was included in the composition beginning on 1 April 1355 (but agreed on 16 June 1355): Capitoli 19, fol. 70v; also in the compositions of 1356 and 1357: fols. 75r, 79v.

33. Capitoli 19, fols. 67v, 72v; A.S.P. Comune A 60, fols. 32r–32v, 7 June, 37v, 11 June 1355.

34. A.S.P. Comune A 60, fols. 36r, 10 June, 40r, 13 June, 41r–41v, 14 June 1355. Other Antelminelli brothers were also threatening Lucchese territory from the Lunigiana: A.S.P. Comune A 60, fols. 12r, 28 May, 14r, 29 May. Altino was handed over to the Pisans by Charles IV and executed: Sardo, pp. 134–135, 136; Sercambi, 1:112–113; M. Villani, V, lii; *Cron. Pis.*, col. 1033; *Cron. Sen.*, p. 582; Mancinelli, "Carlo IV," pp. 456–458, 472–473; Tommasi, "Storia di Lucca," pp. 221–222.

35. M. Villani, V, lxi, lxiv, lxix; Sercambi, 1:113–114; *Cron. Pis.*, cols. 1033–1034; *Cron. Sen.*, p. 583; Civitali, *Storia di Lucca*, fols. 293v–294v; Tommasi, "Storia di Lucca," pp. 222–223. For service in the army against Castiglione: *Regesto* nos. 703–704; also

These threats had caused Pisa to strengthen its defence measures. Immediately after the rising in Lucca Pisa had sent reinforcements to the garrison there, replacing any forces whose loyalty was suspect. The threats from the Antelminelli led to a further tightening of defences in the *contado*.[36] The Pisan Anziani received warning from their rectors in Lucca and from various other sources that there were still dangers in Lucca, and they authorised the rectors to send as many of the most suspect Lucchese as they thought necessary to Pisa without the need to refer back to Pisa first.[37] They seem to have done this again at the time of the Antelminelli threats against Capraia and Castiglione, and they also provided for the arrest of all those, both Pisans and citizens and *contadini* of Lucca, who were named in the confession of Altino Antelminelli.[38] But there were no general reprisals. Indeed, attempts to

---

series Imposte Diverse e Straordinarie no. 10. There were threats by exiles and armies had to be sent to parts of the *contado* later; *Regesto* no. 795, 23 Nov. 1356: Pisa asked Lucca for thirty good crossbowmen for six to eight days. There was an army against Verrucchio, 3–29 May 1358: Anz. Av. Lib. 39, fols. 88r–89r, 28 Sept. 1358; against Coreglia apparently in November 1359: Anz. Av. Lib. 41, fols. 58v–59v, 18 June 1361 (referring to an earlier expedition); Anz. Av. Lib. 40, fol. 75r, 16 Jan. 1360.

36. A.S.P. Comune A 60, fols. 7r, 25 May, 8r–9v, 25 May, 12r, 28 May, 14r–14v, 29 May, 29r–29v, 5 June, 31v–32r, 7 June, 36r–37r, 10 June, 48r–48v, 20 June 1355; Mancinelli, "Carlo IV," doc. XIX, pp. 494–497. Pisa also took over for a while direct rule of the vicariate of Coreglia from Tobia, the widow of Francesco Castracani and her sons, because her men were "male dispositi" and because of the disturbances: fol. 37r, 10 June, also fol. 40v, 14 June 1355. Messer Francesco had been murdered by his nephews, the sons of Castruccio Castracani in May: M. Villani, V, xxvii; Sercambi, 1:111–112; Sardo, pp. 125–126; *Cron. Pis.*, cols. 1032–1033; *Cron. Sen.*, p. 582; Tommasi, "Storia di Lucca," p. 221; Mancinelli, "Carlo IV," p. 347. There were proceedings against them *in absentia* in the *podestà*'s court: Potestà di Lucca, Inquisizioni 4841, fols. 91r–91v.

37. A.S.P. Comune A 60, fol. 29r, 5 June 1355: "Anthiani sentiunt per licteras rectorum Luce et alias quamplures licteras subditorum et amatorum pisani comunis quod suspicant et timent quod Luce non fiant in proximo novitates nocive et periculose comuni pisano"; Mancinelli, "Carlo IV," doc. XIX, pp. 496–497; also A.S.P. Comune A 60, fol. 14r, 29 May 1355. The Pisan Anziani also confirmed the Lucchese Anziani of April and May in office for another month: A.S.P. Comune A 60, fol. 17r, 1 June 1355; and fol. 48v, 20 June: they provided for the election of Lucchese named by ambassadors who had just returned from Lucca. These Lucchese were to be Anziani in July and August 1355 and were presumably regarded as reliable from the Pisan point of view. There was also provision for the election of "amici et devoti pisani comunis et presentis status" as vicars of Camaiore and the other Lucchese vicariates, "et aliter dicti rectores ipsas electiones fieri non permictant."

38. M. Villani, V, lxi, lxiv; A.S.P. Comune A 60, fol. 40r, 13 June; Mancinelli, "Carlo IV," pp. 472–473 and n. 2, p. 472. Proceedings against nine Lucchese in Pisa by the Pisan *podestà* for leaving Pisa without permission: A.S.L. Potestà di Lucca, Inquisi-

reassure the Lucchese and negotiations for a new composition with a reduced annual payment from Lucca continued at the same time as Pisa was trying to reinforce its defences and was at its wits' end to pay the garrison in Lucca.[39]

But there was no question of Pisan rule coming to an end in 1357, when the fifteen-year custody originally agreed to expired. Pisa now held an imperial vicariate over Lucca and Lucchese territory several times confirmed. In agreeing to accept Marquandus, bishop of Augsburg, as imperial captain for a period after the departure of Charles IV, Pisa made it clear that he was not to interfere in the custody or jurisdiction of Lucca, emphasising Pisan authority over the offices and revenues of both cities.[40] In 1357 the league between Lucca and Pisa was formally renewed for a further twenty years, though with the stipulation that this was not to prejudice the imperial vicariate over Lucca granted by Charles IV. The same day the Lucchese Anziani elected the Anziani of Pisa as captains general, governors, and defenders of Lucca for twenty years from the day of the expiry of their previous term. Though it was stipulated that this election was not to prejudice the renewed league of Pisa and Lucca or the imperial vicariate, there was no saving clause for the rights of the Lucchese Anziani as there had been in the similar election of 13 September 1352.[41]

---

zioni 4845, fols. 25r–25v, 14 Aug. 1355. For the deportation of suspect citizens in other cities in times of danger: P. Silva, "Pisa sotto Firenze dal 1406 al 1433," *Studi storici* di A. Crivellucci, 18 (1909–1910), pp. 142–145 and A. Bonardi, "I Padovani ribelli alla repubblica di Venezia," *Miscellanea di storia veneta* ser. 2, 8 (1902), pp. 437–445.

39. A.S.P. Comune A 60, fol. 39v, 12 June 1355: "comune pisanum est in magnis debitis cum masnadis ab equo et pede pisani comunis Luce existentibus et cum aliis masnadis et officialibus pisani comunis. Et in camera comunis vel alibi non est aliqua quantitas pecunie unde predictis satisfieri possit. Et propter nova que noviter occurrerunt comuni pisano non solvere masnadis Luce existentibus id quod recipere debent a comuni pisano portat magnum periculum." Pisa provided for obtaining money from the goods of Pisans condemned for treason in May 1355. Earlier it had had to promise special rates of pay for its forces involved in the suppression of the Lucchese revolt: fol. 31v, 7 June 1355. The same day it had agreed to a reduction of the sum Lucca paid each year: fol. 32v, and fol. 37v, 11 June it had pointed out that the Lucchese were responsible for the increased expenses, while at the same time agreeing to a reduction of their payment.

40. A.S.P. Comune A 60, fols. 23r–23v, 2 June 1355; Mancinelli, "Carlo IV," pp. 463–465 and doc. XVII, pp. 489–491.

41. Renewal of the league: A.S.P. Comune A 29, fols. 117r–118r; election of the Pisan Anziani as captains general, governors, and defenders: fols. 118v–119r, both dated 19 May 1357. For the terms of the election of 1352: Anz. Av. Lib. 34, fols. 60r–61r, 13 Sept. 1352. The renewed league of 1357 specifically grants Pisa the right to garrison

The fall in 1355 of the Bergolini, who had remained on friendly terms with Florence, led to a gradual deterioration of relations between Florence and Pisa and the eventual renewal of war between them in 1362. One of the main causes of the war was disputes over the terms for the use of Porto Pisano by the Florentines. Florence had in fact already abandoned Porto Pisano in favour of the Sienese alternative of Talamone, with considerable loss to Pisa.[42] Florence had also not forgotten its claims to Lucca, and Pisa's continued possession of the city was another cause for resentment as relations deteriorated.[43] Though the event that sparked off the war was the seizure by Florence of the Lucchese border fortress of Pietrabuona,[44] Lucchese interests would be in no way forwarded by a war with Florence. Nevertheless under the terms of the league with Pisa, recently renewed, Lucca was necessarily involved in the war. Lucca had to pay a share of the financial levies and contribute men and supplies for operations against Florence, and its territory was open to attack, though in fact much of the fighting was on Pisan or Florentine territory.

The war consisted mainly of harrying raids, and both sides had their successes. Pisa and Lucca recaptured Pietrabuona on 5 June 1362, despite Florentine efforts to defend it.[45] In 1363 Pisa took Altopascio

---

all the fortresses of Lucca and its *contado,* not just the few that were mentioned in the league of 1342. The Lucchese Anziani in making these agreements state that they are acting under powers granted them in the league of 4 July 1342 and also according to an authorisation by a council held on 16 May 1357. There is no other record of this council meeting. See also Sercambi, 1:111, for mention of the renewal of the league, but with inaccurate details.

42. M. Villani, X, lxxxiii; Sercambi, 1:114; *Cron. Pis.,* col. 1034; *Cron. Sen.,* p. 583.

43. Speakers in the Florentine *consulte* occasionally voiced demands that Lucca should be freed or even handed over to Florence: A.S.F. Consulte e Pratiche 3, fols. 95r–98r, 29 July 1361, 150r, 29 Dec. 1361; Consulte e Pratiche 4, fols. 8r, 12 Jan., 67r, 15 June 1363; Consulte e Pratiche 5, fols. 4v, 10 Jan., 52r, 10 April 1364.

44. Strictly speaking it was raised in rebellion by a pro-Florentine party, secretly assisted by Florence: Marchionne di Coppo Stefani, *Cronaca Fiorentina,* R.I.S. n.s. (Città di Castello, 1903), rubr. 690; *Cronichetta d'incerto,* ed. D. M. Manni in *Chronichette antiche di vari scrittori del buon secolo della lingua italiana* (Florence, 1733), pp. 181–182; M. Villani, X, lxxxiii; Sercambi, 1:115.

45. Sercambi, 1:115–116; M. Villani, X, ci; *Cron. Pis.,* cols. 1037–1038. There are many references to Lucchese contributions to the army of Pietrabuona. *Balistarii* were sent: Anz. Av. Lib. 41, fols. 133v–134r, 22 Dec., 135r–135v, 29 Dec. 1361; Anz. Av. Lib. 42, fol. 8r, 17 Feb. 1362. Pisa allowed citizens and *contadini* of Lucca to be replaced by hired footsoldiers, for whom however Lucca had to pay: Anz. Av. Lib. 42, fols. 2r–2v, 7 Jan. 1362. There are many references to raising the money for this: Anz. Av. Lib. 42, fols. 3r, 7 and 8 Jan., 4r, 11 Jan., 16r, 19 March 1362. An *imposita* of 1,000 florins was decreed: Anz. Av. Lib. 42, fol. 3r, 8 Jan., and one of 3,700

and harried and burnt Florentine territory almost up to the gates of the city, running *palii* at Rifredi as a sign of contempt and defeating the Florentines at Ancisa.[46] Lucca contributed forces and supplies to these expeditions and joined in the celebrations for victories against the Florentines.[47] Florence had made similar raids on Pisan territory and had also hired galleys to blockade Pisa, capturing the island of Giglio and carrying off to Florence the chains that ran across the harbour of Porto Pisano.[48] There had also been operations in the Garfagnana, where Florence had held Barga for a year against a Pisan force laying siege to it and finally defeated the Pisans with heavy losses.[49]

---

florins, eventually raised to 4,300 florins: Anz. Av. Lib. 42, fols. 36v-37r, 9 and 10 May 1362. Pisa asked for 300 good, well-armed *balistarii* to be ready when called upon: Anz. Av. Lib. 42, fols. 21v-22r, 31 March 1362; and more citizens were serving in the army in April and May: Anz. Av. Lib. 42, fols. 36r, 9 May, 43v, 24 May 1362. The courts were suspended until 1 June because of this: Anz. Av. Lib. 42, fol. 40r, 13 May 1362. There were also operations to defend S. Gennaro, Medicina and other places: Anz. Av. Lib. 42, fols. 28v, 13 April, 47r, 10 June 1362, p. 319 (no foliation at this point), 14 Dec. 1363. Accounts for the payment of those serving against Pietrabuona: Ragionieri 10, fols. 14v-15r, 34r-35v, 38v-43r, 47r-49v, 5r, 40r-43v (various foliations); and for supplies for the army: fols. 19r-21v, 75r, 91v, 114r-115v. Also Anz. Av. Lib. 42, fols. 28v, 13 April, 55r, 20 June 1362.

46. *Cron. Sen.,* pp. 600-601; *Cron. Pis.,* cols. 1040-1043; *Cronichetta d'incerto,* pp. 184-185; F. Villani, XI, lxviii-lxx.

47. Lucca sent forces to Fosso Renonico, July 1363: Anz. Av. Lib. 42, fol. 56v, 10 July 1363; Ragionieri 10, fols. 35r-36r; well over a hundred Lucchese citizens were paid for this. Also Sercambi, 1:116. Expenses for men in the army against Figline: Ragionieri 10, fols. 154r-155r. The Lucchese *podestà* and his whole *familia* and also a number of Lucchese citizens were fighting at Pontedera in the Pisan *contado* in March: Anz. Av. Lib. 42, fols. 114r-114v, 15 March, 122v, 17 April, 129v-130r, 16 June 1363; Ragionieri 10, fols. 101v, 111r. There were arrangements for the *conservatore* to make a *tasca* of Lucchese citizens to be sent on expeditions when Pisa needed them: Anz. Av. Lib. 42, fols. 142v-143r, 25 Aug. 1363. *Palii* on Florentine territory: Anz. Av. Lib. 43, fol. 38r, 23 July 1363; Ragionieri 10, fols. 120v, 124v, (authorised 28 Aug. 1363). Bonfires in Piazza S. Michele, ringing bells for joy, and other celebrations, "de felicibus novis et prosperis successibus abitis de Anglicis et eorum exercitu contra Staggia": Ragionieri 10, fol. 122v; "de obtentu Fighini contra Florentinos per exercitum pisani comunis," "de Florentinis conflittis apud castrum Ancise": fols. 126r, also 126v, 122r, and Anz. Av. Lib. 42, fol. 139v, 4 Aug. 1363; Anz. Av. Lib. 43, fol. 38v, 2 Aug. 1363, and Sercambi, 1:115, 121-124. There were also Lucchese in the army defeated at Cascina in August 1364: Sardo, p. 158.

48. *Cronichetta d'incerto,* pp. 182-183; *Cron. Sec.,* pp. 596-597; M. Villani, XI, ii, vii, xiii, xvii-xx, xxiv, xxviii, xxx, liv; Sercambi, 1:116-117; *Cron. Pis.,* col. 1041.

49. M. Villani, XI, xlv, xlix, l, lviii; F. Villani, XI, lxxv; *Cronichetta d'incerto,* pp. 184-185. Lucchese serving and Lucchese *contadini* providing supplies against Barga: Anz. Av. Lib. 42, fols. 122r-122v, 17 April, p. 326 (no foliation), 29 Dec. 1363. Payment to *balistarii* sent against Barga: Ragionieri 10, fols. 101r, 111r, 145v, 146r; celebrations for a victory there: fol. 107v.

In 1363 the Pisans had the upper hand, doing great damage to Florentine territory, but in 1364 the tide turned in favour of Florence. In May there was a raid on Pisan territory almost up to the gates of the city, and the castle of Livorno was taken and merchandise there plundered. In July a Florentine raiding force inflicted a heavy defeat upon the Pisans at Cascina, only a few miles from Pisa itself.[50] When peace was made on 29 August 1364 it was therefore on terms unfavourable to Pisa. Though Pisa recovered the island of Giglio, Ghizzano, Peccioli, and other places it had lost, it had to recognise Florentine possession of Pietrabuona, Altopascio, Sorano, and Lignana, which had once been Lucchese, and agree to the payment of an indemnity of 100,000 florins over the next ten years.[51]

Lucca therefore found itself involved in heavy financial levies and contributions of men and supplies for a war that had ended in defeat and an unfavourable peace. But the war also seems to have resulted in the imposition of greater restrictions on the Lucchese and to have caused Pisan rule to become harsher. Lucca was a source of weakness to Pisa during the war with Florence, for the Lucchese could not be relied upon. Not only was it probable that Lucchese efforts on the Pisan side would be reluctant and half-hearted, but there was also the danger that certain elements in Lucca might actively assist Florence. By this time Lucca's best hope of liberation from Pisan rule probably did lie in an understanding with Florence. Some Lucchese certainly hoped that the war might provide an opportunity to free themselves from Pisan rule with Florentine assistance. While realising that the acceptance of Florentine aid might mean merely exchanging one master for another, they nevertheless preferred to take the risk of finding themselves under Florentine rule, hoping that it might at least be less onerous.

Pisa was aware of these dangers and tooks steps to counter them, forbidding meetings of more than four Lucchese without a licence.[52] Though Pisa's need for forces was too great not to make use of the Luc-

---

50. F. Villani, XI, xc, xcvii; *Cron. Pis.*, cols. 1044–1046; *Cron. Sen.*, pp. 608–609; *Cronichetta d'incerto*, pp. 186–187; Sardo, p. 158; Sercambi, 1:124–126.

51. A.S.P. Comune A 29, fols. 120v–127v; printed by D. Catellacci, "La pace tra Firenze e Pisa nel 1364," *Archivio storico italiano* ser. 5, 2 (1888), pp. 145–165. There were also clauses about the release of prisoners and the pardon of *banniti,* some of them Lucchese. Sardo, pp. 161–162; *Cron. Sen.,* p. 610. Sercambi, 1:127–128, says that the Pisans forced Lucca to pay the indemnity, but there is no confirmation of this in any document and Lucchese *proventus* were in Pisan hands at this time. His assertion that the Pisans allowed the Florentines to devastate Lucchese territory is also unconfirmed. F. Villani, XI, cii: on the honourableness of this peace to Florence.

52. Sercambi, 1:115–116.

chese both in the field and in the garrisoning of villages and fortresses, it distrusted them as guards of Lucca itself. The Pisans therefore arranged that some of the more reliable Lucchese should be sent to Pisa as guards, while the men of one of the quarters of Pisa went to Lucca.[53] Rumours of unrest in Pisa caused the *conservatore* in Lucca to take even more extreme measures. He issued a proclamation ordering that all Lucchese between the ages of fourteen and seventy were to leave the city and remain a distance of at least 1,000 *canne* away. The only Lucchese exempt from this were the ghibellines, who were warned in advance to remain, though they were to make a pretence of leaving. Although Sercambi's account of the proclamation is confirmed by Matteo Villani with various circumstantial details, there is no mention of it in any official document. It cannot in any case have been intended to be more than very temporary.[54]

Either because they were provoked by such measures or because they in any case preferred the risk of Florentine rule to that of Pisa, a group of Lucchese did conspire with Florence. The plan was for the Lucchese to throw down a part of the wall to admit a Florentine force of 1,500 men approaching from Pescia. The Lucchese were then to join with the Florentine force in driving the Pisans out of the city.[55] The plot was discovered on 11 April 1363 before it could be put into effect, and the Pisans hastened to take defensive measures. In order to obtain information about the full ramifications of the plot, Pisa at first promised that those involved would be punished by fines, not put to death. But their number was found to be large, and according to Sercambi certain pro-Pisan elements in Lucca urged that there must be executions if the city was to be held securely for Pisa in the future. Pisa tried to avoid openly breaking its promise by imposing impossible fines of sums like 10,000 florins, payable within a very short period and with the death penalty for those who failed to pay in time.[56] There are no official records of any of these arrests and trials, but Sercambi relates that eleven Lucchese, whose names are not given, were executed on 25 April 1363.[57] The Luc-

---

53. Sardo, pp. 153, 158; Sercambi, 1:116–117; *Cron. Sen.*, p. 597.
54. Sercambi, 1:117; M. Villani, XI, xvi. Villani relates that a candle was placed on each gate and that everyone, men and women, citizens and *forestieri*, had to leave the city before the candles had burnt out. He estimates the Lucchese ghibellines as numbering about 100. A *canna* was just over 2 1/3 metres: *Inventario*, 2:69.
55. Sercambi, 1:118; M. Villani, XI, xlvi; *Cron. Pis.*, col. 1040; *Cron. Sen.*, p. 605.
56. Sercambi, 1:118–119.
57. There are no documents concerning this plot among the records of the *podestà*, captain of the people, or the rectors, and none of the names of those involved is known. But other chroniclers confirm that there were a large number of arrests and some executions. Matteo Villani says that 42 Lucchese were arrested and many of them be-

chese were also obliged to decree that the anniversary of the discovery of the plot and the happy delivery of the city be kept as a day of public celebrations in the future.[58]

---

headed and some exiled: Lib. XI, xlvi. The Pisan chronicler says that over a hundred people were involved and suggests a greater number of executions: *Cron. Pis.*, cols. 1040–1041. Also *Cron. Sen.*, p. 605.

58. Anz. Av. Lib . 42, fols. 120v–121r, 17 April 1363. A curious detail is a payment in the account of the *camarlingo generale* for April and May 1363, but not precisely dated, to Berto de Casentino "qui die revelationis tractatus quod fiebat in civitate lucana . . . pro honore lucani comunis venit Lucam cum aquila dominorum Anthianorum pisani populi et ibi stetit aliquibus diebus": Ragionieri 10, fol. 106v. This eagle and its bearer are also mentioned by Sercambi, 1:122.

Lucca under Giovanni dell'Agnello

WHEN ON 13 August 1364, in the aftermath of the unsuccessful war against Florence, Pisa elected Giovanni dell'Agnello doge, this election apparently applied to Lucca also.[1] In September 1364, at the request of the Pisan Anziani, Lucca elected him for life as captain-general, governor, and defender of Lucca, the position previously held by the Pisan Anziani,[2] and the next year Lucca authorised him to appoint his sons captains, governors, and defenders of Lucca with the same authority that he himself held. This authority could continue after his death if he wished.[3] The Lucchese were also obliged to send an embassy to Emperor Charles IV to second his attempts to obtain an imperial vicariate over Lucca for himself and his sons.[4]

---

1. Letter from the doge to the Lucchese Anziani announcing his election over both Pisa and Lucca, 13 Aug. 1364, in Anz. Av. Lib. 51 and no. 950 in *Regesto*. On 14 August Lucca sent an embassy to Pisa "ad recomendandum sibi civitatem et cives lucanos": Ragionieri 10, fol. 148v. Sercambi, 1:126–127; Sardo, pp. 158–160. N. Caturegli, *La signoria di Giovanni dell'Agnello in Pisa e in Lucca e le sue relazioni con Firenze e Milano* (Pisa, 1921), pp. 43 et seq.; G. Mamo, *Alcune ricerche su Giovanni dell'Agnello, doge di Pisa e governatore di Lucca, 13 agosto 1364-6 settembre 1368* (Pescia, 1911), p. 20.

2. Letter of 5 Sept. 1364, in Anz. Av. Lib. 51 and no. 954 in *Regesto*. The election is recorded in A.S.P. Comune A 29, fols. 128r–128v, 8 Sept. 1364, where the Lucchese Anziani state that they are acting under authority granted to them in the agreement of 4 July 1342 and by virtue of a council held on 7 Sept. 1364. The election is on the same terms as that of the Pisan Anziani 19 May 1357: A.S.P. Comune A 29, fols. 118v–119r. Anz. Av. Lib. 44, fol. 2r, 22 Oct. 1365, records another election on the same terms. Caturegli, *La signoria di Giovanni dell'Agnello*, p. 123, n. 1, on the problem of this apparent double election. That there was a second election appears to be demonstrated by a provision for expenses on the occasion of the election of the doge "ad capitaneum lucane civitatis," 26 Oct. 1365: Ragionieri 10, fol. 176v. Also Mamo, *Giovanni dell' Agnello*, pp. 36–39.

3. Anz. Av. Lib. 44, fol. 3r, 5 Aug. 1366. Cianelli prints part of this in *Memorie e documenti*, 1:395; Sercambi, 1:131. The doge sent his nephew, Gherardo dell'Agnello, to Lucca as his deputy; Sercambi, 1:128–129.

4. Anz. Av. Lib. 44, fols. 7r–8r, 20 Aug. 1367; no. 982 in *Regesto* and partly printed in *Memorie e documenti*, 1:396–397. But Charles IV had been offended at his assumption of the title of doge: Anz. Av. Lib. 44, fol. 16r, 11 July 1366 (but should perhaps be dated 1367; see *Regesto* no. 978). Also Anz. Av. Lib. 44, fol. 16v, 1 Aug. 1367. Caturegli, *La signoria di Giovanni dell'Agnello*, p. 179. He was eventually granted an imperial vicariate over Pisa and Lucca in August 1368: Mamo, *Giovanni dell'Agnello*, p. 82; Sardo, p. 167.

Lucca's position seems to have deteriorated under Giovanni dell'Agnello. Sercambi, punning on his name, says that dell'Agnello behaved like a wolf rather than a lamb, and describes him as "mai satio della pompa mondana." He records increased oppressions and financial exactions in general terms and gives some particular examples. He says that Gherardo dell'Agnello, administering Lucca on behalf of his uncle, "cominciò a opressare, e villanegiare i ciptadini oltra l'uzato modo." Giovanni dell'Agnello had promised not to levy any *imposite*, and, observing the letter but not the spirit of this undertaking, he imposed a *sega* of 20,000 florins a year instead.[5] When this expired the Lucchese were obliged to make compositions individually, and a Lucchese supporter of the doge, Niccolò Genovardi, named the sum each citizen should pay, so that everyone paid half as much again as he could afford.[6] The Lucchese were obliged to make gifts of as much as 10,000 florins to the doge on ceremonial occasions, such as his visits to Lucca and the appointment of his sons as captains and governors. Sercambi also records that one leading citizen of Lucca, Francesco Guinigi, fled to Genoa on being asked for a loan of 6,000 florins, which he knew would never be repaid and would not be the last such demand. After that no Lucchese was allowed to leave Lucca without a pass, and many were fined for failing to obtain one.[7]

It is difficult to find confirmation for most of this in Lucchese sources. Lucchese revenues were still being administered by Pisa, so that

5. For these and other promises: Sardo, p. 161; *Cron. Pis.,* col. 1046; Sercambi, 1:129-130. A *sega* or *seca* was a recurrent levy, assessed at so much per day or per month, such as the £933 per day for six months decreed in August 1362. The imposition of as large a sum as 20,000 florins over as long a period as a year makes it clear that this levy was in all but name an *imposita.*

6. Sercambi, 1:133-134. There is some confirmation that Niccolò Genovardi played a role in Pisan finance in Lucca. Three documents record compositions between Gherardo dell'Agnello and individual Lucchese citizens, under which they were to pay a certain sum each year for three years and during that time were to be free of any other financial levies or personal services, except for gabelles and the salt tax. The money was to be paid each year to "Nicolao Genovardi lucano civi exactori ad predicta specialiter deputato." But there is no indication that he played any role in fixing the sum to be paid and the sums themselves, three florins in two cases and one florin in the other, are so low that the compositions should probably be regarded as privileges rather than impositions. The documents in fact refer to them as "immunitas": Diplomi, Spedale 21 July 1367; Archivio di Stato, Tarpea 29 July 1367; S. Romano 31 July 1367. Cf. Mamo, *Giovanni dell'Agnello,* p. 44. They are paralleled by earlier grants of the right to pay a fixed sum each year and be free of any other dues, except gabelles and the salt tax; these were granted on the petition of the eventual beneficiary and clearly represent privileged treatment: Anz. Av. Lib. 35, fols. 80v-81r, 24 Sept. 1353; Anz. Av. Lib. 37, fols. 59v-60r, 24 July 1354; Anz. Av. Lib. 41, fols. 116v-117r, 20 Oct. 1361; Anz. Av. Lib. 42, fols. 6v-7r, 14 Feb., 37r-37v, 9 May 1362.

7. Sercambi, 1:126-137.

the *ragionieri* accounts deal only with the few hundred florins a year that passed through the hands of the *camarlingo generale*. The council records for these years are very meagre and there is nothing at all for the period from November 1367 to March 1369.

There are, however, some records of expenditure on ceremonies when the doge visited Lucca and on gifts to him and his sons. When he visited Lucca in December 1364, the sum of 150 florins was authorised for the celebrations.[8] A further 79 florins and £712 11s. 6d. *picc.* was spent on repairs and embellishments in the palace in Piazza S. Michele, where he was to stay, furnishings for his room, a banquet, and ceremonial robes for a number of Lucchese citizens.[9] When he and the dogaressa made another visit in November or December 1365, 250 florins and more were authorised for gifts to him, and further sums were spent on ceremonies.[10] There were further gifts and celebrations when the doge's sons were made captains and governors. Lucca sent some of the Anziani and other leading citizens to Pisa at public expense to take part in the ceremonies there, made gifts of velvets and silk cloths, and had the bells rung for joy and a bonfire lit in Piazza S. Michele.[11] There are records of further gifts of silks to the doge in 1367, and on at least one occasion the Lucchese made him a gift as an inducement to grant a favour.[12] Though this kind of expenditure might amount to several hun-

---

8. Ragionieri 10, fol. 165r, a provision of the Anziani, 19 Dec. 1364.

9. Ragionieri 10, fol. 164v. An additional £13 19s. was spent on painting the doge's coat of arms on the palace of the Anziani "iusta imagines imperatorum": fol. 165v.

10. More than this seems to have been spent. Ragionieri 10, fol. 181v: 97 florins of the 150 florins authorised were paid on 4 Dec. (and 56 florins were spent on wax, candles, etc.); fol. 183v: another 60 florins of the 150 florins were paid; and fol. 184r: another 13 florins on 5 Jan. Another 100 florins were authorised on 20 Jan.: fols. 187v, 189v. Sixty florins were spent on two pieces of *baldacchino* of silk and gold given to the dogaressa in December: fol. 183r.

11. Expenses of sending the Lucchese to Pisa: Ragionieri 10, fols. 196v, 198r, 199v, 200v. A total of 224 florins and £12 6s. 9d. *picc.* is recorded as having been paid for this. Sixty florins were paid "pro veglutis et drappis de seta . . . pro dono facto per comune lucanum magnificis dominis Gualterio et Francischo Achus novellis dominis": fol. 201v; and further sums totalling 359 florins £5 4s. *picc.* later: fol. 202r. Gifts to the doge had also been authorised on 29 July 1366, perhaps in the same connection (fol. 195r, 30 florins were paid), and there were various minor expenses: fol. 198r. The cost of running *palii* may belong to this occasion, though some seem to belong to 1365: fols. 173v–174v, 196v, 198r. For these ceremonies and Lucchese participation in them: Sercambi, 1:131–132; Sardo, pp. 164–165.

12. Ragionieri 10, fol. 202v for "drappo de seta dicto camuccha misso ad magnificum dominum ducem pisanum," 119 florins £2 11s. 6d. *picc.* Further sums of 20 florins, £1 19s. *picc.*: fol. 203r; 9 florins: fol. 203v; and 10 florins: next folio (unnumbered). Gift in connection with a request: fol. 183r, provision of 23 Dec. 1365.

dred florins—a serious burden in view of the modest sums at Lucca's disposition—there is no evidence of gifts of 10,000 florins in cash such as Sercambi claims that Lucca made on ceremonial occasions. Sercambi was a contemporary, just beginning his active political life at this time, and he asserts that he was present at a ceremony in 1366,[13] but one must doubt the reliability of some of his more extravagant claims. It is difficult to believe that gifts of the order of 10,000 florins could have been made without leaving some trace in the *ragionieri* accounts. As in the case of special efforts to raise *imposite* between 1362 and 1364, one would expect to find references to the raising of loans or to payments to *impositatores* for assessing contributions, to treasurers for collecting the money and converting it into florins, or to notaries for writing the documents.

The absence of such records is especially noteworthy given the fact that there are some references in the *ragionieri* accounts to special levies and increased gabelles under Giovanni dell'Agnello. It is difficult, however, to know quite what weight should be given to these references, as they are very brief. There had already been increases in the gabelles early in 1364,[14] and it is unclear whether the increases under Giovanni dell'Agnello were additional to these or merely an extension of the same increases for a further period. The increases under Giovanni dell'Agnello seem themselves to have been only temporary, for an embassy was sent to the doge, apparently in October 1365, "ad inpetrandum ab eo ut augmentatio nuper facta super gabellis et introitibus lucani comunis differetur usque ad Kalendas Novembris presentis et quod finito termino temporis augmentationis dicte gabelle et introitus reducerentur ad statum pristinum."[15] It was perhaps again to help ensure that the increase did not become permanent that an embassy was sent to ask that the *proventus* should not be sold at all and to press particularly that, if the doge decided they were to be sold, the increase should not be included in the contract with the old gabelle.[16] This was in 1365 and the response to these requests is not recorded. There are, however, some references in Pisan sources to increases in the Lucchese gabelles. A private citizen of

---

13. Sercambi, 1:132.
14. Anz. Av. Lib. 51, no. 1014 in *Regesto*, and above, Chapter IV, pp. 81–82.
15. Ragionieri 10, fol. 177r. The payment of the ambassadors was authorised 27 Oct. 1365, but the precise date of the embassy is not given. Mamo, *Giovanni dell'Agnello*, p. 42.
16. Ragionieri 10, fols. 181v–182r. Two ambassadors were sent to the doge "occasione petendi quod introitus lucani comunis que videbantur velle vendi cum augmentatione facta de dictis introitibus venderentur more pristino," provision of 27 March 1365. *Regesto* no. 971 (original in Anz. Av. Lib. 51) perhaps represents the instructions to these ambassadors.

Pisa invested 300 florins "ne la compra delentrate di Lucha le quale entrate ae vendute messer lo dogio in nome del comune di Pisa per pregio di fiorini XX^m."[17] Subsequently a further hundred florins was invested "ne le dicte entrate per lo radopiamento de le gabelle di Lucha,"[18] but it seems doubtful whether this meant that all the Lucchese *proventus* were now twice what they had been, since the "radopiamento" is elsewhere referred to as having been sold for 7,000 florins.[19]

The level of the gabelles for the next few years is, therefore, unclear, but in March 1369, a few weeks before Lucca regained its freedom, some gabelles at least were being levied at rates above what was customary, and it seems possible that this had been the case since October 1365 or even early in 1364. On 24 March 1369 the General Council authorised a *balia* of eighteen citizens to make provision in view of the possibility that Lucca would soon regain control of its own *proventus*. Together with the Anziani, they issued a series of decrees "volentes intendere ad modificationem et ordinationem infrascriptarum gabellarum que hucusque fuerunt incongrue et excessive." The decrees are not as informative as one could wish; either they lay down what the gabelle should be without detailing the rates charged hitherto or they simply say that it is to be levied according to the statutes of the Lucchese gabelle. Nor is the list of gabelles involved by any means comprehensive. But it does seem that in the last few years of Pisan rule there had been increased gabelles on the retail sale of wine, on cloth if sold by measure, on legacies, on the import of wine, flour, oil, vegetables, and firewood, and on animals butchered in the *contado*.[20]

---

17. A.S.P. Archivio del Opera del Duomo 1281, fol. 15r. The date is 1 Oct. 1365, but this is presumably Pisan style and therefore 1364.
18. A.S.P. Archivio del Opera del Duomo 1281, fol. 15v.
19. "Item misse ne la suprascripta compra . . . per lo radopiamento che messer lo dogio ae facto et vendute de le suprascripte gabelle per pregio di fiorini VII^m a di xxiii doctobre 1366" (presumably Pisan style and therefore 1365): Archivio del Opera del Duomo 1281, fol. 19r. An investment of 100 florins in addition to an earlier 300 florins would be roughly proportionate to an increase of 7,000 florins on an earlier 20,000 for the Lucchese *entrate*. Cf. Caturegli, *La signoria di Giovanni dell'Agnello*, p. 146. There is also mention of a sale of the Lucchese "intrate e diricti" for thirteen months for a price of 20,700 florins. It is not clear what year this refers to, as an investment of 300 florins in this is recorded for November 1365 (presumably Pisan style and therefore 1364), but the sale is to begin "in Calende octobre prosimo che viene," which could mean either 1365 or 1364, if the investment were retrospective: Archivio del Opera del Duomo 1281, fol. 19r.
20. Also one or two other minor increases: Anz. Av. Lib. 45, fols. 1r–1v, 24 March, 2r, 29 March, 3r, 2 April, 25v, 28 June 1369. The new rate given for flour was 2s. 6d. *picc.* a *staio*, itself higher than the rate customary earlier, though lower than the 3s.

The only evidence for the amount that the ordinary Lucchese revenues produced in these years comes from Pisan sources. Neither the 20,000 florins nor the 27,000 for which Lucchese revenues were said to be sold seems large enough to represent Lucca's full revenues, and the same source indicates the possibility that some Lucchese *proventus* were being administered separately. There is a reference to a group of citizens buying "lentrate e diricti di Camaiore," which had earlier been part of the receipts of the Lucchese *camarlingo generale,* for 6,000 florins.[21] More important is a document in the Deposito Raù in the Archivio di Stato in Pisa, which records the sums paid to Pisa by ser Piero Raù, who had held the post of official of the gabelles and *proventus* of Lucca for the year 1 December 1366 to 30 November 1367. He paid the Pisan *camarlingo* a total of 35,540 florins and 28s. 1d. *pis.* in twenty-eight separate payments between 22 December 1366 and 30 December 1367, and a further 317 florins 3s. 6d. *pis.* subsequently, making a total of 35,857 florins 31s. 7d. *pis.*[22] This is remarkably close to the 36,000 florins Pisa had got from Lucca in 1355 and less than it had obtained in 1360–1362.[23] It provides interesting negative evidence in that it does not show that Pisa was drawing a larger sum from Lucca in these years, but it is not entirely conclusive. It simply records the sums paid and the coinage in which the payment was made on various dates with no indication of the Lucchese sources from which they were drawn. It certainly represents all the sums that ser Piero Raù paid to the Pisan *camarlingo* for his period of office, but one cannot exclude the possibility that some Lucchese *proventus* were excluded from his administration or that he had made some payments of salaries and expenses directly, even though the Pisan *camarlingo* was responsible for many such payments. If this sum does indeed represent the whole of the amount that Pisa was receiving from Lucca, it would

---

Lucca had complained of in 1364: Anz. Av. Lib. 51; no. 1014 in *Regesto.* There also seem to have been new gabelles imposed on the export of wine, oil, and cereals from the vicariate of Camaiore in 1367. Lucca sent three embassies in June and July about this and "de modo extrahendi vinum et bladum civium lucanorum sine solutione gabelle": Ragionieri 10, fols. 202r–202v. For increased gabelles and the imposition of new ones in Pisa and also *prestanze* there under Giovanni dell'Agnello: Caturegli, *La signoria di Giovanni dell'Agnello,* p. 139.

21. A.S.P. Archivio del Opera del Duomo 1281, fol. 17r, 17 Feb. 1364. This may have been for more than a year, as the *proventus* of Camaiore had not been producing anything like 6,000 florins a year.

22. A.S.P. Deposito Raù, Pergamena, 19 Jan. 1369 (Pisan style).

23. Most recently Frammuccio di messer Frammuccio had undertaken to pay 40,800 florins for the year on Lucca's behalf: A.S.P. Comune A 206, fol. 124v, 26 June 1361.

appear to demonstrate a further decrease in Lucchese revenues and must have meant problems in covering the necessary expenditure.

There is, however, also evidence of special levies in these years. In March 1365, there seems to have been an *imposita* in Lucca assessed on each hearth. As the only references to it are incidental ones in the *ragionieri* accounts, there are no details of how it was worked out, but payments were being authorised in March "pro impositatoribus elettis de presenti anno ad inponendum focos civitatis lucane."[24] That this was for a specific levy and not just a more general census of hearths appears to be demonstrated by a payment for ambassadors to the doge "ad impetrandum ab eo ut summa vel imposita que videbatur velle esse a floreno medio supra reduceretur et esset quartus unius floreni."[25] It may have been levied more than once, as another embassy was sent to the doge later, "occasione focorum civitatis lucane nuper solvi in dicte pro dimidia impetraturis ab eo ut super exactione ipsius imposite supersedeatur de mense Januarii."[26] Without knowing whether the lowest rate was half a florin or a quarter, whether the poor were exempt, how many hearths there were in Lucca, whether the *burgis* and *subburgis* were included, how high the top rates went, and how many people paid these, it is impossible even to begin to guess how much this *imposita* may have produced or how burdensome it was. But rates as low as half or even a quarter of a florin suggest that it affected large sections of the population. If it included all hearths in Lucca and was levied more than once, it may well have produced significant sums and have been a serious burden to the poorer classes.[27]

Lucca could still make petitions after 1364 as before, and hope for grants of relief. The doge abolished the office of captain of the *contado* as

---

24. Ragionieri 10, fol. 178r, 29 March 1365, another reference fol. 166v. Mamo, *Giovanni dell'Agnello,* p. 50 and n. 4.

25. Ragionieri 10, fol. 181v, authorised on 10 April 1365. Pisan sources mention a "prestantiam focorum nuper impositam" in Pisa, 12 Sept. 1364: A.S.P. Comune A 37, fols. 39r–39v.

26. Ragionieri 10, fol. 187r. This is in the account of the *camarlingo generale* for Feb. and March 1366. The ambassadors were in Pisa for three days and payment of their salary was authorised on 6 Feb., but the precise date of the embassy is not stated.

27. The clergy were also obliged to pay gabelle during the rule of Giovanni dell'Agnello, though this had not been customary hitherto and it was discontinued soon after his fall: A.S.P. Comune A 207, fol. 7v, 26 Sept. 1368. Also Caturegli, *La signoria di Giovanni dell'Agnello,* pp. 148–150. There was also a change in the coinage in these years, though nothing is known of the details of this or its effects. In or before December 1366 two Lucchese ambassadors were sent to the doge "occasione mutationis monete videlicet ut debentibus recipere solvatur ad illam monetam que expendebatur tempore debiti contratti": Ragionieri 10, fol. 202r. Also Caturegli, *La signoria di Giovanni dell'Agnello,* pp. 150–152.

a relief measure for the inhabitants of the Lucchese *contado,* "quia comitativi lucani comunis pluribus sunt vexati ponderibus et ipsorum saluti mitique levamini providere quantum comode possumus." The removal of Totto da Bozzano from the office of the roads seems to have been in response to requests from Lucca and may have had a similar motive.[28] There seem in fact to have been a number of relief measures for the inhabitants of the *contado,* who perhaps had particular need. Sometime before the end of 1364 or in 1365 they were granted a temporary alleviation of the salt gabelle, and this may have been extended later.[29] In November 1365 the doge approved a series of decrees, drawn up by a commission of Lucchese citizens, granting relief to parts of the Lucchese state, especially the Six Miles, that had suffered in the recent wars. The inhabitants were freed from any obligation with regard to animals held in *soccida* or *collaria,* provided that they could prove they had been robbed of them by the enemy. Many communes were freed from two thirds and others from one third of rents in cereals for 1364, and they were required to pay only two thirds for 1365. Individuals were granted a year's immunity from arrest for debt and two years' freedom from proceedings for anything owed to the *camera* of the doge or Pisa.[30] But perhaps even more important was the authorisation of a new *estimo* for the whole of the *contado.* The initiative for this perhaps came from Lucca, and the Lucchese certainly seem to have been strongly in favour of it, for they sent two ambassadors to ask that it be done and to make the doge a gift.[31] Gherardo dell'Agnello with the knowledge and consent of the doge authorised the Lucchese Anziani to have it done, making all the necessary arrangements.[32] A new *estimo* had already been declared to be

28. Anz. Av. Lib. 44, fol. 12r, 23 Oct. 1365 (*Regesto* no. 975), fol. 10r, 6 Aug. 1365 (*Regesto* no. 973). Lucca had sent an embassy to the doge "ad inpetrandum ab eo ut officialis elettus super viis in comitatu lucano relevaretur et ut comitativi lucani non gravarentur ad solvendum tersiam partem focorum ad quod solvendum nunc molestabantur." The ambassadors were there three days, but the date of the embassy is uncertain. Payment was authorised for this and also "pro littera remotionis officialis viarum," 23 Oct. 1365: Ragionieri 10, fols. 176v–177r.

29. Anz. Av. Lib . 51, no. 971 in *Regesto,* undated but see above n. 16. Lucca asked among other things "che lo sale che si levò alli contadinghi per li tempi che verranno come al presente a loro è relevato, si rilevi."

30. Anz. Av. Lib. 44, fols. 10v–12r, 29 Nov. 1366 (Pisan style), *Regesto* no. 973.

31. Payment authorised on 23 Dec. to two ambassadors who had been in Pisa for three days "ad faciendum eidem certum donum nomine lucani comunis ad impetrandum ab eo quod reficiatur extimum et impositam salis lucani comitatus": Ragionieri 10, fol. 183v. Payment was also authorised on 13 Dec. 1365 for an embassy from Lucca to the doge for three days "occasione extimi lucani comunis et imposite salis reficiendi": Ragionieri 10, fol. 182r.

32. Anz. Av. Lib. 44, fol. 12r, 15 Dec. 1365.

urgently needed in November 1362 because of the decline in the population due to wars, plagues, emigration, and the many changes in the
resources of communes and individuals since the last *estimo*.[33] Unless
they were granted special relief the inhabitants of a commune remained
bound for the full *estimo* of their commune even if it had declined in
wealth, and they also had to pay the sum due for any of its inhabitants
who had died without heirs or who had emigrated. A new *estimo* that
would correspond accurately to their numbers and resources was
therefore an important relief measure in view of the condition of the
Lucchese *contado* in the 1360s. The new *estimo* thus authorised seems to
have proceeded regularly, if slowly. Provision was made on 12 March
1367 for payment to four *gite* of three Lucchese citizens each as
"estimatoribus lucani comitatus qui iverunt in dicto comitatu ad in-
quirendum de hominibus et personis dicti comitatus" and their notaries,
and the *estimo* must have been completed in the next few months.[34] But if
the compilation of a new *estimo* was likely to be well received in Lucca,
the same cannot be said of another measure taken in these years. That
was the formal incorporation into the Pisan *contado* of the vicariates of
Pietrasanta and Massa Lunense and the lands the Pisans held in the
Garfagnana. These territories, once part of the Lucchese *contado,* had
been in Pisan hands since their recovery in 1345, but the final extinction
of their special status and their incorporation into the Pisan *contado* must
have been unacceptable to the Lucchese, though there is no record of
any protest.[35]

Gherardo dell'Agnello, as the doge's rector and vicar, had authorised the Lucchese to have a new *estimo* made without calling any council, as would have normally been the case. This measure was paralleled
by a number of others that show a tendency to dispense with the need for
conciliar authority or the observation of strict statutory requirements
and to rely on the arbitrary authority of the doge or his deputy. Gherardo dell'Agnello authorised the Lucchese Anziani to make mandates for
the spending of Lucchese money without observing the relevant
statutes[36] and to elect without the authorisation of any council at all of-

33. Anz. Av. Lib. 42, fols. 79v–80r, 28 Nov. 1362.
34. Ragionieri 10, fol. 201r. For the problems of the Lucchese *contado* in these years:
    Caturegli, *La signoria di Giovanni dell'Agnello,* pp. 159–165. The only fragment of this
    estimo to survive is in series Estimi no. 39, but there is a reference to it in Consiglio
    Generale 7, Riformagioni Pubbliche, fol. 54v, 22 June 1379.
35. A.S.P. Comune A 37, fol. 2r, 18 Sept. 1365. The change in their status was noted by
    Caturegli, *La signoria di Giovanni dell'Agnello,* pp. 166–167, but he was unable to ex-
    plain its significance.
36. Anz. Av. Lib. 44, fol. 10r, 9 June 1365.

ficials whose election was normally reserved to the General Council.[37] Some offices for judges and notaries were excluded from this measure and were to be filled according to the decree of Giovanni dell'Agnello himself,[38] and there are also examples of Gherardo dell'Agnello's making appointments.[39]

The doge also concerned himself with the readmission of *banniti* and with grants of citizenship, both of which normally required conciliar authorisation. At the request of the Lucchese Anziani Giovanni dell'Agnello authorised them to grant Lucchese citizenship to two *contadini*, which he had apparently earlier forbidden, but at the same time he insisted that they accept a grant of citizenship he had already promised to one of his servants.[40] Gherardo dell'Agnello authorised the Anziani to grant citizenship to a Lucchese *contadino* and to one of his sons, but not to another who apparently still lived in the *contado*.[41] No council was consulted in either case. Gherardo dell'Agnello authorised the Lucchese Anziani to elect without consulting the General Council or any other body a *balìa* to make compositions with *banniti* to cancel their sentences and enable them to return, provided they had made peace with the injured party. Similar compositions were to be made with men who were absent because they had not been able to pay *imposite*. This was to apply only to men who owed fines or unpaid *imposite* to Lucca, but Gherardo also appointed a Pisan and a Lucchese to make similar arrangements for fines and other sums owed to Pisa or the doge.[42] In addi-

---

37. Anz. Av. Lib. 44, fols. 10r–10v, 22 Nov. 1365, 14r, 19 Nov. 1366, 18r, 9 Nov. 1367.
38. Anz. Av. Lib. 44, fols. 10r–10v, 22 Nov. 1365, 14r, 19 Nov. 1366, 18r, 9 Nov. 1367. Giovanni dell'Agnello did make appointements of officials: fol. 14r, 20 Aug. 1366, 15r, 2 April 1367, 18r, 16 Aug., 3 Sept. 1368.
39. Anz. Av. Lib. 44, fol. 12v, 7 Oct. 1366.
40. Anz. Av. Lib. 44, fols. 12r–12v, 29 Jan. 1366; no. 976 in *Regesto*. Payment to the doge's chancellor "pro lictera autoritatis concesse per ipsum dominum ducem Anthianis lucani comunis faciendi quosdam cives lucanos" was authorised on 23 Dec. 1365: Ragionieri 10, fol. 182r.
41. Anz. Av. Lib. 44, fol. 17r, 30 Aug. 1367.
42. Ans. Av. Lib. 44, fols. 12v–13v, 12 Oct. 1367. He had authorised the Anziani to cancel banns where the fine came to Lucca, provided the *banniti* had made peace: Anz. Av. Lib. 44, fol. 17r, 30 Aug. 1367. The General Council continued to exist. Their names for the year beginning 1 January 1365 are recorded in Anz. Av. Lib. 44, pp. 141–150 (modern pagination; no foliation), and this council is stated to have met at least once. Pages 151–160 record the names of another General Council, probably for the next year, which met at least twice. Libro di Corredo alle Carte della Signoria 33 shows that many offices were filled as usual for the years 1365 and 1366. The names of the Council of Fifty for the semester beginning 4 November 1368 are recorded in Anz. Av. Lib. 45, p. 5 (modern pagination; no foliation) and it met at least six times, though this was of course after the fall of Giovanni dell'Agnello.

tion to these general measures, he also authorised the Anziani to deal with the banns of individuals without consulting any council, in one case specifically empowering them to reduce the fine.[43] Giovanni dell'Agnello himself authorised the cancellation of a number of banns, in some cases only on payment of the fine and on condition that the guilty party had made peace with the victim. But in others, including some involving death sentences, he ordered the cancellation of banns without any fine, and in one case he ordered the readmission of *banniti* who had not made peace.[44]

The doge not infrequently interfered in lawsuits that had yet to be decided. When he received a petition from the men of the commune of Orbicciano, pieve di Mostesgradi, concerning the claims of Franceschino Martini against them, he sent it to the *podestà*, despite the fact that a civil suit was already proceeding in the *podestà*'s court. His letter to the *podestà* stated that "quatenus de comprehensis in petitione predicta veritate comparata ad nichil aliud habendo respectum nisi ad solam et lucidam veritatem summarie facias quod est juris ne quisque lamentari possit contra veritatem opprimi vel gravari."[45] The doge does not seem to have been favouring one party over another, and his interventions were directed to speeding up decisions and preventing delays from legal cavils and excuses; he stressed the need to discover the truth as quickly as possible and then act on it. He always seems to have insisted on the careful observance of Lucchese statutes, ordering things to be done only if permissable under Lucchese statutes or not contrary to them.[46] He was apparently particularly concerned to give men acccused of capital offences every chance to make their defence. In the case of Francesco Vite of Carciana he wrote five letters extending the time limit and then granting him a further extension because his advocate had

43. Anz. Av. Lib. 44, fols. 18r–18v, 10 Nov., 14 Nov. 1367.

44. *Regesto* no. 957; without fine: nos. 963, 964, 967, 969, 970; without peace: no. 962. In at least some cases the fine waived would have come to Lucca. Series Potestà di Lucca, Inquisizioni no. 4898, fol. 52r: pardon of six men for any offences committed before 13 August without any fine, 6 Nov. 1364. He had ordained a general "taxa" for offences committed before 13 August 1364, extended by decree of 30 Oct. 1364 in Anz. Av. Lib. 51. Also Mamo, *Giovanni dell'Agnello*, pp. 31–33 and appendices 6 and 7.

45. Potestà di Lucca, Curia Civile, no. 424, fol. 6r, also 6v.

46. Other cases where he urged a quick decision: Potestà di Lucca, Curia Civile 432, fol. 2r, 10 July 1365, fol. 80v, 9 Dec. 1365. Insisting on the observance of Lucchese statutes: Potestà di Lucca, Curia Civile 426, fol. 103v, 3 May 1365; Curia Civile 432, fol. 81r, 19 Nov. 1365; Inquisizioni 4902, fols. 89v–90r, 27 Jan. 1366, 93v–94v, 31 March 1366.

been sent on an embassy.[47] Nevertheless all this certainly constituted interference in cases for which Lucchese statutes and Lucchese courts already provided remedy. He wrote three letters in less than a week in one case, giving the *podestà* various instructions about assigning time limits for one of the parties to present his case, allowing the parties to compromise, and allowing appeal from the sentence of the *podestà*, if Lucchese statutes permitted this.[48]

A measure with particularly serious implications was a decree of 29 November 1364 in which Giovanni dell'Agnello authorised *forenses* living in Lucca or the Lucchese *contado* to buy property and possessions there. Though this applied only to *forenses* resident in Lucchese territory and was specifically stated to be designed to attract outsiders to Lucca in order to increase the population,[49] it was a serious breach of the statutes forbidding *forenses* to buy land or possessions in Lucca. The decree might have opened the door to Pisan investment in Lucchese territory, eventually leading to the development of a powerful group of Pisans with interests in Lucca, influential enough to exercise pressure in Lucchese

47. Potestà di Lucca, Inquisizioni 4899, fols. 40r–42r: letters of 26 Aug., 1 Sept., 7 Oct., 9 Oct., 17 Oct. 1365.

48. Potestà di Lucca, Curia Civile 426, fols. 103r, 28 April, 103v, 30 April, 3 May 1365. For these and other references: Caturegli, *La signoria di Giovanni dell'Agnello*, pp. 143–144. Many of the doge's interventions began with petitions addressed to him: Mamo, *Giovanni dell'Agnello*, pp. 53–54. There are occasional indications of intervention in lawsuits by the Pisan Anziani before 1364. They ordered the rectors to speed the execution of a sentence in a case between two Lucchese in the Curia di S. Cristoforo, "in favorabile faciatis iustitia suadente": A.S.P. Comune A 206, fol. 46r, 13 March 1361, also fol. 46v, 14 March. The *podestà* in Lucca was instructed by virtue of his office to induce two Lucchese litigating over a house in Lucca to appoint arbitrators, and if they would not agree, to appoint the arbitrators himself: A.S.P. Comune A 206, fol. 46r, 14 March 1361.

49. Potestà di Lucca, Inquisizioni 4898, fols. 34v–35r: "Affectantes civitatem nostram lucanam eiusque comitatum bonis incolis et habitatoribus uberari in ipsis habitare volentibus dare materiam residendi volumus et hoc nostro decreto decernimus et salubriter providemus quod universis et singulis forensibus undecumque existant habitantibus et habitatoribus imposterum in civitate comitatu et districtu lucano cum familiis et massaritiis suis liceat eis facultatem et licentiam concedentes emere sue alio quovis titulo adipisci quascumque possessiones et predia in comitatu civitate et districtu lucano a quibuscumque tam civibus comitativis et districtualibus lucanis quam forensibus cum quibus in concordia fuerint. Et quod tam vendentes quam ementes seu quovis alio licito titulo accipientes et concedentes a quacumque pena contra eos vel ipsorum alterum imposita occasione et causa vendictionis vel emptionis fiende liberi sunt et esse intelligantur penitus et immunes non obstantibus in predictis vel aliquo predictorum aliquibus brevibus statutis ordinibus provisionibus consiliis reformationibus in contrarium factis vel editis seu aliis contrarietatibus quibuscumque," 29 Nov. 1365 (Pisan style).

economic and political concerns and erode the degree of local autonomy that the Lucchese still enjoyed. In the few years between this decree and the recovery of Lucchese independence not many Pisans seem to have acquired real property in Lucca. In fact the only example so far found is the purchase by Giovanni di ser Jacobo Scarso de Comitibus of Pisa, said to be living in Lucca, of a piece of land with trees and vines in the *contrata* of S. Donato outside the gates of Lucca from Jacobo Sercambi.[50] But the reality of the danger is clear in a gift by the doge to Filippo Nardini of Pescia, apparently intended as a reward for fidelity to himself and to Pisa, of houses and land in Collodi, Villa Basilica, and the vicariate of Valdilima.[51]

Some historians have seen the period of Giovanni dell'Agnello as a time of improvement for Lucca, in certain respects at least, and have even contrasted his rule of Lucca favourably with his régime in Pisa.[52] In part this rests on a misinterpretation of Pisan rule before 1364. Lucca had always enjoyed a measure of autonomy in internal affairs. When Giovanni dell'Agnello authorised the Anziani to appoint officials or spend Lucchese money without consulting the usual councils, he was not giving them power in matters previously outside their sphere; he was merely authorising them to do alone what they had previously done in consultation with other bodies. Their power to deal with these matters alone was a departure from statutory regulations and derived from the doge's grant, which was usually temporary or even for a single occasion only. He probably preferred to use the Anziani rather than the General Council or the Council of Fifty because they were easier to control. But he was in no way increasing the powers of the Anziani; their scope for independent action seems rather to have diminished in these years.[53] While the doge seems to have tried to govern efficiently and humanely, for example in speeding up procedure in legal cases or granting relief to the *contado*, he was also gathering power more firmly into his own hands.

It is possible that financial burdens increased in these years, though it was a time of peace when the Lucchese might have hoped for some

50. Series Archivio de'Notari no. 151, Protocolli of ser Bartolomeo Bianchi, 24 Jan. 1366 (no foliation).
51. A.S.P. Comune A 37, fols. 3v-4r, 29 Sept. 1364. Also Mamo, *Giovanni dell'Agnello*, pp. 51-52, quoting a *pergamena* in the Archivio di Stato in Lucca, Diplomatico, Tarpea, 29 Sept. 1364.
52. Cianelli, *Memorie e documenti*, 1:394, interprets the grant of the power to elect officials without consulting any council as a concession to the Anziani, and Caturegli, *La signoria di Giovanni dell'Agnello*, p. 126, seems to take the same view. He felt that Lucca was better treated than Pisa in matters of justice and the administration of the *contado*, though not in financial affairs (pp. 152-154, 163-168; also Chapter VI).
53. Caturegli, *La signoria di Giovanni dell'Agnello*, p. 146 n. 8, also p. 131.

relief. Sercambi's claims about the gifts Lucca was obliged to make may be exaggerated, but the doge certainly seems to have had a weakness for elaborate and costly ceremonial, and on at least one occasion he accepted a present in connection with a request Lucca was making. There are hints, too, of moves that would have reduced still further Lucca's cherished autonomy. The decree permitting *forenses* resident in Lucca to acquire real property there was a measure with serious implications for the future. The incorporation of the Lucchese vicariates of Pietrasanta, Massa Lunense, and the lands in the Garfagnana into the Pisan *contado* extinguished the last trace of their special status. All in all the Lucchese of the 1360s were probably at least as conscious of being subjected to arbitrary government as they were of being offered good government.

Conclusion

LUCCHESE TRADITION saw Pisan rule as harsh and tyrannical. There are naturally enough no judgments on it before 1369, but those written after Lucca had recovered its independence are virtually unanimous. The harshness and tyranny of Pisan rule is a theme that runs through Sercambi's chronicle, and he reproduces a poem in which it is claimed that the Pisan rulers of Lucca

> Questa terra più bella de'christiani
> Facta avean diventar luogo selvaggio;
> Tractando i ciptadini sì come cani,
> Con ongni villania & ongni oltraggio.[1]

A similar view is reflected in official Lucchese records. There were specific complaints that men had been forced to sell houses in the Augusta for less than their true value[2] or had been unjustly condemned for crimes "tempore detestandi regiminis Pissanorum [sic]."[3] Formulations such as "in del tempo tiranpnico de Pisani"[4] or "tempore dominationis Pisanorum quando ut est omnibus notum publicum et notorium quod negotia gubernabantur et ducebantur sub eorum tirannica dominatione"[5] were commonly used even when no very specific or serious complaint was being made about Pisan administration. A more considered statement of the Lucchese attitude to Pisan rule came at the end of the century, when the Gonfaloniere said:

> Dele più care cose che dio ponesse al mondo fu libertà, la quale si conosce per lo suo contrario, cioè per la servitù, la quale servitù quanto sia dura et aspra molti citadini viveno li quali per prova et experientia ne possono rendere et rendeno vera testimonanza. Certo veramente si tiene che ciascuno virtuoso citadino prima la morte volesse che nele mani de crudeli et perfidi pisani ne daltri ritornare.[6]

1. Sercambi, 1:198, also 108–109, 115–117, 142, 199.
2. Consiglio Generale 3, Riformagioni Pubbliche, fol. 85r, 30 Dec. 1371.
3. Consiglio Generale 1, Riformagioni Pubbliche, fol. 24r, 20 Aug. 1369.
4. Consiglio Generale 6, Riformagioni Pubbliche, fol. 37v (various foliations), 16 Feb. 1378.
5. Consiglio Generale 6, Riformagioni Pubbliche, fol. 54v, 22 June 1379.
6. Consiglio Generale 13, Riformagioni Pubbliche, fol. 19v, 18 June 1397.

Since he made these remarks in the course of a speech designed to induce his fellow citizens to accept financial sacrifices at a time when Lucca was again at war with Pisa, he presumably felt that these views would be widely shared.

This traditional view of Pisan rule was adopted by later writers. The sixteenth-century chronicler Civitali writes of "la tirannide loro, che mai o di rado fu la più crudele et insupportabile per l'estreme gravezze e severissime leggi che sopra la città di Lucca sovente essi imponevano" and of "atrocissimi supplicii senza pietà o compassione alcuna,"[7] and Andrea Boccella claims that "mai fu tirannide più crudele."[8] The same view is reflected in more recent works. Tommasi speaks of Lucca "mentre gemeva sotto strettissima servitù" and of "l'abietta e dura servitù dei nostri."[9] Bongi speaks of Lucca under the "assoluto governo de'suoi vicini" and of Pisa ruling Lucca "con ogni crudeltà e immoderatezza; composizioni del tutto usurpate, poiché i Lucchesi soprafatti dai loro vicini, non ebbero altra parte in queste che di accettarle e di sostenere il peso."[10] Fumi too speaks of "l'esodo degli oppressi . . . le esazioni si erano rese insupportabili" and of "la docilità imposta della paura."[11] Even as recently as 1950 Augusto Mancini described Pisan rule as "una vera servitù."[12] Nor was it only Lucchese who took a harsh view of Pisan rule. Matteo Villani speaks of it as "grave giogo, e servaggio de'Pisani" and of "la loro usata crudeltà,"[13] and Pietro Silva, writing from a Pisan point of view, nevertheless speaks of Pisan rule in Lucca as "duro servaggio."[14]

No doubt for most Lucchese commentators, whether contemporary or more recent, Pisan rule in itself constituted tyranny and servitude. Probably no institutions or methods of government could have rendered it really acceptable; any Pisan officials would have been regarded as oppressors and any financial arrangements as extortion. But it is necessary to look at Pisan rule in context—to examine the particular problems that

7. G. Civitali, *Storia di Lucca*, Lucca, Archivio di Stato, Biblioteca Manoscritti 38, fols. 280v–281v.

8. He also speaks of the Lucchese as "soggetti alli crudeli Pisani, la cui tirannia fu acerbissima." Summary of this chronicle in B. Baroni, *Miscellanea*, MS 925, Lucca, Biblioteca Governativa (no foliation).

9. G. Tommasi, "Sommario della storia di Lucca," *Archivio Storico Italiano* 10 (1847; repr. 1969), pp. 210–211.

10. *Inventario*, 1:104, also pp. xiii, xiv, and 2:91.

11. *Regesto*, 2, part 1, preface, pp. ix–xi; 2, part 2, preface, p. iii.

12. A. Mancini, *Storia di Lucca* (Florence, 1950), p. 153.

13. M. Villani, V, xxxiv; XI, xvi.

14. P. Silva, "Il governo di Pietro Gambacorta," *Annali della Reale Scuola Normale Superiore di Pisa*, sez. Filosofia e Filologia 23 (1912), p. 46.

Pisa had to face in trying to rule Lucca and the solutions that it found—
before one can see whether its administration was harsher than it need
have been.

There can be no doubt that Pisa had to face a particularly difficult
situation. Pisan conquest of Lucca came suddenly. It was undertaken
only when Pisa realised the danger it would face if Lucca fell to Florence.
Many cities that established their rule over a neighbour did so gradually
as the result of a long period of preparation, building up a party
favourable to their rule or giving their support to an internal faction.[15]
Pisa had had no time to prepare such a party and could rely on no such
internal support. Pisa and Lucca were long-standing enemies, and Lucca's party allegiances, though probably somewhat blurred by the vicissi-
tudes the city had suffered in the earlier fourteenth century, were guelf,
not ghibelline. It is true that Sercambi says that in 1341-1342 the Pisans
counted on the aid of the ghibellines and *dughali,* that is, the supporters
of Castruccio Castracani and his descendants, but the same writer later
speaks of the difficulty of distinguishing ghibellines from guelfs.[16] Many
of such ghibellines as there were in Lucca were supporters not of Pisan
rule but of the descendants of Castruccio Castracani, whose ambitions
further complicated the situation. Pisa perhaps had the support of some
timeservers and quislings,[17] and more Lucchese may have preferred
Pisan rule to that of Florence, or at least were prepared to acquiesce in
Pisan rule when they could see no alternative. But Pisa cannot have had
many really whole-hearted supporters in Lucca.

This was the more serious since Lucca was too large and strong to
be ruled easily. Rule of another city presented fewer problems where the
ruling city was very much stronger than the subject city. This was not
the case for Pisa and Lucca. Though Pisa was certainly larger and
stronger than Lucca, the difference was not great enough to enable Pisa
to hold Lucca easily. Pisa therefore found itself trying to rule a city that
was quite strong and fundamentally hostile, a city where it had little internal support and which it had acquired by conquest.

Did Pisa treat Lucca like a conquered city? In some respects one can
perhaps argue that it did. Pisa certainly did not long observe the original
generous terms. Contrary to the agreements of 1342, it garrisoned not

15. G. Romano, "Delle relazioni tra Pavia e Milano nella formazione della signoria
    viscontea," *Archivio storico lombardo* 19 (1892), pp. 566-575; S. Favale, "Siena nel
    quadro della politica viscontea nell'Italia centrale," *Bollettino senese di storia patria* 43,
    n.s. 7 (1936), pp. 316-318; J. K. Hyde, *Padua in the Age of Dante* (Manchester, Eng-
    land, 1966), pp. 221-224.
16. Sercambi, 1:89, 117.
17. Sercambi, 1:108-109.

only Lucca itself but all the fortresses of the *contado*. Pisa kept under its own direct administration the part of Lucchese territory that had been recovered after 1342, in violation of an undertaking that such territory would be returned to Lucca. The area in question was incorporated into the Pisan *contado* under Giovanni dell'Agnello. The forces that Pisa stationed in Lucca and in Lucchese fortresses constituted an army of occupation. It is also clear at quite an early date that Pisa saw its rule in Lucca as permanent. The agreement of 1342 was in the nature of a protectorate and limited to a period of fifteen years, but Pisa saw its rule as more extensive and clearly had no intention of restoring Lucca to freedom after the fifteen years were over. The Bergolini and Raspanti were united in a determination to hold on to Lucca, and they were prepared to sink their differences when Pisan possession of the city was threatened.[18] Pisa insisted in 1355 that Charles IV should recognise Lucca as "omnino sub gubernatione et regimine pisani comunis" and not allow it to be under any other rule.[19] Such evidence indicates that the Pisans were thinking of their position in Lucca as Pisan rule, not just as a league or an alliance or a protectorate, and that they saw it as permanent, although by that time the original agreement had little over two years to run.

There are no general statements of principle with regard to Pisan policy in Lucca in either Pisan or Lucchese sources. These principles must be deduced from decisions in particular cases and from Pisan policy in general. It seems, however, that Pisa put the security of its position in Lucca first, but apart from that was prepared to allow Lucca autonomy in local and internal affairs. Most of the more serious infringements of Lucchese autonomy—the presence of Pisan rectors, the insistence on Pisans in the offices of *podestà, conservatore,* and chancellor, and Pisan control of the selection of Lucchese Anziani and interference in other offices—probably sprang from fear of some situation arising in Lucca that might threaten Pisan hold on the city. It is difficult, in fact, to conceive of one city ruling another without placing some of its own citizens in important posts and vetting the selection of men holding offices and sitting in councils in the subject city.[20]

18. *Cronaca di Pisa,* R.I.S. 15, col. 1030.
19. A.S.P. Comune A 60, fols. 2r–2v, 10 May 1355, 5r, 21 May 1355; Mancinelli, "Carlo IV," docs. V and VIII.
20. For examples of this in Venetian *terraferma* cities: B. G. Kohl, "Government and Society in Renaissance Padua," *Journal of Medieval and Renaissance Studies* 2 (1972), pp. 215–217; A. Ventura, *Nobiltà e popolo nella società veneta del '400 e '500* (Bari, 1964), chapter 2; for Florence: M. E. Mallett, "Pisa and Florence in the Fifteenth Century," in *Florentine Studies,* ed. N. Rubinstein (London, 1968), esp. pp. 439–441; D. Herlihy, *Medieval and Renaissance Pistoia* (New Haven and London, 1967), pp. 223–231.

Apart from that Lucca was allowed much autonomy. It was always administered separately from Pisa, and there seems to have been no attempt to assimilate it to the Pisan state.[21] There was little or no attempt to promote closer relations between Lucca and Pisa on an institutional or personal basis. The Lucchese acquired no special position in Pisa as Pisan subjects, as did the inhabitants of some Florentine subject cities, and there was no question of their holding offices there or becoming Pisan citizens on terms more favourable than those offered to immigrants from anywhere else outside Pisa. There was no attempt to promote immigration from one city to the other, and nothing more is heard of efforts to encourage intermarriage between Pisans and Lucchese. Prohibitions of the acquisition of land in the Lucchese *contado* by non-Lucchese were maintained until 1364, and there is no sign of the development of a group of Pisans with special economic interests in Lucca comparable with those of Florentine families like the Medici, Capponi, and Ridolfi in Pisa after Pisa came under Florentine rule. Nor was there any apparent attempt to influence the Lucchese economy in a direction favourable to Pisa by such things as insisting that Lucchese merchants ship their goods through Pisan ports.

Although at least one Pisan rector was normally present at council meetings to keep an eye on events, Lucca was left free to deal with its own citizens and subjects as it thought fit. Pisa did not normally intervene in internal affairs, refraining from taking advantage even when Lucchese subjects addressed petitions to it. Pisa was not entirely consistent about this—absolute consistency is perhaps too much to expect of any medieval government—but basically Lucca appointed most of its own officials and regulated its own internal affairs.

In some respects Lucca was unusually well treated. Its freedom in economic affairs contrasts favourably with the position of Florentine subject cities or the cities of the Venetian *terraferma*.[22] In finance, too, it seems to have been fairly, even generously, treated. Tax farming and the actual collection of taxes at the local level remained in the hands of Lucchese. Obviously Lucchese resources were expected to cover Lucchese expenses, but in assessing the amounts it was to pay efforts were made to balance revenues against expenses. Both Pisa and Lucca were in difficulties at this time.[23] Certainly Lucchese revenues seem to have

21. Cf. Milan: D.M. Bueno de Mesquita, *Giangaleazzo Visconti* (Cambridge, 1941), pp. 45-58.
22. Mallett, "Pisa and Florence in the Fifteenth Century," pp. 413-439; A. Pino-Branca, "Il comune di Padova sotto la Dominante nel secolo XVº," *Atti del Reale Istituto Veneto* 96 (1936-1937) and 97 (1937-1938).
23. N. Caturegli, *La signoria di Giovanni dell'Agnello* (Pisa, 1921), p. 128.

declined a great deal, and if Lucca could count on perhaps only half the revenue it had earlier required for local needs, there were bound to be problems. Nevertheless the sums Lucca was called upon to pay do not seem disproportionate to the expenditure they were to cover. There was no definite upward trend,[24] and Lucca seems to have been in a stronger bargaining position than one might expect, able to extract financial concessions and win acceptance of conditions it desired. If for part of the time Lucchese revenues were in Pisan hands, it seems to have been the Lucchese who desired this system. Though Lucca sometimes had to levy *imposite* from its subjects, extraordinary financial demands by Pisa were rare until the outbreak of war with Florence in 1362. Then the division of *imposite,* with Lucca paying a quarter to Pisa's three-quarters, seems decidedly generous. Lucca might be paying large sums in extraordinary levies, but its subjects were treated no worse than those of Pisa, and often better. Certainly Pisa cannot have been drawing large sums of surplus revenue from Lucca and seems at times to have been out of pocket.

Of course Pisan rule brought abuses. There were times when Pisa intervened directly in Lucchese internal affairs, demanding the appointment of its candidates to offices in Lucca and even selling such offices. The Lucchese can never have been quite sure whether Pisa would intervene or leave them to deal with a matter themselves. There were occasions, too, when Pisa refused to allow officials of whom the Lucchese had complained to be dismissed. But there are many examples of Pisa's attempting to maintain an orderly and decent administration. The rectors had a court to deal with offences committed by mercenary soldiers. Pisa often seems to have looked up precedents or checked the Lucchese statutes or the customs of local communes when appealed to on some disputed point. It also tried to discipline its officials and prevent them from encroaching on each other's authority or intervening in matters which under the compositions belonged to the Lucchese.

Many of the worst consequences of Pisan rule sprang from Lucca's involvement in Pisan foreign policy. Lucca was certainly obliged to follow all the fluctuations of Pisan internal and external affairs. A change in government for Pisa meant a change in the officials Pisa sent to Lucca, but even more serious for Lucca was its involvement in Pisan foreign affairs, which dragged it into the disastrous war with Florence. Pisan rule could, of course, have meant no less. Even the loosest rule of one city by

---

24. Cf. the treatment of Florentine subject cities in this period: Becker, "Economic Change and the Emerging Florentine Territorial State," *Studies in the Renaissance* 13 (1966), pp. 34–35 and *Florence in Transition* (Baltimore, 1968), 2:187–188, 191.

another must have involved the subject city in the alliances, enmities, and wars of the ruling city. But it was this involvement in Pisan foreign affairs that led to the worst period of Pisan rule.

It seems justifiable to distinguish, as earlier Lucchese historians have done, between Pisan rule up to about 1362 and after that date.[25] The last years were almost certainly the harshest. First there was the exceptional situation of the war with Florence with the material destruction and financial hardship that it brought. This might have been no more than temporary, had it not been followed by the rule of Giovanni dell'Agnello, itself a consequence of the war. The years after 1364 are unfortunately the most obscure period of Pisan rule in Lucca. It does, however, seem possible that there were increased gabelles and extraordinary levies, although these were years of peace when the Lucchese might have hoped for a return to normal levels. The rule of Giovanni dell'Agnello brought relief measures for the *contado*, but it also saw the relaxation of the prohibition of the acquisition of lands in the Lucchese state by non-Lucchese, more intervention in lawsuits, and a more arbitrary form of government at the expense of the traditional councils. It is, however, important to note that much of this applied to Pisa as well as Lucca. Indeed in some ways Pisa fared worse. The changed nature of the régime in Lucca should perhaps be regarded as a consequence of signorial rule, rather than Pisan rule. Unfortunately the last few months of Pisan rule after the fall of Giovanni dell'Agnello were so heavily overshadowed by the expedition of Charles IV, the efforts of the Pisans to maintain their hold on Lucca, and the attempts of the Lucchese to induce the emperor to free them, that it is impossible to say whether or not Pisa would have reverted to its old methods of government.

Throughout the period of Pisan rule Lucca had retained some degree of civic life. Lucchese continued to participate in the administration of their city as Anziani, members of the General Council and of the smaller councils of Fifty and Twenty, or as holders of the many lesser offices. It is true that Pisa maintained control directly or indirectly over their selection, but they cannot all have been Pisan tools. The General Council in particular had 250 members and since they could not sit for two consecutive years, at least 500 citizens, and in practice many more, had the opportunity to take some part in public life. It is highly improbable that Pisa numbered that many supporters in Lucca. Evidence from after 1369 makes it clear that, although some citizens may have been newly returned, many of those sitting in councils or holding office after 1369

25. Tommasi, "Storia di Lucca," p. 226. Cianelli, *Memorie e documenti,* 1:386, saw the turning point as coming a little earlier, in 1355 or 1358.

were the same men or came from the same families as had held office under Pisan rule.[26] The old republican institutions survived and continued to function to some extent even under Pisan rule. All that was required after 1369 was for independence to breathe new life into them.

The continued vitality of Lucchese civic life is best shown by Lucca's efforts to regain its freedom and the ease with which it resumed its character as a self-governing republic after 1369. The uninterrupted functioning of the councils gave a precious continuity which explains the relative smoothness of the transition. There was no break in continuity. The Anziani and councillors who were in office during the last stages of Pisan rule completed their terms after Lucca was declared independent.[27] The ease of the transition is in fact remarkable and demonstrates the superficial nature of Pisan rule. Although some institutions had been developed for Pisan rule in Lucca, most obviously the office of rector, and there were clearly numerous posts in the Pisan forces and administration, this structure was not really deep-rooted. When it was swept away in 1369 it left no gap. Pisa had ruled mainly by securing the appointment of its own citizens to the old communal offices such as those of the *podestà*, *conservatore*, and chancellor and by controlling the selection of Lucchese for the Anzianate and other offices, not to mention maintaining a garrison to overawe the citizens. Had there been greater institutional changes, or had the Pisans attempted to unify the two cities and establish joint institutions, it would have been much more difficult to set up an independent republican régime after 1369. On the social level, too, Pisan rule in Lucca had not taken deep root. Had Pisan families established themselves in Lucca economically and socially, setting up businesses and marrying into Lucchese families, the upheaval in 1369 would have been much greater.

Nothing Pisa could have done would have rendered its rule really acceptable. The Pisans were right to be concerned with security and to fear some turn of events that might be exploited by the Lucchese to throw off their rule. After all, that was exactly what did happen in 1369, after two earlier attempts—the rising of 1355 and the plot of 1363—had been unsuccessful. Considerations of security dominated Pisan rule and were behind the harshest measures. Although Lucca suffered all the disadvantages of having a superior which might intervene at any time

26. For a fuller discussion of this see my *Lucca 1369-1400: Politics and Society in an Early Renaissance City-State* (Oxford, 1978), pp. 179–193.

27. For the circumstances of this transition: O. Banti, "Un anno di storia lucchese (1369-1370), dalla dominazione pisana alla restaurazione della libertà," in *La "Libertas Lucensis" del 1369, Carlo IV e la fine della dominazione pisana*, Accademia Lucchese di Scienze, Lettere e Arti, Studi e Testi 4 (Lucca, 1970), pp. 33–53.

and to which the disgruntled might appeal, it was allowed a measure of autonomy. Pisan rule may have been irksome and difficult for a proud and independent city to tolerate, but it does not seem to have been intentionally harsh or cruel or extortionate. From the Pisan point of view firm measures were necessary if it was to keep its hold on Lucca, but it does not normally seem to have gone beyond that. The mere fact that Lucca was ruled by Pisa may have constituted servitude for the Lucchese, but the rule itself does not seem to have been tyrannical.